MW00830670

V

SECONDARY EDUCATION

IN THE

NINETEENTH CENTURY

SECONDARY EDUCATION
IN THE
NINETEENTH CENTURY

BY

R. L. ARCHER

PROFESSOR OF EDUCATION IN THE
UNIVERSITY COLLEGE OF NORTH WALES,
BANGOR

CAMBRIDGE
AT THE UNIVERSITY PRESS
1921

CAMBRIDGE UNIVERSITY PRESS
Cambridge, New York, Melbourne, Madrid, Cape Town,
Singapore, São Paulo, Delhi, Mexico City

Cambridge University Press
The Edinburgh Building, Cambridge CB2 8RU, UK

Published in the United States of America by Cambridge University Press, New York

www.cambridge.org
Information on this title: www.cambridge.org/9781107622326

First published 1921
First paperback edition 2013

A catalogue record for this publication is available from the British Library

ISBN 978-1-107-62232-6 Paperback

PREFACE

THE period of which we commonly think when we hear or speak of the nineteenth century began in 1789 and ended in 1918. The landmarks of educational history coincide very conveniently with those of wider history. The year 1918 might well be chosen as our terminus by reason of the passing of Mr Fisher's bill even if it had not been the year of the Armistice. Even if the years from 1789 to 1815 had not witnessed the Napoleonic wars, they might have been chosen as our starting-place because they saw the foundation of the monitorial schools and the re-awakening of our ancient universities. These two disconnected sources of educational energy for a long time distributed power over distinct areas; it was not till the middle of the century that even a "ladder" was suggested as a means of ascent from the region served by the one to that served by the other; it was not till the Act of 1902 that elementary and higher education were treated as parts of a single whole; and it was not till the Act of 1918 that universal education from fourteen to eighteen—the years which the children of the wealthy had throughout the nineteenth century spent at a public school—was brought into sight.

Here then the work of the preceding century has reached a definite landmark. The history of twentieth century education will not naturally fall into two divisions. That of the nineteenth century does. In the one story the universities are the centre from which activity radiated. In one direction it spread to the old public schools and from them to the newer public schools and the grammar schools; in a second direction it supplied the driving power for adult education by means of working men's colleges, extension lectures, and finally tutorial classes; in a third it was converted into a demand for modern universities and university colleges, which in their turn required new types of school, the Welsh county schools and the municipal secondary schools, to prepare their future students. This is the story of which the present volume tries to give an outline. The other story starts with the monitorial schools; it shows the elementary leaving-age rising slowly from ten to fourteen, till finally a demand is created for a further education of their pupils. In Wales the Intermediate Education Act of 1889, in England the Act of 1902, link the two systems of influence together.

The following pages deal only with England and Wales. Though foreign education exercised considerable influence in this country, the nineteenth century was far more national than the sixteenth. The English Renaissance represented the effect of a self-conscious civilisation on a people which felt the inferiority of its own culture, whereas in the nineteenth century Englishmen, in consequence of their industrial supremacy, were led to an undue depreciation of other nations. English education in Tudor times can only be treated as a branch of the tree whose roots were in Italy: from whatever quarter the seed of our nineteenth century education was brought, it had a life which was all its own. Moreover, the translation of ideas into practice followed quite different lines in England and abroad. In France and Germany educational systems were created by the State; in England institutions grew up with a minimum of State intervention. Comparative education is a study of the greatest importance, but it is based on the recognition of a difference in educational development in different countries rather than on an attempt to find a unity between them.

Though English higher education is most conveniently discussed by itself, it is not for a moment suggested that educational thought can be based on anything less than a study of all forms of education both here and abroad. At present we fear that the majority of men are of necessity restricted, as regards first-hand knowledge, to some one particular type even of secondary or higher education. Other types may be known through returns, blue-books, and discussions; but there is something sadly unreal about such an acquaintance. There is a strong reason for a more comprehensive view; it is this. Continental systems are in their very nature highly stratified; English policy seeks to avoid stratification. But stratification is with us all the same; it is a legacy of the past. The more the origin and growth of different types of educational institution are known to the alumni of other types, the more will this isolation tend to disappear. They will soon discover that, however segregated were the children of different classes in the nineteenth century, influences spread from one class to another in the most astonishing manner. The spread of games from the public schools to the nation is no isolated instance. Underfeeding was as marked at Eton as in Mr Squeers's school; to-day it would be impossible anywhere. Artisans studied science before Cambridge undergraduates knew of it; now Cambridge is in the forefront of scientific study. The educational ideals of the twentieth century will have their root in those of the nineteenth, but the good features which in the nineteenth century were peculiar to specific types of institution will in the twentieth century tend to become the common property of all. The teachers of fifty years hence will not trace back their spiritual pedigrees separately to Arnold or to Huxley, to F. D. Maurice or to Ruskin; they will be descended from them all.

R. L. A.

February, 1921.

CONTENTS

TABLES OF DATES

SOME PROMINENT HEADMASTERS

Goddard, Winchester ... 1796–1809
Samuel Butler, Shrewsbury 1798–1836
Keate, Eton 1809–1834
Russell, Charterhouse ... 1818–1832
Arnold, Rugby 1827–1842
Hawtrey, Eton 1834–1852
Moberley, Winchester ... 1835–1866
Prince Lee, Birmingham ... 1837–1848
Vaughan, Harrow ... 1845–1859
Cotton, Marlborough ... 1851–1858
Thring, Uppingham ... 1853–1887
Pears, Repton 1854–1874
Bradley, Marlborough ... 1858–1870
Benson, Wellington ... 1859–1868
A. G. Butler, Haileybury... 1861–1867
Philpotts, Bedford ... 1862–1874
Percival, Clifton 1862–1878
Almond, Loretto (full time) 1862–1883
Howson, Gresham's ... 1900–1919

Miss Buss 1850
Miss Beale 1858

FOUNDATIONS OF SCHOOLS AND COLLEGES

1807 Mill Hill School.
1823 Mechanics' Institutes.
1827 University College, London.
1828 King's College, London.
1831 Durham University.
1834 Liverpool Mechanics' Institute.
1836 London University.
1841 Cheltenham College.
1843 Marlborough College.
1844 Rossall School.
1847 Queen's and Bedford [Women's] Colleges
1848 Williams's Secular School.
1851 Owens College, Manchester.
1853 Cheltenham Ladies' College.
1854 Working Men's College.

1862 Malvern College.
1869 Hitchin College for Women.
1872 First higher grade school.
1872 Girls' Public Day School Company.
1872 Aberystwyth College.
1873 Girton College.
1874 Yorkshire College, Leeds.
1875 Newnham College.
1877 Maria Grey Training College.
1879 Oxford women's colleges.
1879 Camden Road Girls' School.
1880 Victoria University.
1880 City and Guilds Institute.
1880 Mason College, Birmingham.
1880 Regent Street Polytechnic.
1883 Cardiff College.
1884 Bangor College.
1884 Toynbee Hall.
1890 University Training Departments.
1893 University of Wales.
1900 London University reorganised.
1900 Birmingham University.
1903 Victoria University defederalised.
1905 Sheffield University.
1907 Workers' Educational Association.
1909 Bristol University.

BOOKS WHICH INFLUENCED EDUCATION

1798 Edgeworth, *Practical Education.*
1810 Copleston's defence of Oxford against the *Edinburgh Review*
1822 The Hills' book on self-government in schools.
1827 George Combe begins writing.
1830 Attack on public schools in *Edinburgh Review.*
1835 Whewell on reform of Cambridge.
1839 Dickens, *Nicholas Nickleby.*
1849 Phillips's book on *Welsh Education.*
1852 Newman, *Idea of a University.*
1853 Ruskin, *Stones of Venice.*
1854 Huxley, *Educational Value of the Natural History Sciences.*
1857 Thomas Hughes, *Tom Brown's Schooldays.*
1859–1861 Herbert Spencer, *Education.*
1867 Farrar, *Essays on a Liberal Education.*
1868 R. H. Quick, *Educational Reformers.*
1869 Matthew Arnold, *Culture and Anarchy.*
1883 Thring, *Theory and Practice of Teaching.*
1901 Report of British Association on teaching of geometry.

LEGISLATION AND STATE ACTION

1818–1837 Brougham Commission.
1849–1853 Chichester Commission.
1850 Royal Commissions on Oxford and Cambridge started.
1851 School of Mines founded.
1853 Science and Art Department, South Kensington.
1853 Charitable Trusts Act.
1854 Oxford University Act.
1856 Cambridge University Act.
1859 Science grants reorganised.
1867 Public Schools Commission, report.
1868 Public Schools Act.
1868 Schools Inquiry Commission, report.
1869 Endowed Schools Act.
1871 Universities Test Act.
1872 Reorganisation of Schools of Science.
1873 Second University Commission, report.
1875 Devonshire Commission on Science, report.
1877 Second University Act.
1884 Technical Education Commission, report.
1889 Welsh Intermediate Education Act.
1889 Technical Instruction Act.
1895 Bryce Commission on Secondary Education, report.
1899 Board of Education Act.
1902 Education Act (county and municipal schools).
1907 Free place system required in grant-earning schools.
1912 Teachers' Register instituted.
1918 Fisher's Education Act.

OTHER EDUCATIONAL EVENTS

1801 New Examination system at Oxford.
1805 Leeds Grammar School case.
1831 British Association founded.
1833 Tractarian movement at Oxford.
1848 Christian Socialist movement.
1851 New triposes instituted at Cambridge.
1853 Science and history honours schools at Oxford.
1858 London degrees given purely on examination.
1858 Cambridge Local Examinations started.
1863 Unofficial use of Local Examinations for girls.
1873 University Extension lectures recognised.
1873 Women admitted to tripos examinations.
1878 New London charter to give women degrees.
1892 Women admitted to degrees of Scottish Universities.
1897 Central Welsh Board instituted.

CHAPTER I

THE DAWN

ENGLISH education is very old—older than the State, older than every national institution save the Church. Yet so completely had its antiquity been forgotten that, till a few years ago, it was believed to go back only to the Renaissance. Mr Leach has changed all this: we now know that the supply of grammar schools was greater, in proportion to the population, in the Middle Ages than at any subsequent period up to the Education Act of 1902. The past has come to its own again; and there is some danger that we may under-rate the work of more recent times. Institutions are not like plants which grow from a seed into a pre-determined shape: they are transformed into something radically different by a creative period, and such a period was the nineteenth century. The mediaeval State did not spontaneously develop into modern democracy, but was reshaped by the ideas of the French Revolution: mediaeval religion did not evolve into the beliefs held by the majority of Englishmen to-day, as Newman claimed that it developed into modern Romanism, merely by making explicit what had previously been implicit. Both State and Church have been changed by the influence of new ideas; and these new ideas have been due to original thinkers, to the influence of other nations, and to the effects of changes in one compartment of life upon another. So it has been with education. If we took away either from present-day educational ideals or from their realisation in schools and universities all that is due to influences which have become operative since 1789, how little would be left as an inheritance to the twentieth century from the eighteenth! A mere enumeration of these modern influences would be a long task. Changes in political and religious thought, changes in social life and

aspirations; the French Revolution and the Liberal movement; Evangelicalism, the Oxford movement, and Broad
Church views; the discoveries of modern science; the
Industrial Revolution, and the revolution in means of communication; the fuller understanding of ancient thought,
the growth of national self-consciousness, and the altered
outlook on the universe created by modern geology and
biology; the increasing knowledge of hygienic and psychological principles; a fuller consciousness both of the value
of the individual and of the possibilities of the State:—all
these influences have been brought to bear on education
either for the first time or with increased force during the
last hundred and thirty years.

There is a peculiar difficulty in studying a recent period
that these broad influences may elude our grasp. We may
lose the wood in the trees. Particular events, acts of
parliament, prominent individuals, may attract our attention too much. The very nearness of the period makes the
details stand out too closely; we may fail to appreciate the
general structure of the building. But it is only by recognising the broad influences that we are able to interpret
as well as to know past events, and it is only by interpretation that we can use the past as a guide to the future.

This danger of laying over-much stress on events which
can be named and dated is particularly insidious in the
present case because it tends to put State action in the
forefront of the changes which have taken place in education during the last century. State action is now peculiarly
in favour; and large numbers of persons are brought into
contact with education as holders of administrative posts
or as members of administrative committees. They are
therefore inclined to look at education as a machine built
by the State and driven by the bodies controlling local
government. The history of education, provided it be truly
the history of education and not the history of educational
legislation, should help to rectify any such one-sided view.
It should reveal the vitalising forces which were the true
source of educational energy; it should endeavour to
establish the extent to which education has been affected

by the work of individual men and women; it should show
by what forces legislators and administrators have been
driven.

A study of English higher education in the nineteenth
century involves then keeping the balance even between
three kinds of topic; intellectual and social movements
which have affected education, the work of individual
endeavour, and the action of the State. Three of the
chapters which follow take great movements as their
starting-point. Two[1] of them are concerned with the intellectual movements which affected the two great divisions
of study, the humanities and the natural sciences; one[2]
deals with movements which are more of a social character.
The humanistic movement in education which revived the
older universities and schools was a meeting-point of the
new political, religious, and aesthetic enthusiasms of the
early part of the century; the scientific movement in
education which created new subjects of study and new
institutions to teach them was the outcome of the great
advances in science itself. The social movements produce
their effect later, and we have grouped them round the
well-known names of Matthew Arnold, Ruskin, Maurice,
and Kingsley. In the early part of the period these movements were brought to bear on education almost entirely
by the creative genius of individuals; and four chapters
are devoted mainly, but not entirely, to their work. In
each case one or two individuals have been peculiarly
originators, though many persons have taken a share in
the building. These chapters[3] deal with the revival of the
public schools in the thirties and forties, the creation of
new types, the work of individual endeavour in boys'
schools after the middle of the century, and the reform of
girls' and women's education. Finally the part played by
the State is examined in two chapters[4], of which one deals
with the reform of old institutions as a result of the Royal
Commissions which sat during the fifties and sixties, and
the other with the great extension of educational facilities

[1] chs. II, v.   [2] ch. VII.
[3] chs. III, IV, VIII, IX.   [4] chs. VI, XII.

by more recent legislation: and another chapter[1], on popular and technical education, is largely of the same character[2].

It may be well to indicate at the beginning the part which the reader will probably judge at the end that each of these three factors has played. The State cannot create ideas, and rarely has it been the first agency to realise them in concrete institutions. Its main function has been to multiply copies of the successful experiments which have been made by individuals. Though a State official who was also a creative genius in educational matters is conceivable, no example can be produced from English history during the nineteenth century[3]. The creative work of devising new types of educational institution, new curricula, and new methods of teaching and government has been mainly the work of individuals, such as Birkbeck the founder of Mechanics' Institutes, Maurice the author of the Working Men's College, Hogg the originator of polytechnics, Thomas Arnold who discovered how the elder boys could transmit the headmaster's influence to the younger, Thring who discovered how the aesthetic and practical subjects could be made a vehicle of education, or Miss Beale the creator of the first public school for girls[4]. State-created institutions have been either copies or failures[5]. But the individuals who built up the institutions have been largely inspired by ideas which originated outside the scholastic circle; hence such men as Ruskin or

[1] ch. x.

[2] The chapters on Welsh education (xi) and on changes in curriculum and method do not fall under any of the three headings.

[3] Matthew Arnold seems to "prove the rule." He was an educational official and he was a great force in changing educational ideals: but he exercised his main influence not through what he did as an inspector, but by his leisure occupation as a literary critic!

[4] If the volume took in elementary education, we should add the names of Robert Owen, Dr Barnardo and Baden-Powell (Froebel and Montessori being foreigners).

[5] Had it not been for "schools of science" the last two words could be omitted, as there is nothing distinctive in any other State-created institution.

Huxley claim as large a part in the history of education
as the great teachers or founders of schools and colleges.

Probably the nearest approach which the State has
made to originality in the sphere of education is to be
found in the activities of the various Royal Commissions.
Not even the most pronounced individualist would deny
the capacity of the State to choose a number of the most
thoughtful men in the country, to induce them for a limited
time to devote their concentrated attention to a particular
topic, and to give them facilities for collecting all available
evidence and for coming into contact with all opinions
worth having. It is probable too that these bodies of
enquirers reached conclusions in their corporate capacity
which no single member would have attained for himself.
But it must be remembered that such conclusions only
crystallised the thought of half-a-century on the problems
concerned; and that their effect was produced quite as
much by their influence on public opinion and through
the subsequent action of individuals as through the legislative and administrative changes to which they gave rise.

*   *   *   *   *   *   *

A comprehensive glance at the state of British universities and secondary schools between 1789 and 1815
reveals one outstanding feature. They do not reflect any
ideals of their own age. No new driving power had come
to them for a century and a half. To understand them we
have to go back to the Renaissance. As early as the first
half of the seventeenth century there had come a loss of
faith in the educational ideals of classical humanism; by
the second half of that century intellectual and moral
enthusiasm was exhausted; and low-water mark was
reached in the middle of the eighteenth century. After
that point moral energy was gathering power, but it was
still unable to cope with the tremendous force of inertia.
Existing higher education, then, at the beginning of the
nineteenth century represented tradition. It was there
because it had been there for two centuries and no one had
arisen to alter it.

We will consider the state of the universities first. In the days of Queen Elizabeth they seemed about to enter on a period of new vigour. These hopes were not destined to be fulfilled. Many explanations have been given. Controversialists[1] in the first half of the nineteenth century found the reason in the changes which took place in their constitution, by which the powers hitherto exercised by the whole body of resident masters of arts were transferred to a council of heads of colleges. Others, anxious to point a moral to modern times, have explained it as due to State intervention. The dissipation of energy in religious controversies has been put forward with a greater show of probability as the reason. None of these explanations appears to go to the root of the matter. A system of studies which possessed an inherent vitality should have been able to offer a more vigorous resistance to external circumstances. A fervid belief in the worth of classical pursuits would not have allowed itself to be overwhelmed by religious quarrels. We are more likely therefore to find the true explanation of the stagnation which crept over the English universities in some lack of stimulating power in the new curriculum. Two features give us the clue. The first is the *exclusiveness* of humanism. Its literary ideal appealed only to the few. In spite of its claims to be a guide of life, it never touched the hearts of Englishmen. It did not, like the older Scholasticism, offer a rational explanation of the universe which would support their religion. Content was entirely subordinate to form. There was no study of ancient history. Classical scholarship advanced, but it was left to the Germans of the late eighteenth century to discover the true significance of Greek literature. The second feature is the character of post-Renaissance philosophy. The universities, when they abandoned Scholasticism, did not, as a thorough-going humanism might have done, abandon philosophy. Nor did they even give up Aristotle: for it was a canon of Renaissance teaching that all knowledge worth acquiring

[1] *E.g.* Sir William Hamilton whose articles are collected in his *Discussions*, 1852.

was contained in the ancient writers. They merely substituted the genuine Aristotle for scholastic Aristotelianism.
The recognition of a single writer as the infallible standard
of philosophic, and for a time even of scientific, truth
substituted a more rigid authority for that measure of
originality which, within fixed limits, stimulated the
student of scholastic philosophy. The Middle Ages trained
the undergraduate in original speculation, though they
forbade him to use the power which they had given him;
the Renaissance Aristotle dulled his mind by bidding him
blindly accept the written text. A revival could only come
with a new inspiration.

The loss of intellectual interests made the way easy for
a lowering of the moral tone. The "poor scholar" had
nothing to attract him to the university. His place was
taken by the sons of the aristocracy whose interest in
study was small. In the Middle Ages the nobility had been
the exception, middle class students abounded, and the
children of the labourer were not unknown. In the course
of the eighteenth century, the poor boy came to be regarded
as a tolerated addition: he was often a "servitor," and was
bitterly conscious of being among his social superiors. The
land-owning class were regarded as the natural denizens.
They entered the university, not to feed on solid intellectual
food, but to enjoy a costly luxury. While they were there,
they naturally did what other young men of their class
were doing elsewhere. So far from being formed by the
ethos of the university, they brought it its ethos. It was
merely the atmosphere of the London coffee-house transferred to Oxford or Cambridge. Extravagance, debt,
drunkenness, gambling, and an absurd attention to dress
became the special forms of irregularity favoured by the
gentlemen commoners, whose ranks were swollen by the
nouveaux riches at the end of the century. Even fellows
of colleges spent much of their time in the tavern.
Work ceased at dinner time, which meant eleven o'clock
at the beginning of the century, and two or three hours
later at the end. By the middle of the century the interest in his pupils which the better type of tutor still

displayed in the days of Whitefield and Johnson had vanished.

The intellectual decadence was greater at Oxford than at Cambridge. Vicesimus Knox's account of the tests for the Oxford degree is well-known[1]. In form they were a combination of the mediaeval disputation and an oral examination. There were three stages: the first constituted the candidates "sophs," the second conferred the bachelor's degree, and the third the master's. For the sophomore test two candidates were paired off as "opponent" and "respondent" in a disputation. The arguments, Knox tells us, "consisted of foolish syllogisms on foolish subjects" of which the candidate knew nothing, "handed down from generation to generation on long slips of paper." Armed with these the two disputants betook themselves to a "large dusty room" where "not once in a hundred times does any officer enter; and, if he does, he hears one syllogism or two and then makes a bow and departs." For the rest of the time the candidates read a novel or carved their names on the desks. Passing was a matter of course. The bachelor's degree involved a *viva voce* examination; but this was conducted by three masters of arts of the candidate's own choice, and it was "considered good management to get acquainted with two or three jolly young masters of arts and to supply them with port previous to the examination." It was indeed usual to obtain little cram-books containing "forty or fifty" traditional questions on each subject and to spend three or four days in memorising them, and there was a perfunctory construe of a passage from a classical author; but the turning of familiar English phrases into Latin which ended the proceedings seems merely to have fulfilled the rôle of the satyric play which followed an Athenian trilogy. "I have known," says Knox, "the questions to consist of an enquiry into the pedigree of a race-horse." The test for the master's degree involved both a disputation and an examination, which were no better than those at the earlier stages, as well as a "declamation." Originally the M.A. degree had

[1] *Essays, Moral and Literary*, vol. i, Essay 77.

been at the same time a license and an obligation to teach
within the university, and the declamation was the proof
of the candidate's ability to lecture. In Knox's day, however, "it was always called a wall lecture, because the
lecturer had no other audience than the walls," though he
"gets a sheet or two of Latin from some old book" to read
should the proctor come in. Knox is clearly no favourable
critic, but he is supported by the evidence of men of such
different standpoints as Gibbon, Adam Smith, Malmesbury,
and Eldon, while no effective defence has ever been put
forward. If we wish to picture Oxford in the year when
George III ascended the throne, we must imagine a
university in which professors had ceased to lecture, where
tutors regarded an enquiring student as a nuisance, and
where work was the last thing expected.

Cambridge never sank quite so low as Oxford, and the
revival came earlier. The causes of decay were the same;
but Cambridge received a stimulus from the genius of
Newton which Oxford lacked. It may be observed in
passing that the call of Bacon, the herald of experimental
science, did not seriously affect either university; for the
non-mathematical sciences had no point of contact with
the old curriculum, nor did they satisfy the demand for
logical certainty, to which four centuries of training in
dialectic had habituated the academic mind. But mathematics was part of the old quadrivium, and its development
and application supplied just that stimulus which was
suited to the time. It proceeded on strict syllogistic lines,
yet it was progressive and yielded new truths; further, it
gave a comprehensive explanation of the material order
of the universe through astronomy, which men had in
different directions been long seeking. Unfortunately
Newton lived in a slack age and three-quarters of a century
was needed to reveal the full force of the new driving
power. But by the second half of the eighteenth century
mathematics was established as the dominant study in
Cambridge. This necessitated the substitution of a new
type of exercise for the old disputation and between 1766
and 1833 the modern type of written examination was

gradually evolved. In 1800 Oxford adopted the same kind
of test, and the revival of the university was believed to
date from that event. Later, the written examination,
which originated simply as the easiest means of testing
the power of solving mathematical problems, was everywhere adopted as an educational panacea.

Since the system was long regarded, not merely as a sign
of returning life, but as its cause, it is desirable to trace its
growth a little more fully. Dr Jebb of Trinity describes it
as it existed in 1772[1]. Disputation and examination were
still combined, and the latter was mainly oral. The disputations were begun in the second term of the candidate's
last year, when the "moderators," as the examiners were
called, conducted them on five afternoons a week. The
candidates received a fortnight's notice. One acted as
"respondent" and three as "opponents." The respondent
submitted in advance three propositions which he was
prepared to maintain, and read a short Latin thesis on one
of them. He then disputed with his three opponents in
turn, the discussion commencing in strict syllogistic form,
but "sliding into free and unconfined debate" as it proceeded. Marks were recorded, on the strength of which
the candidates were divided into groups for the examination. This was conducted in English. All candidates were
questioned orally on the first six books of Euclid, elementary
algebra, trigonometry, mechanics, hydrostatics, astronomy,
and optics; and "a very superficial knowledge in morality
and metaphysics" was expected, involving a few questions
on Locke, Butler, or Clarke. The colleges took a share in
the examination, each appointing one of its tutors as
"father." The university moderators and the college
fathers met at breakfast and dinner to discuss the merits
of the candidates, the best of whom were eventually
divided into three classes. The best twenty-eight usually
formed the first two classes, Wranglers and Senior Optimes,
and the next twelve the Junior Optimes. The system was
obviously not the farce which Knox describes at Oxford;

[1] Whewell, *A Liberal Education*, Part I, chapter 3, sect. 1, §§ 192–
209.

but it must be borne in mind how small a part of the university was included in the list of forty candidates who were awarded honours and how small was the ground covered in two years almost exclusively devoted to mathematical study. Moreover Jebb goes on to tell us that "so alarming is the apprehension" of this half-year "that the student frequently seeks to avoid the difficulty or disgrace by commencing fellow-commoner"; for in those days social position and higher fees were officially recognised as entitling to easier examinations!

Changes were inevitable. Owing to the difficulty of combining the marks for the disputations with those for the examination, it was soon found that the candidate's place in the class-list was in fact determined almost solely by the examination; and the importance of problems in mathematical work emphasised the written part of the examination. It was not, however, till 1838 that the division of candidates into groups on the strength of the disputations and the setting of different questions to these groups were finally abandoned; and the disputations and the *viva voce* examination maintained a moribund existence for a little longer.

The revival at Oxford began during the last thirty years of the eighteenth century. An energetic type of college tutor once more arose[1], and Gibbon[2] assures us that learning had once more "become a fashion." To encourage work among the undergraduates, three heads of colleges, Cyril Jackson, dean of Christ Church (1783–1809), John Parsons, master of Balliol (1798–1813), and John Eveleigh, provost of Oriel (1781–1814), carried the "new examination statute," which introduced a genuine examination for all candidates and the award of honours to the most successful, as at Cambridge. Conservative opposition was allayed by making the change at first purely optional; but the success of the new system was in a few years so obvious that it was made compulsory without a struggle, and there was

[1] This is shown by Godley, *Oxford in the Eighteenth Century*, pp. 213–215.
[2] *Autobiography*, p. 57 ("World's Classics").

a tremendous rush of candidates to take their degrees before the old system finally disappeared. At Oxford classics naturally held the premier place in the examination, with mathematics as second. The *viva voce* examination, being more suited to classics than to mathematics, was for a long time of great importance and it has never entirely vanished. A few more years saw the introduction of three classes, as at Cambridge, the separation of classical and mathematical honours, and the institution of separate examinations for pass candidates. Up to our own day the view has generally prevailed that the revival of serious study is to be mainly attributed to the new statute: yet, great though its influence undoubtedly was, it would have been powerless but for the more serious attitude to life which, under the influence of the religious revival and the struggle with Napoleon, was spreading among the whole of English society. It is doubtful too whether the revival of classical studies would have been permanent had they not been found to have, in their political and philosophical bearings, a close relation to modern life which has quite transformed the studies of the school of *Litterae humaniores*. The rise of this newer humanism will form the topic of the next chapter.

The revival of intellectual life in the universities was followed by a revival in some of the larger public schools which gradually spread. The history of these few schools is therefore for the moment the main thread of the history of secondary education.

The eighteenth century is an obscure period in the history of English schools; but, by comparing their condition at its close with their condition in the middle of the seventeenth century, we can see that many changes had taken place. Nevertheless, as in the case of the universities, the basis of education in the schools was still the curriculum of the Renaissance.

Half of the mediaeval grammar schools perished in the troublous times of the Reformation, but through the generosity of founders the loss was made good in the reign of Queen Elizabeth. With a few exceptions, such as Shrewsbury, these schools, though numerous, were quite small, and the staff regularly consisted of two only, the schoolmaster who took the upper half of the school, and the usher who took the lower. All were day schools except Eton and Winchester: the boys from the country districts lodged in the town. The distinction between the great public schools and the smaller grammar schools had not yet arisen.

Their decline probably set in with the Restoration. Locke takes it for granted that to send a boy to school is "to sacrifice his innocency to the attaining of confidence and some little drill of bustling for himself among others, by his conversation with ill-bred and vicious boys," and declares it to be wholly impossible for a master to supervise "three or four score boys lodged up and down[1]." As time went on, matters grew worse. The bulk of the grammar schools decayed; some disappeared altogether. Governing bodies became lethargic; in some cases they even mis-appropriated the funds which they were appointed to guard; parents no longer showed the old zeal for educa-tion; the universities were no goal to which boys eagerly pressed, nor did they send forth a supply of capable teachers.

By the time when we next have much information on English secondary schools, at the close of the eighteenth century, the distinction between the "public schools" and the rest of the grammar schools is well established. The public schools were merely those of the grammar schools which had increased in numbers and prestige while the rest declined. Two changes had occurred which served to differentiate them; they had increased the numbers of their staff, and they had become boarding-schools. The first of these changes cannot be traced clearly, as it is not usually recorded in the minutes of governing bodies. It seems to have been regarded as a private arrangement of the head-master for the performance of the work for which he alone was responsible to the governors; hence the existing custom

[1] *Thoughts concerning Education*, § 70.

in these schools by which the appointment and dismissal
of assistant masters rest with the headmaster alone. The
boarding system at first took the form of houses kept by
"dominies" and "dames," who were not members of the
teaching staff; headmasters began to keep houses before
their assistants were encouraged to do so. The new system
may well have arisen from a desire to escape from the
laxity described by Locke; but it would be facilitated by
the coming of the stage coach and improvements in the
roads. If it was intended to improve the tone of schools, it
was a terrible failure. It exaggerated the evils, though it
concealed them. Unruly conduct could no longer occur in
the streets where it could be seen; but the herding together
of forty or fifty boys with a low moral tone in barracks
without proper supervision made it impossible for any to
escape the bad influence. The resulting evils will be considered when we come to the attempts of the great reforming headmasters to combat them.

The Public Schools Commission in the middle of the
nineteenth century recognised nine public schools—Eton,
Winchester, Westminster, Shrewsbury, Harrow, Charterhouse, Rugby, St Paul's, and Merchant Taylors'. The last
two were still day-schools, and the number is in consequence usually taken as seven. Of the nine, four were in
London and three comparatively near. Before describing
their common features it may be well to explain briefly
how each of them attained its position.

Eton and Winchester, unlike the others, were boarding-
schools from their foundation. William of Wykeham, in
founding Winchester and New College, Oxford, intended
them to be a new departure, a school and a college on
a larger scale than any which were then in existence.
Henry VI, the royal founder of Eton and King's College,
Cambridge, followed William's lines. In both cases, though
the free scholars were the true foundation, a limited number
of the sons of the aristocracy were from the first to be
admitted as paying boarders: for both founders wished to
encourage the novel desire for book-learning among the
baronial and knightly class. In both cases these boys came

to outnumber the foundation scholars, and the later character of the schools was thus established.

Eton, situated close to the royal residence of Windsor, and zealously patronised by monarchs like Elizabeth, gradually rose almost to the position of a national institution. Such it must have been when Gray wrote his Ode, though its Toryism rendered it, like Oxford, suspect to the Hanoverian kings and their Whig ministers. Towards the end of the eighteenth century it was exercising a direct influence over other schools. James (1778–1794) developed Rugby on Etonian lines, and Butler (1798–1836) transplanted many Etonian institutions from Rugby to Shrewsbury. James's account of Eton, written in 1766, and rendered accessible in Maxwell Lyte's *History of Eton College*, is almost the only living document which gives us a real insight into the school life of the eighteenth century.

Winchester originally not only took its foundationers and ten commensales (young aristocrats), but also dayboys. Leach believes that the day-boys disappeared with the foundation of a rival school by a seceding usher in 1630. The patronage of Charles II emphasised the aristocratic side; new buildings were erected in 1689; and, after a temporary decline due to its high Toryism, it revived under Burton (1724–1766), under whom its numbers reached 204 and its aristocratic character became more pronounced. Dames' houses never existed at Winchester, and the numbers had to be restricted through lack of room in the school itself. From 1775 to 1793 it passed through troublous times and furnishes several instances of the school rebellions which marked that period. The rule of Goddard (1796–1809) revived it, and his experiments in self-government formed the model on which his more famous pupil Thomas Arnold built his system at Rugby.

Westminster in its original intention approximated more nearly to Eton and Winchester than did any of the others. It was refounded in 1560 for forty foundationers who were boarders and for the day-boys of the city, as well as for a few "pensioners" (commensales). The Latin play which it still preserves was a common feature of Elizabethan schools. Its floruit was in the middle of the seventeenth century under its famous headmaster Busby (1640–1695). Dames' houses after the Eton model appear early in the eighteenth century. But it declined to a hundred pupils at the close of the century and did not revive till the appointment of Liddell in 1848.

Shrewsbury was the great school of Elizabeth's reign and of the early seventeenth century, when it contained no less than four hundred pupils. But from the middle of that century it declined, and was only restored by a change in its constitution which was effected by an act of parliament in 1798. The appointment of Samuel Butler (1798–1836) to the headmastership made it for a time a model which other schools followed in the matter of classical teaching, and old Salopians introduced Butler's methods even into Eton.

Harrow, opened in 1615, was intended by its founder purely as a local grammar school for the "poor boys" of the parish, and entered on its career in humble fashion with only thirty boys. But House (1669–1685), an Etonian, set to work to remodel it on Eton lines; dames' houses appear; the proximity to London placed it in an advantageous position; and finally it received the patronage of the Whig nobility who distrusted the Toryism of Eton and Winchester. After a short period of eclipse its position was consolidated by Thackeray (appointed 1746), and the famous classical scholar Dr Parr was one of its ushers. A second period of decline, which set in about 1805, removes it from importance during the great reforming epoch, and it only recovered with the headmastership of Vaughan (1844), who introduced the ideas of Thomas Arnold.

Charterhouse (1611) was intended for foundationers only. The almshouse attached was no peculiar feature, though it has been rendered more familiar than its fellows by the genius of Thackeray.

Rugby (1567) was the last of the seven to win its position. Its founder, Laurence Sheriff, left its endowment in the form of land just outside London. In course of time the

houses extended over these lands, which were let on long
leases. These leases began to fall in during the latter half
of the eighteenth century, and the school suddenly found
itself wealthy. James (1778–1799), its Etonian headmaster,
seized the opportunity, and raised the numbers from 52
to 245. It was James and not Arnold who made Rugby
large and famous; to Arnold was left the greater task of
catching the popular imagination by a picture of an
idealised Rugby which was the pattern for three generations
of great headmasters in other schools.

It may be gathered that there was much mutual influence between these schools. Eton was the model for
James's Rugby, this in its turn for Butler's Shrewsbury,
and Shrewsbury repaid its debt to Eton by the influence
of Butler's pupils. Goddard's Winchester inspired Arnold,
and Arnold's Rugby had an even closer influence on
Harrow, which at an earlier time had been influenced by
Eton. But the influence of these schools was soon not to
be confined to their own circle. From 1840 onwards new
schools sprang up on the same lines; the Arnold tradition
shaped Cheltenham, Marlborough, Haileybury and many
others; and the torch was subsequently handed on till it
reached all the schools which were given new life by the
Endowed Schools Act. It is this which renders the reform
of the public schools so important. The smaller grammar
schools, important as they had been in the past, had
decayed, and their new vigour came to them from the
public schools half a century later. History is concerned
with the germs from which proceeded future growth, not
with the vestiges of decay. For this reason we are not
here concerned with the history of the Nonconformist
Academies, which probably gave the best education that
was known in the eighteenth century: for they underwent
a sudden eclipse and hardly lasted into the new century.

The history of the public schools during the thirty years
which preceded Queen Victoria's accession enables us to
trace the origins of our present secondary school tradition.
The gross evils of this period determined the lines on which
the great headmasters of the next generation had to

proceed in their reforming efforts. The genius of the reformers lay in diagnosing the causes of evil and turning many of them into means of good—indeed into instruments for destroying others which were irredeemably bad. We will begin with the intellectual side and glance at the curriculum of Eton as described by James[1], which, with a little alteration, formed the curriculum of Rugby under James and of Shrewsbury under Butler.

The work of the sixth and fifth forms, which were taken together by the headmaster, gives the best indication of the standard which a classical school of those days aimed at. There were ten construing lessons in a full week: Homer's *Iliad*, 35 lines, two; Lucian, 40 lines, two; Vergil's *Aeneid*, 30 lines, two; *Scriptores Romani*, 40 lines, two; *Poetae Graeci*, 35 lines, one; Horace (hexameters), 60 lines, one; and seven repetition lessons, viz. in the pieces translated from Homer, Vergil, Horace, and the Greek poets, and in the Greek Testament (one) and a book of Latin selections (two). Horace's *Odes* and Greek plays were substituted for some of the other books during a part of the year. Three compositions were written each week, an original Latin theme, a set of Latin elegiacs, and for the sixth a set of Greek iambics or for the fifth of Latin lyrics. Declamations and speeches came at the end of term. This syllabus remained substantially unchanged throughout the long headmastership of Dr Keate (1809–1834); for except that a selection of *Scriptores Graeci* had been added to Lucian, who was till then the only Greek prose-writer read, and that the hours seem to be slightly fewer, it is the syllabus attacked by the *Edinburgh Review*[2] in 1830. James's scheme[3] contains all the Eton writers along with Cicero, Demosthenes, and Juvenal; the Homer and Vergil are read in selections; and there is one hour's history (biblical, classical, and English in turn), and one hour either of Milton or of mathematics. The compositions are the same, but only a few boys took iambics, which were so recent an

[1] Lyte, *History of Eton College*, pp. 319–324.
[2] Vol. LI, No. 101, Article 3.
[3] Butler, *Life and Letters of Dr Samuel Butler*, ch. 3.

innovation that Walter Savage Landor was under the belief that he was in the first batch of boys in any school to do them[1]. Even after Butler had been more than twenty years at Shrewsbury, Tacitus was the only addition[2].

As regards the work of the lower forms at Eton, the first did nothing but Latin grammar; the second the Latin Testament, and catechism, and Phaedrus; the next form began Greek and read Latin selections; the fourth took Ovid, Aesop, Caesar, Terence, Latin selections, and Greek Testament; the Remove did Vergil, Horace's *Odes*, Pomponius Mela, Cornelius Nepos, and the *Poetae Graeci*. The younger boys did some writing and arithmetic, and some of the fifth took geography and algebra as extras.

The *Edinburgh Review* in 1830 mercilessly analysed the old classical scheme of studies. It was essentially linguistic and stylistic. It did not reveal ancient life or thought. Scarcely an author was read consecutively. The authors were illuminated by no systematic course in ancient history. The choice of prose-writers was bad; Lucian was exalted and Thucydides neglected. "It is doubtful if any boy knows what the Persian and Peloponnesian wars were." The *Poetae Graeci* were not arranged in chronological order; the biographical notes were not enough to put the authors in their proper setting. In short "attention is distracted from the really important lessons of history and philosophy to grammatical and metrical trifling." But, setting aside this cardinal defect, even if the stylistic aim were to be accepted, was the study of selections written in all dialects the way to secure a good Attic (or any other) style? What defence could be made for the text-books? The notes in the editions were suitable neither for beginners nor for more advanced pupils. What purpose was served by the Latin translation of the Greek authors? Why were the grammars written in Latin? Even their contents were bad; yet they were used in other schools owing to the prestige of Eton. They had not kept pace with the "recent improvements of critics and philologists"; "they contain

[1] Rouse, *History of Rugby School*, p. 138.
[2] Butler, *op. cit.* vol. I, pp. 196–197.

much that is useless and much that is inaccurate, they exclude much that is useful"; they are badly arranged; in the Greek grammar "needless rules and technical divisions are multiplied without mercy," till there were ten declensions and thirteen conjugations[1]. The compositions were noticeable for the "triteness of the subjects proposed for the Latin themes and the inattention to the mode of treating them." Had the reviewer condescended to discuss the teaching of the lowest form as well as that of the upper school, he might have found a still stronger ground of criticism in the devotion of a whole year's work to the memorising of accidence before the beginner was allowed to apply his grammar to the simplest Latin sentence. The absence of all non-classical subjects save as despised "extras" was too obvious a point of attack to be missed. Only one possible merit is allowed—the compositions stand out above the rest of the work. The Latin prose is very fair, and the verses may even be good.

Can we endorse this sweeping condemnation? Three questions are involved, (1) the almost entire confinement of studies to classics, (2) the purely stylistic aim in teaching classics, and (3) the effectiveness of the teaching in attaining the stylistic aim.

Two lines of defence are conceivable under the first heading. The first is that the schools were bound to confine their teaching to classics by their foundation statutes. One of the local grammar schools, Leeds, made a mild attempt to substitute modern studies and in consequence in 1805 found itself entangled in a law-suit, in which Lord Chancellor Eldon decided that, however desirable the change might be to the community and however much it might be wished by the great majority of parents, it was not the founder's intention and was therefore illegal. To this plea it may be answered that, before the Public Schools Act provided for the revision of founder's statutes, a modicum of mathematics, French, modern history and geography found their way into the regular curriculum of several of the public schools and that no one brought an

[1] As against three and two respectively in modern grammars.

action against them. The second plea is more forcible. No methods had been found of teaching most of the newer subjects save as mere memory work. As taught in the bulk of private schools and girls' schools, they were value-less. Making out the meaning of an author or writing a Latin prose at least involved real mental activity on the part of the pupils: memorising dates and lists of capes did not. But, valid as this argument is against most of the "modern" subjects, it fails against mathematics, which already fulfilled all the requirements of a good school subject. Cambridge sent out a plentiful supply of graduates who could have taught the subject as well as classics was taught. The pupils had an opportunity for using the mathematics which they learned at school in their subse-quent university course. In view of these facts we can only conclude that the schools merely succumbed to the weight of inertia; and the generation which failed to stimulate them must itself share the blame.

The case is somewhat different with the second charge. The historical, political, and philosophical value of the ancient writers had to be discovered before it could be utilised in teaching. Up to 1800 the best exponents of classics were still cast in the scholarly mould of Bentley and Porson. The literary criticism of Wolf, the artistic criticism of Lessing, the insight of Goethe, the historical criticism of Niebuhr, had to wake echoes in the English universities before they could produce an effect on the teaching in English schools. The Reviewers were right in raising the question in 1830. A few years earlier there would have been no one capable even of understanding the issue. And almost immediately afterwards we find Arnold adopting these very lines. But the slowness with which he found imitators is a justification of the Edin-burgh attack.

Finally, narrow as was the aim which the schools set before them, can we say that they were successful in accomplishing it? It is here that modern opinion is apt to be a trifle unfair. We may grant all the defects charged against it; the methods at the early stages were of the crudest, and even at the upper stages Butler had almost everything to teach his contemporary headmasters; still, far more was accomplished than we should have anticipated. The public schools were doing better work than the universities. The freshman of those days went up knowing his Vergil and Horace by heart; he could write a fairly polished Latin prose; and, if we admit that even a good versifier is "born, not made," the number is somewhat surprising. We should probably be wrong if we denied the schools a claim to have made the governing classes of those days more civilised by these means. Pitt's House of Commons would have been out of its depth if any speaker had presupposed an understanding of the political or ethical philosophy of Plato or Aristotle, but it was readily moved by humanitarian appeals; and it does not seem unreasonable to attribute its broad human sympathy, its love of stately oratory which appealed to the nobler elements in our nature, and its dawning consciousness of a national mission for the promotion of liberty, in part at least to its familiarity with a great literature. Canning, Peel, and Gladstone, no less than Chatham, Burke, and Pitt, were products of the old classical course.

We have dealt somewhat at length with the purely intellectual side of public school education because it is the hardest side for us who live in the twentieth century to appreciate, not because it is the most important. The other sides can be passed over more quickly at this stage, as it will be necessary to revert to them again in describing how they were remedied.

1. The boarding arrangements, in so far as they were in the hands of the school, as for instance in the case of the "collegers" or foundation scholars at Eton, were bad. The food was insufficient and had to be supplemented privately[1]. There were no private studies, so that opportunity for work was practically confined to the preparation hours[2]. The

[1] Lyte, p. 376. Living persons who were at other schools say the same as to the poorness of the food at a much later date.

[2] Parkin, *Life of Thring*, vol. I, p. 24. On the other hand at Eton, but not elsewhere, a considerable amount of work and general English reading was done with tutors.

dormitories were badly furnished and damp; it is even said that the snow could drift into "Long Chamber[1]." The household work was left to the "fags[2]." There was no place to wash save at the pump. Matters were better in the dames' houses; Gibbon's account of these is quite favourable[3]. The change whereby boarding-houses tended to come into the hands of assistant masters may not therefore always have been a change for the better.

2. Discipline, judged by modern standards, was intolerable. Assistant masters were not expected to take any part in its maintenance out of school hours; and in school they relied on the terror inspired by the head[4]. Constant floggings could maintain some semblance of obedience for a time; then the suppressed discontent would break out in open mutiny. In two cases, at Winchester and at Rugby, these rebellions reached such dimensions that the military had to be called in. No semblance of confidence existed between masters and boys. Keate expected that all boys would lie to him, and took no pains to conceal his belief from them. The elder boys, on whom a modern headmaster most relies, were the ringleaders in insubordination.

3. The moral atmosphere was never good, and was sometimes indescribably bad. "A boy who passed unscathed the ordeal of a Colleger's life must have been gifted in no uncommon degree with purity of mind and strength of will[5]." There was neither influence to encourage good nor supervision to check evil. Save during class hours or private tuition masters saw nothing of their pupils. If a boy had the extreme good fortune to meet neither impurity, drunkenness, gambling, or open profanity, even so he would meet no elevating influence. His life was that of a slave till he grew strong enough to be a tyrant. Then too often the joy of feeling free was intensified by showing that he could bully his weaker schoolfellows.

4. School games were only taking shape during this

---

[1] Lyte, p. 45.   [2] Ib. p. 459.
[3] Autobiography, p. 30 ("World's Classics").
[4] Lyte, p. 408.   [5] Ib. p. 463.

period; no headmaster yet counted them as a means of training character. In James's school-days battledore, tops, hoops, and a host of forgotten games[1] were as recognised relaxations for an Etonian as cricket, football, fives or tennis[2], and hoops at least survived for another fifty years. By 1830, however, natural selection seems to have done its work. In view of these facts the suggestion that the Duke of Wellington's oft-quoted remark referred, not to the games, but to the fights which took place on the "playing fields of Eton" seems plausible.

This brief account is enough to show that two possibilities only existed; either the public schools must be reformed from within, or the whole system must be swept away, as it was swept away in Prussia by Humboldt and Stein. The evils were too deep-rooted to be eradicated merely by administrative action from without. Nothing but the life-work of men who combined great force of will and moral earnestness with consummate tact and the gift of influencing the boys could suffice for the task.

REFERENCES.

L. M. Quiller Couch, *Reminiscences of Oxford by Oxford Men*, 1559–1850, 1892 (a collection of the chief original authorities).
Vicesimus Knox, *Essays, Moral and Literary*, 1778, vol. I, Essay 77.
Edward Gibbon, *Autobiography*, 1796 (ed. Bury in "World's Classics").
Adam Smith, *Wealth of Nations*, 1776, Book V, ch. I, Part 3, Article 2.
A. P. Godley, *Oxford in the Eighteenth Century*, 1908.
W. Whewell, *Of a Liberal Education*, 1850, Part I, ch. III, § I.
A. I. Tillyard, *History of University Reform*, 1913, ch. I.
Sir William Hamilton, *Discussions*, 1852 (reprint of article written 1831).
Sir H. C. Maxwell Lyte, *History of Eton College*, 1877.
William Cowper, *Tirocinium* (attack on public schools), 1784.
S. Butler, *Life and Letters of Dr Samuel Butler*, 1896, chs. 3, 4, 11, 13.
W. H. D. Rouse, *History of Rugby School*, 1909.
Other histories of public schools; see references at end of ch. III.
Edinburgh Review, vol. LI (No. CI), Article 3.

[1] Lyte, p. 328.   [2] "Real" tennis, of course, not lawn tennis.

CHAPTER II

CLASSICAL HUMANISM

THE enlargement of classical studies, whereby to the old idea of "pure scholarship" was added the conception of opening up the life and thought of antiquity as an avenue to the better comprehension of modern problems, was in point of time the first of the great educational revivals of the nineteenth century. It was largely an Oxford movement, and by reason of the *post hoc ergo propter hoc* fallacy was long believed to be a direct outcome of the new examination statute. That statute was itself the outcome of the more serious attitude to life which became common towards the end of the eighteenth century and which produced a more zealous type of college tutor; this quickening of intellectual activity co-operated with the stimulus and guidance of studies supplied by the new statute, to promote work among the undergraduates, at first on the old scholarly lines; but in course of time, under the influence of the Greek revival in Germany, which took place in the latter half of the eighteenth century, the newer classical humanism emerged. The change took, however, a considerable time, and was not complete till the fifties. But in the long run the new zeal, which, had it not been replenished by a force more potent than linguistic interest, would probably have died down after a short blaze of fiery energy, was rendered permanent by the discovery of the many messages which ancient Greece had to give to modern England. What were these messages and why did they appeal more to the early Victorian age than to preceding periods?

In the first place, modern democracy was coming to birth. Since 1689 the constitutional machinery of parliamentary government had been so worked out that there was prepared a healthy body into which modern democracy could enter as its soul. In France there was no such body and the ideas underlying the French Revolution had remained an aspiration. In England for a time the body refused to let the soul enter. Then it was that democrats turned to ancient Greece and Rome. Here alone were to be found important communities which had long maintained what at least appeared to themselves to be democratic institutions. These democratic communities had, moreover, originated everything except Christianity which was most valuable in modern civilisation. Democratic Greece had created art, science, literature, and philosophy: democratic Rome had laid the foundations on which the Empire built the edifice of law. The democrat could always turn to classical history when he wished to show what his principles could accomplish. Moreover, he could find in it guidance as well as stimulus. Modern Europe appeared to be evolving on much the same lines as Rome or as the Greek republics; and, whereas modern history showed only the first half of the story—the rise of states and their transition towards democracy—ancient history completed it with the decline and fall. By studying the causes, first of the rise, then of the stability, and finally of the decline of the ancient communities, it was possible to acquire a political sagacity which could be applied to maintaining modern states and modern civilisation and to avoiding the dangers to which they were exposed at different stages in their evolution. The stimulus which stirred Grote to write his *History of Greece* was not antiquarianism but zeal for modern liberalism. As Thomas Arnold put it, "Aristotle and Plato, and Thucydides, and Cicero, and Tacitus, are most untruly called ancient writers; they are virtually our own countrymen and contemporaries, but have the advantage which is enjoyed by intelligent travellers, that their observation has been exercised in a field outside the reach of common men; and that, having thus seen in a manner with our eyes what we cannot see for ourselves, their conclusions are such as bear upon our own circumstances, while their information has all the charm of novelty, and all the value of a mass of new and pertinent facts, illustrative of the great science of the nature of civilised man[1]."

In the second place, the French Illumination had striven to undermine the Christian basis of morals. No society can exist without a moral code, and the moral code of Europe had been built on the foundation of the Christian religion. It is true that in England the followers of Voltaire were few in number. Indeed religion was far more potent than it had been a century before. The leaders of thought were now for the most part sincere Christians, whereas in the earlier period belief was often assumed from a notion that religion was a useful restraining force upon the masses. The Wesleyan and Evangelical movements had greatly increased the influence of Christianity over motive. But the more thoughtful Christians saw the danger of sitting still in the hope that, in an age of criticism, young men of enquiring minds would be content to believe in Christianity merely because they had been taught it in childhood. The more thoughtful theists who did not accept or were doubtful about Christianity were equally afraid of bare negation. Eighteenth century France had been destructive; nineteenth century England strove to be constructive. The situation was not unlike that at Athens, when, traditional beliefs having been shaken by the Sophists, Plato turned the tables on the destructive critics by showing the weakness of their own position. Once more Greek philosophy could be studied in the same spirit as that of Plato's original audience, as an antidote to the corrosive power of negation, which appeared to be dissolving the mortar that bound society together. Here was the thought of the most intellectual race that had ever lived, earlier than any of the great Western religions, evolved more from the brain than from the emotions, the result of reflection and not of authority, which nevertheless in essentials supported a belief in the divine ordering of the world, in the inadequacy of purely materialistic explanations, and in the need of an accepted code of morals which should include among other essentials respect for the State.

[1] Article in the *Quarterly Journal of Education*, 1834.

In the third place, a new spirit was animating art and literature. The cold marble statue felt the warm blood in its veins and the warm breath in its nostrils. Formal stately "classicism" might well receive the homage of courtiers accustomed to the palace of a Louis XIV; but men who had not learned to suppress their feelings at the demand of etiquette still felt it to be true that *mentem mortalia tangunt*. The emotions were coming to their own. The "Augustan period" had made an unreasonable divorce between form and the feelings which form exists to express. Romanticism was the reaction, when men rebelled against the restrictions which form appeared to impose. It began to be seen that the so-called "classicism" of the preceding period had caught only one aspect of the genuine classical spirit. The very phrase "Augustan" bewrayed it. The principate of Augustus had produced masterpieces of form, but it was essentially an imitative and not an originative epoch. For originality, for the ideas, aspirations, and feelings which had brought classical literature into being, it was seen that we must look not to Rome but to Greece. It was seen too that these things cannot remain fixed unless they are to become wholly artificial, but that, while they cannot be transferred unchanged from one age to another, they can stimulate another age to ideas, aspirations, and feelings of its own. The Renaissance had erred in this respect. It produced a Shakespeare indeed but it had not aimed at so doing. Its conscious aim was to revive classical modes of thought and the classical forms in which to express them. The newer Renaissance sucked the flowers of Hymettus to make honey that should be all its own. The spirit of independence and originality was of Greek stock even when it was displacing classic architecture by Gothic and seeing Nature with its naked eye and not through the glass of ancient literature. A revaluation of classical authors resulted. It cannot be claimed that the new estimate is true absolutely and for ever; it may in part have been anticipated by some of the thinkers of that many-sided movement, the Renaissance: but it can fairly be asserted that the balance was more correctly adjusted than ever before and that the truer values were more widely accepted. Homer took precedence over Vergil, Aeschylus over Euripides, Plato over Cicero, Thucydides over Plutarch.

Perhaps the common factor in all three new appeals may be expressed by saying that the new age was conscious of unsolved problems whereas the older generation believed that all problems had been solved by the ancients. Both beliefs give a value to literature, history, and philosophy, but the value is different. The old age believed that a full knowledge of religious and philosophic truth, and perfect political institutions, had been attained. Philosophy could therefore be expounded as a formal and logical system. As such it made a cold appeal to the intellect, but, if it were to influence motive, it needed the aid of literature with its concrete examples to stimulate the imagination in matters of personal conduct, and history to fill the same rôle in matters of public conduct. Under such a system art had little to do but to please the taste. But to an age which is conscious of unsolved problems, the values are quite different. The problems of life are not wholly intellectual; it is a sense of values which creates the craving for their solution. Literature or art may be the agency which awakens a sense that a problem exists; they will certainly enhance the feeling of its importance; and it is even possible that they will suggest a solution. This is why Plato, the artistic philosopher, and Aeschylus, the philosophic artist, appealed so much more strongly to the new age than to the old. History too was no longer an exhibition of models for imitation, but a means of suggesting, clarifying and partially solving, problems concerned with human society. Thucydides and Tacitus were the two historians who appeared most "philosophic" to the new age.

England was striving to reconcile political liberty with obedience to law, moral liberty with obedience to duty, and intellectual liberty with religion. Her thinkers were seeking to harmonise to the intellect those principles which her people instinctively seek to combine in their actions.

It was a typically English reaction against the intellectual tendency which had come in from France in the preceding century, dictated by a fear lest the former member of each pair of contending principles was obtaining an undue preponderance. The movement was greatly influenced by contemporary German thought, but only by certain lines of that thought.

It may be therefore useful to distinguish three tendencies in German thought which have manifested themselves in the last century and a half. The first embodies that "divine discontent" with the limitations which necessity imposes on human knowledge and human activity, of which Goethe stands as the representative. From it sprang the efforts to plumb the depths of philosophy, mysticism, and the best of German literature. In its highest form it was inspired by Greece. It was this Graeco-German spirit which inspired Coleridge and became a powerful influence in England. On its dangerous side it became a rebellious spirit, the spirit of Faust, without the restraining power of the Greek αἰδώς. Eventually this side triumphed, and we have the two consummate rebels, Nietsche, rebel against destiny, and Karl Marx, rebel against society. Milton's conception of Satan might have been enlarged to embrace both, had he been alive to witness their deification of the revolt against human limitation. Discontent may be divine or diabolic. The diabolic kind helped to drive men like Newman into the arms of authority.

The second tendency was the analytic or critical, which sought to *understand* the feelings which the first sought to *actualise*. Art, literature, philosophy, and history came to the seers permeated with values; the critics sought to analyse the values, to show how they were transmitted by these media, and to estimate their validity. In each case there was a historical criticism and a philosophical criticism. History, for instance, embraced both an investigation of the truth of records and an interpretation of the significance of the facts thus verified. Philosophy involved both a historical enquiry into the rise of old beliefs and an attempt to construct a new system. Art and literature needed, on the one hand, an enquiry into the authorship of various works and the conditions under which they had been created, on the other, an estimate of their permanent worth. In all of these directions Germany led the way. In many cases England was long content merely to accept the results; but on the whole she was more influenced by the philosophical criticism, or estimate of values, than by the historical. Gradually a tendency arose in Germany to value novelty too highly. There can never be too much criticism so long as it is honestly directed to the search for truth. But it may have another motive, desire for reputation; and academic reputations in Germany came to depend too much on novelty, and too little on soundness of judgment. England's inferiority in original work saved her from this danger. She accepted many of the German contributions to a fuller understanding of the meaning of history, art, and literature, but was cautious in what she accepted. If, for instance, the acceptance of Niebuhr's criticism of early Roman traditions was a gain, a somewhat flippant scepticism as to the later theory which sought to reduce Troy to a sun-myth was no loss, and a non-committal attitude to Wolf's theory that the *Iliad* was formed by the union of numerous lays into one poem proved in the long run to be sound policy. It took nearly a century before the encouragement of original work became a prominent feature in English universities; but, if not original, our universities were at least eminently sane.

The third feature was the careful fostering of education by the State, which we may regard as part of the efficient State control of everything, which was Prussia's special contribution to the life of Germany in the nineteenth century. In organisation, as in the two characteristics which we have been previously considering, there was a good and a bad side, and the good side was apparent first. Germany had a good school in every town a hundred years before England had a moderate one. Two universities long satisfied England, for a similar population twenty would have been considered necessary in Germany. But England has preserved elasticity and liberty. We are tempted to think of the universal admiration which was felt by an earlier age for the efficiency of the Jesuit education; and then to remember that a century and a half later the rigidity of its bonds was seen to be strangling intellectual development. There is a close parallel, though the object of Jesuit education was to maintain a particular theological system and that of Prussian education was to maintain a particular political system.

After this digression we will return to the classical revival. So wide a movement can best be understood by taking typical representatives of its various aspects; we shall therefore group its history round the personalities of three men, very unlike in all other ways, but all shaped by its influence, Thomas Arnold, Newman, and Mark Pattison.

The account which Mr Justice Coleridge wrote of Arnold's undergraduate days for Stanley's *Life*—Arnold entered Corpus when he was only sixteen years of age—gives a vivid picture of the intellectual activity of a small college which had been influenced by the revival of a working spirit, and shows how the mutual intercourse of inquisitive minds led them to connect classical studies with the real problems of life. Such an attitude was still far from common and Coleridge is clearly still under the sway of the older scholarly ideal. He laments that Arnold "did not leave the college with scholarship proportioned to his great abilities and opportunities." "This," he adds, "arose in part from the decided preference which he gave to the philosophers and historians of antiquity over the poets, coupled with the distinction which he then made, erroneous as I think, and certainly extreme in degree, between words and things, as he termed it." Arnold went up in 1811: forty years later the distinction was more fully recognised. The college consisted of twenty fellows, twenty scholars (some of whom were graduates, as bachelors were obliged to reside) and six gentlemen commoners; there were no commoners. Hence workers predominated, and the smallness of numbers threw men of all years together. The scholars had their junior common room; "we lived on the most familiar terms with each other; we might be, indeed we were, somewhat boyish in manner, and in the liberties which we took with each other; but our interest in literature, ancient and modern, and in all the stirring events of that stirring time was not boyish; we debated the classic and romantic question; we discussed poetry and history, logic and philosophy; or we fought over the Peninsular battles and the continental campaigns with the energy of disputants personally concerned in them." Such intercourse, Coleridge points out, had an even greater share in forming the outlook of those who shared it than the college tuition. Knowledge and scholarship may come from good teaching, but to produce thought there is nothing like the free air of a university.

From Corpus Arnold went to join a society which has left a permanent impress on English university life, the senior common room of Oriel. We have seen how the new examination statute was carried by three heads of houses, Cyril Jackson of Christ Church, Eveleigh of Oriel, and Parsons of Balliol. Each of these colleges in turn took an intellectual lead within the university. Christ Church had an extraordinary predominance in the class lists up to 1837[1] and produced the two most famous of our nineteenth century statesmen, Peel and Gladstone: then it fell with a drop. Eveleigh (1781–1814), however, laid the foundation for the predominance of Oriel by inducing his colleagues— no easy task, we may imagine—to throw open fellowships to open competition. Hitherto colleges had restricted their choice to their own members and were in the habit of choosing pleasant companions in preference to men of greater intellectual force. Henceforth Oriel fellowships won a reputation as a surer test of real capacity than even the honours examinations of the university. Mark Pattison writes[2], "For nearly thirty years the examinations for Oriel fellowships were conducted upon the principle of ascertaining, not what a man had read, but what he was like. The prizes or classes which a candidate might bring

---

[1] See figures in Hamilton's *Discussions*, Appendix III *c*.
[2] *Memoirs*, pp. 77–78.

with him to the competition were wholly disregarded by
the electors, who looked at his papers unbiassed by opinion
outside....Perhaps the word which best expresses what was
looked for...is originality."

He goes on to point out that the Noetics, as the famous
band of Oriel fellows in the twenties came to be called,
were rather opinionated; they knew little of continental
thought, of Kant or of Rousseau; but they maintained
a "wholesome intellectual ferment." Brodrick[1] describes
them as "a select body, somewhat inclined to mutual
admiration, producing little but freely criticising everything": they "applied an unsparing logic to received
opinions, especially those concerning religious faith, but
their strength lay rather in drawing inferences and in
refuting fallacies than in examining and settling the
premises from which their syllogisms were deduced." That
independence of judgment prevailed at Oriel is obvious
if we set the names of Whateley, Arnold, and Hampden
against those of Newman, Keble, and Hurrell Froude[2].
Such was Oriel before the Tractarian Movement.

The provost during Arnold's time was Copleston (1814–
1827), who likewise came from Corpus. A stately don of
the old school, he well-nigh ruled the university. He enjoyed a reputation beyond the limits of Oxford and was
consulted by Peel on economic questions; he advocated
reforms which the majority of Oxonians regarded as
dangerous innovations even in the fifties; he put in order
the college finances; and he was afterwards a reforming
bishop. But it is curious to notice how men who are
pushing reforms from within will resent almost identical
criticism from without. *The Edinburgh Review* commenced
a series of attacks, mainly true in substance but hostile in
form, against the English universities. Playfair, Jeffrey
and Sidney Smith were the leaders; and the attack was
directed equally against the classical and the mathematical
instruction. Copleston took up the cudgels and was believed

[1] *History of the University of Oxford*, ch. XVIII.
[2] W. Tuckwell, *Pre-tractarian Oxford*, contains impressions of the
leading "Noetics."

by Oxonians to have routed his opponents. Reply and counter-reply followed; and the language which was used frequently went beyond what would now be considered seemly in academic discussions. Yet the following would appear to be a just description of the attitude which the Noetics were striving to overthrow. "There is a timid and absurd apprehension on the part of ecclesiastical tutors of letting out the minds of youth upon difficult and important subjects. They fancy that mental exertion must end in religious scepticism; and, to preserve the principles of their pupils, they confine them to the safe and elegant imbecility of classical learning. A genuine Oxford tutor would shudder to hear his young men disputing upon moral and political truth, forming and pulling down theories, and indulging in all the boldness of youthful discussion[1]." And the next quotation would appear to express exactly Arnold's objection to the predominance of words over things. "A classical scholar of twenty-three or twenty-four years of age is a man principally conversant with works of imagination. His feelings are quick, his fancy lively, and his taste good. Talents for speculation and original enquiry he has none; nor has he formed the invaluable habit of pushing things up to their first principles, or of collecting dry and uninteresting facts as material of reasoning. He hates the pain of thinking and suspects every man whose boldness and originality call upon him to defend his opinions and prove his assertions[2]." Scholars have come to value "not the filbert but the shell, not what may be read in Greek but Greek itself[3]." The absence of a working atmosphere, the failure of fellows to make contributions to learning, their ignorance of the latest researches, the neglect of mathematics at Oxford, and a tendency to cling to obsolete mathematical methods at Cambridge, were other matters of attack. Copleston's replies are extraordinary evidence how far we have travelled since his day. Indeed to a modern reader they are stronger evidence of the justice of the attacks than anything contained in the attacks themselves. It is hard to realise that

[1] Vol. xv, Article 3, p. 50.   [2] p. 49   [3] p. 47.

a man who was regarded by his contemporaries as among
the ablest Oxonians of his day both intellectually and
practically should, in carrying on a discussion, be so
completely unable to distinguish the wood for the trees.
He spends more time in defending himself from a charge
of a small slip in his Greek than in meeting serious attacks
on the Oxford system; he indulges in trivial attacks on the
opponent's attorney; and he tediously replies to the charges
sentence by sentence when a few decisive thrusts might
have given him the victory. Yet he was all for giving that
training "in seizing the strong point in any subject" which
made argument in the Coplestonian style an impossibility
for the next generation.

In view of the evidence presented by the attacks of the
Edinburgh Review, by Copleston's defence, by Coleridge's
attitude, and by Mark Pattison's account of teaching in
his undergraduate days, we feel justified in holding that
Arnold was the first man, not only in English schools but
in English universities, who realised the opportunity which
classical instruction offered as an introduction of the pupil
to ethical, philosophical, and political problems and who
illustrated it in practice in such a way as to evoke imitation. The Reviewers had the idea; the Noetics *studied*
classics in this spirit; but Arnold was the first man known
to have *taught* them in it. Dean Stanley's account, though
hackneyed, must be quoted[1]. "He was the first Englishman who drew attention in our public schools"—this, we
suppose, is generally admitted—"to the historical, political,
and philosophical value...of the ancient writers, as distinguished from the mere verbal criticism and elegant
scholarship of the last century." "His whole method was
founded on the principle of awakening the intellect of every
individual boy. Hence it was his practice to teach by
questioning;...and his questions were of a kind to call the
attention of the boys to the real point of every subject
and to disclose to them the exact boundaries of what they
knew or did not know....In proportion to their advance
in the school he tried to cultivate in them a habit not only

[1] *Life of Thomas Arnold*, ch. II, pp. 136–142.

of collecting facts but of expressing themselves with facility, and of understanding the principles on which their facts rested. 'You come here,' he said, 'not to read but to learn how to read.'" "Hence also he not only laid great stress on original compositions, but endeavoured so to choose the subjects of exercises as to oblige them to read and lead them to think for themselves." "Style, knowledge, correctness or incorrectness of statement or expression, he always disregarded in comparison with indication or promise of real thought. 'I call that the best theme,' he said, 'which shows that the boy has read and thought for himself, that the next best which shows that he has read several books and digested what he has read, and that the worst which shows that he has followed but one book and followed that without reflection.'" Arnold's work was done in a school, but it was long before pure scholarship became infused with the new spirit in schools generally. Indeed Mark Pattison states that up to 1834 "scholarship" still maintained the premier place at Oxford in the school of *Litterae Humaniores*; and that a period ensued in which what was expected was a "knowledge of the books" "page by page" rather than a critical reflection on them; in fact it was not till the fifties that this school definitely assumed a philosophical bias[1].

The new humanism presented many shapes as it was refracted through the media of different temperaments. Arnold's was the religious spirit cast in a Protestant mould. He is akin to Plato in one of his aspects, as the great Greek puritan. To Arnold the chief revelation of God was to be found in history, and this was why classical history appealed to him so intensely. Progress was divinely directed. Jews, Greeks, and Romans were the three chosen peoples of ancient times. Their history was directed on converging lines with Christianity as their meeting-point. As before Christ States were the appointed means of drawing men nearer to God, so was it God's purpose that they should be afterwards. The sanctification of the State was the goal of progress. Man, as Aristotle held, can only be perfect

[1] *Suggestions on Academical Organisation*, 1868, pp. 289, 306.

in society; hence individual perfection and the perfection of society must go hand in hand. The greater the approximation to perfection, the more do Church and State become identical; for they are composed of the same persons. Their relations to God, which constitute them a Church, determine their attitude to each other, when they are regarded as a State. Education is engaged in showing the purpose of God for the individual and for the world; its chief subjects are therefore (1) the Christian religion, (2) the Jewish, Greek, and Roman civilisations, as revealed in their literature and in their history, and (3) modern history. Such is education on its intellectual side; on the side of will and feeling it acts through a miniature Christian society in school or university, which are training grounds for the larger Christian societies of Church and State. Arnold's practice accorded with his theories.

Newman equally represents the religious spirit, but his temperament was conservative whereas Arnold's was liberal. By this we mean that, if a new movement arose, Arnold's eye was instinctively cast on the opportunities of so guiding the movement that it might increase the sum of righteousness, whereas Newman instinctively looked at the dangers to the cause of righteousness which might accrue from the disturbance of existing opinions or institutions. Hence Arnold remained a Noetic to the end; but Newman, as he saw more fully the directions in which free enquiry might lead, became alarmed. He recognised, like Arnold, a divine guidance of events, but for him it was that kind of guidance which operates by "turning even the madness of men" to fulfil the divine will. Should we liken the forces of change to a river, Arnold saw the Spirit of God in the stream itself, Newman only in some power which should embank it. So embanked it could be made to subserve the good; but in itself it had the nature of evil. From an early period he recognised this regulating power as being the Church; but, whereas in 1833 he looked to the Anglican Church, in 1845 he seceded to Rome. In 1852, in a series of lectures to the "Catholic University of Ireland," he published his theory of the functions of a university[1]. It is a masterly harmonisation of Catholicism and contemporary Oxonianism, and it remains the outstanding and classic exposition of the latter.

As a Catholic, Newman refuses to accept Arnold's view that intellectual education can make a man better or more religious, and that this is its highest aim. The Church alone pronounces on faith and morals; the individual man must believe and obey. Why then is it better to be educated than not to be educated? His answer is that a sound intellectual condition is in itself a good, just as a healthy bodily condition is in itself a good. In what, he goes on to ask, does this healthy condition of mind consist? The English language, he replies, contains no exact word for it; neither *wisdom* nor *knowledge* nor *learning* gives the right idea. It is certainly not professional skill; for that is a means to something else, whereas the healthy mental state is an end in itself—the end sought by a liberal, as opposed to a professional, education. Rather it consists "not merely in the passive reception into the mind of a number of ideas hitherto unknown to it, but in the mind's simultaneous action upon and towards and among these ideas....It is the action of a formative power, reducing to order and meaning the matter of our acquirements; it is a making the objects of our knowledge subjectively our own, or, to use a familiar word, it is a digestion of what we receive into the substance of our previous state of thought....It possesses the knowledge not only of things, but also of their relations; knowledge, not merely considered as acquirement, but as philosophy[2]." The description of the healthy intellectual state is pure Oxonianism; its dissociation from morals and religion is Catholicism.

He next turns to the subject-matter of a healthy intellectual training. Since beliefs true in themselves may be a source of error if not seen in all their relations, specialisation is an evil. Yet it is necessary for professional efficiency: therefore a liberal education steps in as a prophylactic. "Men whose minds are possessed by some one object take

[1] *The Idea of a University*, 1852.   [2] p. 134.

exaggerated views of its importance,...make it the measure of things which are utterly foreign to it, and are startled and despond if it fail them....But the intellect which has been disciplined to the perfection of its powers, which knows, and thinks while it knows,...cannot be exclusive, cannot be impetuous, cannot be at a loss....That perfection of the Intellect which is the result of education...is the clear, calm, accurate vision and comprehension of all things, as far as the finite mind can embrace them, each in its place, and with its own characteristics upon it[1]." The characteristics therefore of a liberal education are, first, that it is a training in this "philosophical" habit of mind which looks for relations and co-ordinates its knowledge; secondly, that it deals more with the "architectonic" sciences, that is, those which best serve to decide the relations of the others to the scheme of knowledge as a whole.—Thus far goes contemporary Oxford; the end is Rome. Man is related to things, to man, and to God; but the last relation is the most fundamental of the three, and the second more important than the first. Theology, as taught by the Church, is therefore the most "architectonic" of the sciences; and other sciences will be good or bad in proportion as they are studied with this background. Arnold on the other hand would have looked on the scheme of knowledge, not as a building of which theology was the cornerstone, but as a flight of steps of which it was the top; our knowledge of the will of God was to be reached by reflection on the physical world and on human history.

The architectonic hierarchy of the sciences determined for Newman that all must be taught in a Catholic atmosphere; it also established a superiority of the humanities over the physical sciences. In arguing this second position he quotes from his old friend Keble[2], who remained an Anglican; and the quotation is as good a statement of the newer humanistic position as could be found. Keble had called the nameless intellectual quality which Newman conceives as the health of the mind by the title of "judgment." Judgment, he affirmed, "lives by comparison and

[1] pp. 137–139.   [2] pp. 174–6.

discrimination"; it gives the student "strength in any subject he chooses to grapple with and enables him to seize the strong point in it." "To do any good to the judgment, the mind must be employed upon such subjects as come within the cognizance of that faculty and give some real exercise to its perception. Here we have a rule of selection by which the different parts of learning may be classed for our purpose. Those which belong to the province of the judgment are religion,...ethics, history, eloquence, poetry, theories of general speculation, the fine arts, and works of wit." All these "are necessary mutually to explain and interpret each other. The knowledge derived from them all will amalgamate." But further, "if different studies are useful for aiding, they are still more useful for correcting each other; for, as they have their peculiar merits severally, so they have their defects, and the most extensive acquaintance with one can produce only an intellect either too flashy or too jejune, or infected with some other fault of confused reading. History, for example, shows things as they are, that is, the morals and interests of men disfigured and perverted by all their imperfections of passion, folly, and ambition; philosophy strips the picture too much; poetry adorns it too much; the concentrated lights of all three correct the false peculiar colouring of each and show us the truth." The defence of the classical course as it was in process of being reshaped at Oxford therefore was that the three means to seeing life steadily and seeing it whole were pure literature, history, and philosophy; and that in the literature of ancient Greece there was ready at hand a combination of great poets and orators, historians and philosophers, which was unique. Their study presented two great advantages; first, it was the best available means of understanding "humanity," if the word may be used to signify all which concerns human relations; secondly, it was a training in the "philosophic" habit of looking for the relations and significance of the facts which are learned, without which any kind of knowledge is worthless.

Newman, writing in the fifties, acknowledges that

natural science, like all kinds of knowledge, possesses a value in itself as knowledge, apart from the specific professional values of separate branches. But the Oriel fellows in the heroic age of the College had been hardly brought into contact with natural science, though one of the most lovable of their number, Baden Powell, was a scientist: but such was the condition of science in Oxford that, when he was appointed Savilian professor of Geometry in 1827, Copleston advised him that it would be useless for him to lecture, as he would not get an audience, and that it would be better for him to devote himself to research[1]. Science was in fact treated as a hobby of a few eccentric dons, such as Buckland, for whom the Prince Regent erected a professorship of geology, or Daubeny, who combined the professorships of chemistry, botany, and rural economy[2]. It was not till the great change in attitude which followed Newman's secession in 1845 that Oxford awoke to the existence of science as a serious claimant to a place within the temple of knowledge, and that Acland carried through his scheme for the building of a scientific museum, to which a band of artists, including Burne-Jones and Morris, devoted unsparing endeavours to make the shrine worthy of the newly deified muse. When we find even Jowett treating these claims as menacing "the higher conception of knowledge and of the mind" and antagonistic to "morals and religion and philosophy and history and language," we are not surprised to learn that Keble led the theologians to an attack on geology as unscriptural, or that Newman considers that the value which he theoretically allows to science might be purchased at the cost of greater evils. But it is at a period later than the thirties that science was sufficiently recognised to become a subject for attacks.

In addition to aim and subject-matter a complete theory of a liberal university education must also embrace a view on method. "If I had to choose," writes Newman, "be-

---

[1] W. Tuckwell, *Pre-tractarian Oxford*, p. 167.

[2] An account of these "pre-scientific scientists" is given by Tuckwell, *Reminiscences of Oxford*.

tween a so-called university which dispensed with residence and tutorial superintendence and gave its degrees to any person who passed an examination in a wide range of subjects and a university which had no professors or examinations at all, but merely brought a number of young men together for three or four years, and then sent them away as the University of Oxford is said to have done some sixty years since, if I were asked which of these two methods was the better discipline of the intellect—mind, I do not say, which is morally the better, for it is plain that compulsory study must be a good and idleness an intolerable mischief—but if I must determine which of the two courses was the more successful in training, moulding, enlarging the mind, which sent out men the more fitted for secular duties, which produced better public men, men of the world, men whose names would descend to posterity, I have no hesitation in giving the preference to that university which did nothing, over that which exacted of its members an acquaintance with every science under the sun[1]." The importance thus attached to intercourse surmounts the difficulty that, while the studies of a university must be encyclopaedic, the teachers at least must be specialists. They are saved from the evils of specialism by contact with specialists in other branches. "There will be this distinction as regards a professor of law or of medicine or of geology or of political economy in a university and out of it, that out of a university he is in danger of being absorbed and narrowed by his pursuit, and of giving lectures which are the lectures of nothing more than a lawyer, physician, geologist, or political economist; whereas in a university he will know just where he and his science stand[2]." Similarly all students will not study theology, but all will be in contact with theological students in a society in which theology is studied.

When we compare Newman's ideal with the account of Oxford given by Sir William Hamilton, by the Edinburgh Reviewers who renewed their attacks in 1830, by Mark

[1] *The Idea of a University*, p. 145.   [2] p. 166.

Pattison in his *Memoirs*, and by the evidence given before
the Royal Commission, we feel at first at a loss to explain
the glaring contrast. Yet it is not hard to explain. The
reformers of 1800 found in existence a state of things in
which the bulk of undergraduates were unaccustomed to
serious study and the bulk of tutors to serious teaching.
Few fellows of colleges kept up their studies by reading,
though intellectual conversation was sometimes studied
as a fine art in common rooms. The idea of making new
contributions to learning, even of following the new contributions which were being made abroad, was unknown.
A minority of intellectual tutors carried the new examination statute; a minority of working undergraduates
occupied the places in the class lists. This minority needed
a new type of instruction; but, before tutors realised how
greatly the position had changed, they were left behind.
When lecturing on authors, they knew nothing to say which
was not to be found in the printed editions; and they were
only awaking to a realisation of the wider philosophical,
historical, and literary topics, for a discussion of which the
authors might be made the text. Hence the demand of
Hamilton and the promoters of the Royal Commission for
specialist professors. The Oriel band were composed of
the first batch of working undergraduates who had been
produced by the new system. Their interests were so wide
that they did not wish to specialise; as tutors they were
restless students; they learned the forgotten art of study,
but they spent their lives in searching for their intellectual
position. A third generation must arise before tutors were
sure enough of their position to work out a system of
instruction. Meanwhile the bulk of undergraduates were
still passmen, of a low intellectual level; and it was for
them that college tuition had been designed. Academic
organisation was lacking in flexibility, and candidates for
honours were still required to attend those lectures, from
which they could derive no knowledge or stimulus whatever. Their real work was done privately or with the new
class of private "coaches" who arose to satisfy the new
demand, till the third generation of reformers united to

demand from Lord John Russell the interference of the State. In the interval the mind of the university had been distracted for twelve years by the controversies arising out of the Tractarian movement (1833–1845).

Still, much was gained. Arnold's effort to popularise Niebuhr was his chief contribution to university study: but his work at Rugby on its intellectual side may be regarded as working out the school basis on which the "philosophising" of the traditional university classical course could be built. Foreign influences took long to penetrate Oxford, but they came. It was the High Church Conservative school who popularised Kant. They found a philosophical leader in their Scottish academic critic, Sir William Hamilton. If lectures lacked originality and were unsuited to the intellectual needs of honours men, yet tutors were beginning to be conscientious on their own lines. A college lecture was conducted exactly like a lesson to a sixth form and was substantially a construing class; and this was precisely the point in which the tutors of those days saw its advantage. The doctrine that the pupil must not be a mere listener, which is a truism of school method to-day, was held and practised by our predecessors in their instruction in universities. In the great struggle between the rival policies of college tuition and a university professoriate, the tutorial party took it for granted that the tutor would continue to teach while the professor would lecture, and it was on this that they based the tutor's claim to be giving superior instruction. Strangely enough, in the older universities, the tutorial system is still preserved, but the modern tutor lectures; while in the modern universities there is nominally a professorial system, but the professor, like his American colleague, often "quizzes."

The Tractarian movement, much as it distracted Oxford thought from academic reform, was itself a sign of intellectual life. It was only by reason of the enlarged opportunities for free thinking that so unconventional a doctrine as the unfettered claim of authority over freedom of thought was rendered possible. Yet to the opposing school of thought which gained the predominance after Newman's secession in 1845, the twelve years of Tractarian controversy appeared to be an age of scholastic barbarism. Under the rule of Hawkins (1828–1874), Oriel undoubtedly lost its old prestige. An autocrat who dreaded to be surrounded by men of superior ability, he dismissed three of his keenest tutors, including Newman, and put in inferior but "safe" men. He damped enthusiasm, became engrossed in detail, and lived in the past. Mark Pattison—no very impartial witness, to be sure—describes the leading tutors of Oriel after 1831 as "steeped in parochialism," as zealous in study but devoting all their study to theology, and as possessing a very limited knowledge of the classics; "the college must have become a seminary[1]."

Newman's secession seemed to the academic liberals as the break-up of an old order; Pattison tells us[2] how a "flood of reform" broke over Oxford, how "in those years everyone was a liberal," how it seemed "a deliverance from the nightmare" of obscurantism. Two new honours schools were instituted in 1852, one of law and history, the other of natural science. The museum was built. The Royal Commission was appointed. Mill replaced Kant as the philosophic guide. The old classical examination was divided into two parts, Moderations in the middle of the undergraduate's career, which should embrace pure scholarship, the poets and orators, and the final school of *Litterae Humaniores*, better known as "Greats," which henceforth became mainly philosophical and historical. Sir William Hamilton's charge that, though parts of philosophical authors are read, they are not studied as "food for speculation," that memorising of the parts and not a view of a work as a whole is what is expected[3], ceased to be true. Balliol took the intellectual supremacy under the long mastership of Jenkyns (1819–1854), who, though neither a great scholar nor a commanding personality, was "an unfailing judge of a clever man[4]," and, unlike Hawkins, showed no jealousy to men abler than himself, but accepted

[1] *Memoirs*, pp. 91–96.   [2] pp. 236–238.
[3] *Discussions*, p. 704.
[4] H. W. C. Davis, *College Histories, Balliol*.

changes promoted by the fellows, even when he personally disapproved. The chief of these was the opening of scholarships to free competition in 1828 which made a "Balliol" the blue ribbon of schoolboy success. In 1842 Jowett became tutor, and in this capacity and later as master consolidated the ground which Jenkyns had won.

Mark Pattison was as much an outcome of the classical revival as Arnold or Newman, but was in every other respect a contrast to them. The son of a commonplace and not very religiously-minded country clergyman, he came up to Oriel as a shy and awkward freshman in 1830, with an ardent love of classical study which his official instructors failed to satisfy. In 1839 he obtained a fellowship at Lincoln, and for a time came under Tractarian influences, which yielded to a profound reaction. His genius was brilliant and versatile, with more than a touch of egoism and a restless desire to be ever reforming something. "It is impossible for me," he confesses, "to see anything done without an immediate suggestion of how it might be better done. I cannot travel by railway without working out in my mind a better time-table than that in use[1]." His defeat in his candidature for the rectorship of his college, which he not unfairly regarded as an act of jobbery, embittered him; and his subsequent election did not undo its effect on his character. Happy in his hours of study; vindictive, melancholy, and pessimistic in his hours of thought; taciturn in society; ardent but bitter under opposition in his attempts at university reform, he became the most brilliant but the saddest figure in mid-Victorian Oxford. Impelled by an insatiable craving for efficiency, he had none of the hope for the future or the love of his fellow men which bestows a blessing on unsuccessful endeavour when it springs from the heart, but could only feel the sting of personal failure when the reforms which his brilliant intellect was ever suggesting were not carried into effect.

We could almost prophesy from his character how Greek literature would affect him, when once his shyness had

[1] *Memoirs*, p. 254.

been sufficiently overcome to let him follow his own lines. Greece was the nation which had first struck out on new paths of thought. Wherever Greek literature went, it had imparted intellectual life. Pre-existing beliefs and conventions were powerless before the keen sword thrusts of its penetrating analysis. Life had become joyous; thought was no longer a burden, but a delightful exercise in a boundless, invigorating fresh air; gloom, superstition, and fear, the poisonous growths of ignorance, had perished when exposed to its health-giving influence. Its restoration at the Renaissance had brought civilisation to Europe. Pattison was a scholar of the fifteenth century condemned to live in the mid-Victorian age. Having turned his back on Tractarianism, he came to feel for the clerical party that bitterness which he was too prone to experience towards all who did not agree with him. His attitude to Greece, his attitude to Christianity, his attitude to opponents, can all be seen in one sentence which he wrote of Newman, "He was inspired by the triumph of the Church organisation over the wisdom and philosophy of the Hellenic world; that triumph which, to the Humanist, is the saddest moment in history—the ruin of the painfully constructed fabric of civilisation to the profit of the Church[1]."

In some ways Oxford has followed Pattison's lead. He tells us how he was appointed an examiner along with colleagues whose paper qualifications were all better than his own, and how he found himself their equal in scholarship and more than their match in seeing the wider bearings of ancient thought[2]. He claims to have been the first lecturer on Aristotle at Oxford who tried to exhibit his philosophy as a whole instead of commenting on his works section by section[3]: and this, which is obviously the right method of dealing with the philosophers and historians of antiquity, is now universal. The reforms instituted as a result of the Royal Commission, and Pattison's support of the professorial system, must be considered in a later chapter. But, generally speaking, we may say that, as

[1] *Memoirs*, p. 96.　　[2] pp. 232–233.　　[3] p. 261.

regards his attempt to follow the German system and introduce the student to specialised research in his undergraduate days, Oxford did not follow him. He was not satisfied with the form which the school of *Litterae Humaniores* was assuming and has since retained. "The quantity of original writing produced in" the three hours allowed for each paper "is in itself surprising. But the quality is more so. The best papers are no mere schoolboys' themes spun out with hackneyed commonplaces, but full of life and thought, abounding with all the ideas with which modern society and its best current literature are charged. So totally false are those platform denunciations of the Oxford classical system which assume that it leads its alumni in old-world notions and occupies them with matters remote from modern interests." Yet he thinks that the system has done its work. "The philosophical has been a transition stage, by which we have risen above the mere 'belletristic' treatment of classical literature." His objection to the "philosophical" stage is that conclusions are reached without examining the evidence. "To glean rapidly the current ideas floating about in the schools, to acquire the knack of dexterous manipulation of the terms which express them, to put himself in the hands of a practised tutor, to be set in the way of writing in the newest style of thought upon every possible subject and inserting the quotations from Aristotle in their proper place, this is all the student has time to do[1]." The cause is that philosophy is taught, not by middle-aged specialists who have thoroughly studied one particular branch of the subject, but by some young tutor who "reads in his vacation or in such moments of leisure as he can snatch the last new book on the subject" and "becomes of course an immediate convert to the theory of the latest speculator[2]." His own desire is to leave Moderations unaltered as an examination in scholarship, and to divide the final school into specialist philological and classical alternatives, banishing philosophy to the Faculty of Law! Thus, having

[1] *Suggestions on Academical Organisation*, pp. 292–294.
[2] pp. 304–305.

as it were laid the last brick of the "philosophical" edifice, Pattison proceeded to propose its total demolition, and no more belongs to the present chapter. Yet we may note that the faults which he finds with it consist in precisely those features which Newman considered its merits, and the issue is virtually between a general education for life and a specialised education for academic teaching and research.

The change from the scholarly to the "philosophic" ideal hardly affected Cambridge. The Classical Tripos was instituted in 1822, but at first only candidates who had taken mathematical honours were allowed to sit. Cambridge, however, maintained and, if anything emphasised, the older tradition of "pure scholarship." Thus, Peacock's desire to abolish verse and Greek prose in order to open the classical tripos to candidates who had not specialised in classics at school[1] would meet with a less favourable reception among Cambridge tutors now than when it was expressed. Indeed there was a marked divergence between the two universities: as far as real influence on the thought of the nation was concerned, Oxford's contributions were mainly humanistic and those of Cambridge mainly naturalistic.

The change in schools was not so marked as at Oxford. The historical and philosophical outlook was only possible with the sixth form, and it has taken a long time to realise that a boy becomes intellectually, though not emotionally, a man at sixteen. Universities influence schools in two ways, by the requirements of scholarship examinations, which determine the syllabus, and by the mental outfit of the teachers who proceed from the universities, which determines the unconscious drift and background of the teaching. The fact that at Oxford scholarship examinations looked more to Moderations than to "Greats" and that at Cambridge there was no equivalent for "Greats" continued to throw the weight into the scale in favour of good composition. It was some time before the essay and the

[1] *Observations on the Statutes of the University of Cambridge*, pp. 157–159.

historical and general questions came to rectify the balance.
But the mental outfit of teachers often produced a profound, though unnoticed, effect. And, as the linguistic side
of classics is being more and more threatened by naturalistic
studies, the historical, philosophical, social, and political
content of the humanities, as a means of training citizens,
and at the higher stages of statesmen, is being more and
more emphasised. It is not unlikely that, when the general
study of the classical languages has passed away, the point
of view as to the aims and methods of study which took
shape in the course of the new humanistic movement will
survive in connection with the study of modern literatures,
modern history, and modern philosophy and political
economy.

REFERENCES

Edinburgh Review, vol. XI, Article 7; vol. XIV, pp. 429–441; vol. XV,
    Article 3; vol. XVI, Article 7; vol. LI, Article 3.
Sir William Hamilton, *Discursions*, 1852.
Rev. W. Tuckwell, *Reminiscences of Oxford*, 1900.
—— *Pre-tractarian Oxford*, 1909.
College Histories, esp. of Corpus, Christ Church, Oriel and Balliol.
G. V. Cox, *Recollections of Oxford*, 1868.
Edward Copleston, *A Reply to the Calumnies of the Edinburgh Review*,
    1810.
Arthur Penrhyn Stanley, *Life and Correspondence of Thomas Arnold*,
    1844.
Thomas Arnold, article in the *Quarterly Journal of Education*, 1834
    (reprinted in J. J. Findlay's *Arnold of Rugby*, 1898).
John Henry Newman, *The Idea of a University*, 1852 (references to
    1889 edition).
Mark Pattison, *Suggestions on Academical Organisation*, 1868.
—— *Memoirs*, 1885.
George Peacock, *Observations on the Statutes of the University of
    Cambridge*, 1841.

CHAPTER III

THE REVIVAL IN THE PUBLIC SCHOOLS

I N the first three decades of the century the public schools were in a parlous state. Their low moral tone, their narrow classical curriculum, their poor intellectual results, their roughness and bullying, their bad feeding and housing, were no longer likely to be tolerated merely because they were established institutions. The era of the Reform Act knew how to "mend or end" institutions which were not fulfilling their purpose. Evangelicalism was not tolerant of societies which appeared to encourage profanity and vice. Outside the circle of parents who were accustomed to send their boys to public schools were utilitarians demanding a "modern" curriculum, nonconformists objecting to clerical control, and democrats looking for schools which should be open to parents of smaller means.

In Prussia a situation in many respects similar had led to the suppression of the old boarding-schools and the establishment of a system of first-grade day-schools. The work had been carried out in the first decade of the century, and the new Gymnasien, as they were termed, had already proved themselves a success. In England, in the heyday of Individualism, such drastic action by the State was impossible; but, if no reform had come from within, it is hard to believe that the public schools could have survived another fifty years. Demands for their supersession were already beginning to be heard. It has been suggested that it would have been better in the long run had they not reformed themselves and had they been ultimately abolished. It may well be that the needs of the present day would be better met by an efficient system of local day schools with an atmosphere of work and a strong *esprit de corps*. But could such schools have been erected on the ruins of a discredited system? Bedford Grammar School may be taken to represent the type of school demanded. To produce several hundred Bedfords would require several hundred first-rate headmasters; and, had they existed, they would be almost certain to have reformed the existing schools. Probably it was a much smaller number who actually achieved the latter task.

During the years which immediately followed the reform, tradition assigned the major portion of the credit to Thomas Arnold of Rugby. As in the case of many other great reputations, a reaction followed; and to-day it has become fashionable to speak of the "Arnold myth." The discussion has not been free from bias. Alumni of great schools which can boast their own famous headmasters can be pardoned for seeking to revise a version of history which ignores their names. But the pure question of fact is capable of objective historical determination. The question of pure fact is how far the existence of Arnold brought about the reforms. It is when we ask how much credit is to be given to Arnold for what he did, how much greater a man (if at all) was he than other contemporary headmasters, how far he was merely a product of his times, whether if he had not done what he did someone else would not have done it, that we enter on a sphere where conjecture is hardly capable of proof or of disproof.

It is necessary in the first place to set out clearly the reforms which are admitted to have taken place. The moral tone of the schools was vastly improved; discipline was changed, largely by a new bias given to the prefect system; the curriculum was somewhat widened by making French and mathematics regular subjects instead of "extras"; teaching became more efficient and industry more common; an improvement took place in diet and housing; "dames," where they existed, were replaced by house-masters; and the school chapel became a powerful influence. In consequence of these internal changes public confidence was restored; the middle class was attracted to the public schools; a number of new schools were set up on the same lines; some of the old grammar schools became indistinguishable from the original seven; nonconformists came to approve of the clerical headmaster; and the rise of a "religious difficulty," such as that which has done so much to hinder the progress of elementary education, was obviated.

Next it may be noticed that these changes differ considerably in the extent to which they require a strong personality for their attainment. Changes in curriculum, diet, housing, and the position of assistant masters are matters of organisation which can be effected by committees or by headmasters of ordinary capacity, if only public opinion demands them. Improvements in teaching are more dependent on the human factor; but they call, not for a few outstanding personalities, but for an adequate supply of well educated teachers, such as were sure to become available so soon as the universities began to take their duties seriously. But a sweeping reform of moral tone required individuality of a high order; and it is to the changes which took place in this sphere, the changes which did more than anything else to conciliate public opinion, that Arnold's admirers look for their main proofs of his influence. None of these reforms can, however, be overlooked; for they all represent a change of opinion in the nation at large, to which the public schools responded.

The roughness of the material provision for schoolboys was a mediaeval tradition dating from the old monastic days when the mortification of the flesh, whether voluntary or compulsory, was regarded as a means of purifying the spirit. Pecuniary motives of course entered; in the days of the Renaissance, Erasmus and Vives hint that to starve your pupils was the quickest road to fortune in the scholastic profession. Then too Locke's hardening theory reflected a widespread belief, which seemed to give educational sanction to the dictates of economy. But, above all, no one before Thring realised the inevitable effect of external conditions on character. Dr Johnson once remarked that, because a man happened to be born in a stable, he was not therefore a horse; but it is equally true that, if a boy be brought up in a pig-sty, he will tend to become a pig. However, the Platonic view that beautiful surroundings implant in the soul an unconscious love of beauty, which later in life will develop into a conscious striving after the ideal, had no meaning for the early Victorians. Their ideas on such matters savoured of Sparta rather than of Athens. It is from the seventies that most housing legislation dates; the early Victorian placed his workpeople in slums and his own children in bare class-rooms and uncomfortable boarding-houses. Glaring evils, however, began to be remedied. At Rugby, in the interests of work, James gave the boys separate studies, and Butler followed his example at Shrewsbury[1]. At Eton the headmastership of Hawtrey (1834–1852) saw sweeping changes. But, even in 1838 "a deputation which waited upon the authorities with a request that a supply of water might be laid on in College was dismissed with the rebuff:—'You will be wanting gas and turkey carpets next[2]'"; and, a few years earlier, a suggestion of including potatoes in the dietary evoked from one of the fellows the enquiry, "But who is to peel the potatoes?[3]" Only in 1846 were a heating system and a water supply introduced, and tea and breakfast provided. At the same time the boys were given small separate rooms; suitable furniture was provided; sick rooms and lavatories were built; and a "proper staff of servants was engaged to do all menial work under the supervision of a resident matron[4]." Complaints as to food were a frequent cause for school mutinies. The Public Schools Commission completed the sweeping away of the old barrack life in the seven schools; but it was left for Thring to raise the matter to a higher plane by proclaiming the effect of the "almighty wall" on character. Arnold was brought into little connection with these troubles; however, he superseded the Rugby "dames" by house-masters, a change which was going on elsewhere. At Eton Lyte puts its beginning about 1824, but it was not completely effected till fifty years later[5]. Governors would naturally favour the change as

[1] Butler, *Life of Samuel Butler*, vol. I, p. 83.
[2] Lyte, *History of Eton College*, p. 460.
[3] *Op. cit.* p. 464.   [4] *Op. cit.* p. 473.
[5] *Op. cit.* pp. 377, 544.

giving masters an income independent of that derived from the school funds; but it was only the changed attitude of masters which made it an advantage; it might easily have become an incentive to profiteering.

Changes in curriculum before the Royal Commission were slight. Arnold made French and mathematics regular subjects instead of "extras" for which special fees were charged; but James had been extremely fond of teaching mathematics, and Butler, following him, had included it as a regular part of the Shrewsbury studies. It was only in 1851 that Eton[1] elevated the senior mathematical master, Stephen Hawtrey, a relative of the head, to the full status of an assistant master, and his six assistants remained in a subordinate position till the Commission. They were in fact the lineal successors of the visiting teacher of writing and arithmetic, usually a scrivener's clerk, who in the seventeenth century had been allowed to teach the boys out of school hours. So persistent were archaic survivals that, even at a time when Cambridge, with one of whose colleges—King's—Eton was most closely connected, reserved its highest honours for mathematicians, mathematical masters were neither allowed to wear gowns nor to take a share in the general discipline of the school, received lower salaries and could not become housemasters! The attitude of headmasters towards mathematics is illustrated by a story of an interview between a newly-appointed mathematical master and his chief. The assistant's attempts to extract from the head any expressions of opinion on the mathematical syllabus were cut short by the brief answer, "That's as you please"; and, when he went on to make enquiries as to his status and disciplinary powers, as for instance whether the boys would be expected to cap him, he received the equally curt reply, "That's as they please." The attitude of all headmasters, however, was not like this; Charles Butler of Harrow (1805–1829), for instance, was himself a wrangler, and made a little mathematics compulsory, and French soon followed. French was everywhere taught like a dead

[1] Lyte, *History of Eton College*, p. 490.

language; indeed Arnold insisted in the interests of discipline that it should not be taught by foreigners but by the ordinary form master, and up to very recent times experience has justified his view. We have seen that history was taught for one hour a week during one term in the year at Eton, Rugby, and Shrewsbury, and that some geography, chiefly ancient, was taught at Eton. The Eton Atlas of those days had modern maps opposite the ancient maps; but countries which lay outside the Graeco-Roman world, such as Scotland, Ireland, and Russia, were unrepresented. Arnold wrote: "Although some provision is undoubtedly made at Rugby for acquiring a knowledge of modern history, yet the history of Rome and Greece is more studied than that of France and England"; and he defended the procedure on the ground that ancient history could be studied from original authorities who were at the same time first-rate historians and in the front rank of literature, which is not the case with modern history. Arnold was a historian, and the historical bias which he gave to classical studies is perhaps the most noteworthy feature of his curriculum; in other schools ancient history was almost as completely ignored as modern. Non-classical subjects in fact made less progress in the older schools than in newer schools like Cheltenham; and it was only after the Royal Commission that they began to receive serious attention. We must not, however, forget that most of the intellectual stimulus of Eton was supplied not by the class teaching, but by the tutorial system; and that tutors often induced their pupils to do an amount of serious general reading in history and in English, and even in foreign, literature which might sometimes astonish our examination-ridden generation.

We next turn to improvements in teaching, which were very general. Butler of Shrewsbury (1793–1836) stands out at the head of the reformers. The school had sadly declined from its former high estate; and in 1798 an Act of Parliament was passed to reform the statutes and, in particular, to abolish the provision that the headmaster must be a burgess of Shrewsbury and an old Salopian. Butler was the first head appointed under the new scheme, and entered on his duties at the early age of twenty-four. He was one of the foremost scholars of his time and an excellent organiser. His system of periodical examinations and promotion by merit rather than by seniority was hailed as a striking novelty. His great triumph came when Kennedy, while still a pupil of the school and only a scholar-elect of Trinity, won the Porson Prize. Butler's improvements in method consisted largely in diminishing the old "grammar grind." For generations it had not been considered enough that boys should understand and apply the rules of syntax; they must learn them by heart in the exact Latin words of the text-book. Even in sixth forms every word of the author was parsed and the rule for its construction given in Latin[1]. If the reader wishes to realise the procedure, let him read examples from a famous schoolmaster of the seventeenth century, Richard Brinsley[2]. It was not enough that boys should learn the declensions and conjugations; they must also know by heart rules, of course written in Latin, which were supposed to teach how to form the various cases or tenses, though in reality the rule was unintelligible save by reference to the forms themselves! Greek grammar, in particular, was a labyrinth of technical terms, of separate conjugations and declensions which had no real existence, and of endless complications of which the modern schoolboy has never heard. Correct Attic was at a discount, and forms were gathered indiscriminately from every dialect. Butler and his successor Kennedy (1836–1866), being at once first-rate scholars and first-rate teachers, could see what was needed and could supply it; and in the course of fifty years intelligible grammars resulted. Butler's old pupils carried his methods to other schools. But, entirely apart from Butler's influence, a new type of assistant master was arising; we all know Tom Brown's "young master[3]"—Cotton—who "seemed to have

[1] I have been assured by Mr Oscar Browning that the parsing of every word survived up to his own day at Eton.

[2] *Ludus Litterarius*, ed. E. T. Campagnac, 1917, pp. 70–88.

[3] Part II, ch. 5.

the bad taste to be really interested in the lesson and to be trying to work them into something like appreciation of it, giving them good spirited English words, instead of the wretched bald stuff into which they rendered poor old Homer; and construing over each piece himself to them after each boy, to show them how it should be done."

Maxwell Lyte gives two passages[1] supplied to him by a correspondent whose name he does not quote, which give a detailed description of classical teaching at Eton, first under Keate and then under Hawtrey. Keate was for his time an excellent scholar, but he attempted the impossible task of teaching 120 boys at once—the whole of the sixth and fifth forms. Hawtrey introduced organisation; he withdrew with the thirty top boys into the library, abandoned the idea of personally supervising a number of assistants teaching in the same room, divided the rest of the school into a number of parallel forms of manageable size, gave to each a form master for the whole of its work, and, having carefully selected his men, left them a large amount of liberty. The result was that, though he was himself a believer in the older methods, the younger assistants introduced Butler's reforms. At first this produced a chaos of older and newer methods, but in the long run the new methods triumphed.

One sign of the increasing intellectual energy of the schools is to be found in the magazines which began to appear. That of Harrow began in the last year of Charles Butler's headmastership; A. H. Clough had much to do with one at Rugby; while several short-lived attempts were made at Eton, some of a higher literary quality than are usually to be found at the present day.

In spite of improvements, the seven public schools, with the exception of Eton and Rugby, were never lower in public favour than in the thirties and forties. Moberley (1835–1866) was by no means the least of Winchester's masters, but by 1855 the number of commoners had fallen to 68. Harrow dropped to 127 under Charles Butler and to 69 under Wordsworth (1835–1844). Charterhouse stood

[1] pp. 391–395 and 447–455.

at 104 in 1832 and had only risen to 121 in 1863. West-minster, which in 1818 had numbered 324, fell to 100 in 1835 and below 80 in 1841. Even Shrewsbury under Kennedy only numbered 133 in 1841 and scarcely rose for twenty years. The persistence of bad housing arrange-ments at Shrewsbury and the reputation of Winchester for hardship and bullying have been put forward as reasons.

We now reach the vital question of school tone. It may be well to approach causes by way of symptoms. The most astonishing of these symptoms to modern times is the constant recrudescence of mutinies and lock-outs. At Winchester there were several mutinies between 1775 and 1793, the most serious arising from a refusal to let the boys attend a performance by a military band in the Close. For two days the boys held the College buildings under the red flag, and the episode was terminated only by numerous expulsions. Goddard had some insight into the use of self-government as a corrective; but things went back under his successor, and in 1818 a rising was put down by two companies of soldiers with fixed bayonets. At Rugby in 1797, the headmaster having ordered the boys to pay for damages done to a tradesman against whom they had a grievance, they blew up the door of the head's study and made a bonfire of his books and the school desks. On the appearance of a body of special constables and the reading of the Riot Act, they retired to an island in "the Lake"; again soldiers were called in, and the island was taken by assault. George III's standing question when he met Eton boys was, "Have you had a rebellion lately, eh, eh?" Keate was as powerful in suppressing rebellions as he was powerless to produce an administration which would remove the rebellious spirit. Most modern headmasters would think it time to resign when rotten eggs had flown round them on several occasions. Not so Keate; each time he saw it through, and half a dozen expulsions and forty or fifty floggings testified to his triumph. After one occa-sion when he was so occupied from lock-up on Saturday night to the early hours of Sunday morning, he reigned in peace. Even Butler of Shrewsbury had his windows broken and put a stop to insubordination only by three expulsions. The last serious rebellion was at Marlborough in 1851.

This chronicle of mutinies is but the most striking evidence that discipline, as now understood, was non-existent a hundred years ago. Assistant masters were only just beginning to be expected to help the head in discipline outside their own class-rooms. James at Rugby was often warned of impending disorder by notes thrown in at his window, though he was one of the first headmasters to think it unfair to expect boys to give information against their schoolfellows[1].

Unfortunately these external disorders were indicative of worse evils which rarely came to the knowledge of the staff. Readers of these pages will hardly need to be told of these. For every one person who is acquainted with most of the sources of information on the schools of this period, a hundred know *Tom Brown's Schooldays*. The salt water, tossing in a blanket, and roasting; the drinking, gambling, and loose talk; the profanity which was much more than a mere mannerism, are all familiar. Tom Brown's Rugby was bad enough; the record of Long Chamber at Eton throws a more ghastly light still on what was probably common. "Parents who wished to avoid the worst evils of Long Chamber and yet secure the advantage of the scholarships entered their boys as oppidans and allowed them to remain such until the extreme limit of age was reached at which they could enter upon the foundation" of Eton and so of King's afterwards[2]. "Cruel at times the suffering and wrong; wild the profligacy. For after eight o'clock at night no prying eye came near till the following morning; no one lived in the same building; cries of joy and pain were equally unheard; and, excepting a code of laws of their own, there was no help or redress for any one[3]." Thring is here writing from his own memories.

Before asking how these evils have been remedied, it is

[1] Rouse, *History of Rugby School*, p. 147.
[2] G. R. Parkin, *Life of Edward Thring*, p. 16.
[3] *Op. cit.* p. 23.

necessary to ask whether they really have been remedied.
We may ignore the class of croakers who believed that a
Spartan discipline was an actual benefit to character. The
war has surely exploded them and their theories for ever.
The British boy, from whatever class he come, who was
held by these *laudatores temporis acti* to have been "spoilt"
by comfort, has shown that he can undergo a physical and
nervous ordeal to which no previous generation since the
age of the early martyrs had been subjected without a
thought of drawing back unless or until he had "seen it
through." The doctrine of Thring (and of Plato) is
"justified of her children." But it is a more plausible
contention that only the material side has improved, that
bullying and misery have ceased, but that the true moral
tone is no better. The life of an oriental slave gang, it may
be argued, has been exchanged for the luxury of Imperial
Rome; vice has become attractive instead of abhorrent;
public schools are not more virtuous but only more civilised.
A true answer would probably be somewhat as follows.
There are now about a hundred schools, great and small,
conducted "on public school lines," whereas there were
formerly but seven. At any given time there will be a few
of these in which the worst influences are at work. Gambling tends to appear more often than of old in a few of the
wealthiest; occasionally drinking becomes prevalent, but
less than in the old days. As long as we think only of
positive vices we may be tempted to take too gloomy a
view. But, if we think of the good that there is in these
hundred schools and compare it with the amount which
could be found a hundred years ago, our pessimism
vanishes. Far more boys, when they reach the university
and are free to order their own life, order it on lines of
which their headmasters would approve. The improvement may have been mainly in mid-Victorian days; there
may have been even a retrogression in the wealthier schools
in more recent years; but the gain, on the whole, stands.
We have now to consider how it was achieved.

Organisation undoubtedly played some part. Separate
studies, smaller dormitories, supervision, removal of

grievances, and other points which have been already noted did much to suppress the influence of the worst boys, and to develop a cheerful outlook which is itself of great help to the promotion of a healthy mind. Men and boys who are well-treated themselves are more likely to be considerate for others; the brutal soldiery who ravaged Belgium were themselves the product of brutal treatment. Cruelty means selfishness; and selfishness is the ally of sensuality.

But organisation has its limitations. Good policing and good opportunities give the decent boy a chance. Most boys have generous instincts, healthy tastes, and even a desire to use their mental powers, though not always on the subjects which their teachers desire. But there is in every boy a relic of the ape and tiger, and of the savage. In a good home the good is brought out and the bad is atrophied by disuse. Thus each new generation rises to the level which its predecessor has attained. But "a society formed exclusively of boys, that is, of elements each separately weak and imperfect, becomes more than an aggregate of their separate defects; the amount of evil in the mass is more than the sum of the evil in the individuals; it is aggravated in its character, while the amount of good, on the contrary, is less in the mass than in the individuals, and its effect greatly weakened[1]." Personal influence is therefore needed in a school to take the place of parental influence at home.

This personal influence is exercised both by the head-master and his assistants. It was not till long after Arnold's time that the present friendly relations between boys and masters became common. We get just a trace of it at the end of *Tom Brown*, in the conversation between Tom and the new master; but Cotton was no ordinary assistant master. Mr Rowbothom, in his *History of Rossall*[2], tells us that "with a few single exceptions the natural enemy theory" between masters and boys held the field till the

---

[1] Arnold, at the end of his letter to the *Journal of Education*, 1835, reprinted in Findlay's *Arnold of Rugby*, p. 235.

[2] p. 131.

headmastership of H. A. James (1875–1886). Edward
Bowen, who took a post at Harrow in the sixties, lamented
that the master had nothing to do with the boys[1], though
he himself became a typical example of the changed relations. Almond of Loretto, who managed his school almost
like a family, was regarded as an eccentric (1862). But,
even if masters had not yet learned to mix with boys on
easy terms out of school and if boys still looked on their
masters as distant gods on Olympus, masters began to
be really intent on boys' well-being, and boys replied with
admiration, though not yet with affection. The new type
of master likewise stimulated intellectual activity; and
intellectual activity reacts on character. To quote Arnold
once more, "Experience has led me more and more to
believe in this connexion, for which divers reasons may be
given. One, and a very important one, is that ability puts
a boy in sympathy with his teachers in the matter of
his work and *in their delight in the works of master minds*;
whereas a dull boy has much more sympathy with the
uneducated, and others to whom animal enjoyment is all
in all[2]."

When once good traditions have been established, the
influence of men of ordinary sound common-sense and
character is sufficient to maintain them. Schoolboys' in-
tense conservatism makes them, like certain States mentioned by Macchiavelli, hard to win but easy to hold when
won. But the first establishment of good traditions needed
men of that inexplicable power of winning over opposition
which is very rare, coupled with the tact which gains
positions by working round them when they seem to
present insuperable difficulties to direct assault. Almond
of Loretto and Thring of Uppingham, who both built up
schools almost out of nothing, had an easy task compared
with the headmasters of the thirties, who had to pierce
through a barbed wire entanglement of hostile traditions.
Such work could only be accomplished by the headmaster,
since a particular tone penetrates the whole school; and

---

[1] W. E. Bowen, *Memoir of Edward Bowen*, p. 59.
[2] Stanley, *Life*, vol. I, p. 131.

the headmaster, in virtue of his position, finds it harder to bridge the gap between himself and the boys than do his assistants. These considerations may explain why the headmasters who are credited with producing most improvement in the moral tone of their schools were men rather of forceful and dominating than of winning and lovable personalities.

The school chapel gave these powerful characters an opportunity for direct assault. Dean Stanley and the author of *Tom Brown* both represent it as a scene of Arnold's triumphs. The chapel was there before; but Arnold was the first headmaster of Rugby to get himself appointed chaplain: this was essential to his conception of the pastoral relation in which a headmaster should stand to his pupils. In the next generation a school chapel came to be considered as an essential feature of a boarding-school; but it was not so earlier. Charles Butler had no chapel at Harrow and probably never preached a sermon to his boys. Though a chapel existed at Shrewsbury, the governors insisted, against Samuel Butler's wishes, that the boys should attend the parish church on Sunday mornings, in order that any one-sidedness in his preaching might be counteracted by the sermons of the parochial clergy[1]. Most headmasters of the period agreed with Arnold, but the influence which they exercised from the pulpit of course differed enormously.

The chapel was the only place where, on ordinary occasions, the headmaster was brought into direct touch with his school as a whole. Otherwise his immediate influence was brought to bear almost exclusively in the class-room, and on the sixth form only. But the right treatment of a sixth form was discovered earlier than that of the middle parts of the school. The reason is easily seen. We commonly speak of sixth form "boys"; but these "boys" are intellectually men, and at other ages of the world would have been so considered. While the art of understanding boys was still to be learned, a headmaster had only to treat his sixth "as gentlemen," to apply, that

---

[1] Butler, *Life of Dr Samuel Butler*, vol. I, pp. 81–83.

is, to them canons of behaviour with which he was well
acquainted outside the class-room walls, and the way was
clear to bring to bear on them whatever influence as man
to man he possessed. Boys would be kept aloof by the
very dress of a headmaster who, till Temple (headmaster
of Rugby, 1858–1869) set them the example, never doffed
their clerical robes; but young men could tell a man
beneath the uniform. It is curious how this simple plan
of behaving inside the sixth form room as they did outside
was discovered simultaneously by a number of headmasters
who had no model to follow. Hawtrey, Arnold, Moberley,
and Charles Butler none of them ever saw any of the others
teaching; yet the contrast which Lyte's correspondent
draws[1] between Hawtrey and Keate would not be in-
appropriate to any of the four. "Hawtrey may be said
to have done by encouraging what Keate tried to do by
threatening. If there is any truth in that melancholy
caricature by which Keate is known to most men, if his
battle-cry really was 'I'll flog you,' it is no less true that
Hawtrey's characteristic utterance was, 'Very well, very
good exercise,' said with a gracious emphasis which never
lost its charm. Men have almost grown old who still feel
thankful that they once lived with a man who, though
quite at home in the most brilliant circles, did as truly as
Lacordaire 'love young people.'" Or contrast these two
passages: "Keate had as lower master acquired a rooted
distrust in the honour of boys in general, and he used to
make point blank charges quite at random....The effect
of this was to encourage the very evil which he wished to
check[2]." "There grew up a general feeling that 'it was a
shame to tell Arnold a lie—he always believes you[3].'"

As headmasters had the opportunity and the power of
influencing directly only their young men of the sixth form,
we see the importance of that bias given to the prefect
system by which it was made the vehicle for transferring
the headmaster's influence to the rest of the school. The
sixth form, still sufficiently fresh from boyhood not to have

[1] *History of Eton College*, p. 453.
[2] *Op. cit.* p. 402.   [3] Stanley, *Life of Arnold*, p. 113.

forgotten the nature of boys, with no "natural enemy" tradition to break down, mixing freely with the boys, and regarded by the boys as the *élite* of their own number, could do what the masters did not yet know how to do, and had a hundred-fold more opportunities to do it. No one believes that Arnold invented prefects. They had descended from the early grammar-schools where the monitors were used to eke out the resources of a staff consisting of the headmaster and an usher. In the old days they marked attendances, heard accidence, inspected tidiness, and exercised some sort of supervision in church, at meals, and out of school: in fact we may call them the non-commissioned officers of the school. Their teaching functions seem to have vanished with the provision of a more adequate staff, and only one effort was made to revive them. The result was an interesting interlude which, however, exercised no influence on the subsequent development of education. At the time when the monitorial system of Bell and Lancaster was believed to be a panacea for all the difficulties in elementary education, Russell (1818–1832) introduced it at Charterhouse, taking the 120 top boys himself for part of the time, while they taught the lower forms for the rest. So great was public confidence in the monitorial system that the numbers rapidly rose from 233 to 480 in seven years. Even then he had only eight masters. But experience soon condemned the system; the numbers fell back to 103, and Russell resigned. Seeing that Russell's monitors were of the same age as the later pupil teachers, the experiment cannot be considered as intrinsically unpromising, in spite of its failure.

This incident is strong evidence of the fluid character of educational institutions at this period. Russell overlaps Arnold. Arnold's modification of the prefect system was superficially small compared with Russell's. Prefects already supervised, reported, and punished in every public school. In the same sense the functions of king, lords, and commons are the same now as they were in the reign of Queen Anne. But James's lament that his house was the hardest to manage because it contained the largest pro-

portion of older boys shows the change in working. So does
Keate's action in flogging his whole sixth form in front
of the assembled juniors, who viewed the performance
much as we might imagine a Prussian battalion watching
its N.C.O.'s sent to the guardroom in a body[1]. What kind
of influence could Keate imagine his prefects would possess
after this?

Tradition credits Arnold with setting the example of
the way in which prefects became the means of transmitting
the headmaster's influence. A vague hazy public impression may assign to him all the reforms which occurred in
public schools during half-a-century: in this sense there
truly is an "Arnold myth." But for this myth Stanley
and Tom Hughes are not responsible. They make this
one definite claim; and Arnold himself defends his use of
the prefect system exactly as we should expect its acknowledged author to defend it. Can the claim be brought to
the definite test of evidence? We think it can. The change
is not one of those reforms, like improved scholarship or
greater keenness or greater urbanity, which are natural
outcomes of the spirit of the age. It was a discovery—
a very simple discovery it appears, like Columbus's treatment of the egg; but no one discovered it before, and
everyone used it afterwards. These are the two propositions
which need to be proved.

Fortunately the number of public schools was so small
that the first proposition can be proved by the process
of direct enumeration. The only shadow of a counter-claim
is that made by Leach for Winchester. Arnold himself,
in a spirit common amongst English, and especially among
Whig, reformers, seeks to base his reform on the traditions
of the past, and to minimise the change. He contends that
the prefect system was in existence at Winchester when he
was a pupil there under Goddard. If so, the tradition had
been completely forgotten at Winchester, so far as the
real Arnoldian spirit of the institution was concerned; for,
after Goddard's time, came a period when rowdyism
reached its height, and Leach himself admits that Win-

[1] Lyte, *History of Eton College*, p. 405.

chester had a peculiar reputation for bullying throughout the reign of Arnold's contemporary Moberley (1835–1866). The impression which Moberley leaves is that of a humane and scholarly man, fearfully Victorian in decorum, too clerical to be understood by boys or young men and too sedate to understand them, and too conventional to be an originator[1]. Keate's flogging exploit shows how completely absent the spirit of Arnold's prefect system was at Eton; and Hawtrey's reforms were those of an efficient administrator rather than of a leader of men. Charterhouse tried to modify the prefect system on quite different lines. Butler of Shrewsbury had on one occasion expelled all his prepostors, though he subsequently took them back; and Kennedy, though an excellent teacher, was too impulsive and violent in temper to exercise a steady influence. Westminster was undergoing a period of eclipse. At Harrow Goldwin Smith described the form of government as "moderate anarchy[2]"; and C. S. Roundell definitely asserts[3] that the Harrow sixth consciously attempted to follow Arnold's lines, as depicted in Stanley's *Life* (published 1844), under the guidance of Charles James Vaughan, one of Arnold's pupils, who transformed the school between 1845 and 1859.

Vaughan's reform of Harrow brings us from the proof of the negative proposition that the Arnoldian working of the prefect system is found missing in every one of the seven schools before his time to the positive proposition that its spread was directly due to his influence. Vaughan found Harrow with 69 boys and, when he resigned because he held that a headmaster had contributed all the ideas he had to give to a school in fourteen years, he left it with 469. Harrow was the only school of the old seven which was revived by one of Arnold's disciples; but, when we remember that, with the exception of Eton, the other public schools sank during the Arnoldian epoch to the

---

[1] F. D. How's *Six Great Headmasters*, 1904, contains short biographies of Moberley, Hawtrey, Kennedy, Vaughan, and Bradley.

[2] E. W. Howson and G. T. Warner, *Harrow School*, 1898, p. 99.

[3] *Op. cit.* p. 107.

position now occupied by the smallest members of the Headmasters' Conference, we see that the evidence of Arnold's influence has to be sought rather in the new schools which were rapidly founded on public school lines than in the ranks of the seven[1].

Three of these schools were founded during the forties. Cheltenham, the earliest, was a definite attempt to found a new type of school. Marlborough aimed at providing an education less costly than that of the public schools for sons of parish clergymen, but without any specific views as to the type of government which should prevail. Rossall had somewhat similar aims, but the first headmaster was a fervid Arnoldian with more faith than discretion, whose ideas almost anticipated the modern American experiments in self-governing communities. Yet in twenty years all came to be of the uniform public school type, as it is now understood. Marlborough led the way; its happy-go-lucky system of the first decade broke down the most completely; and it was deliberately reformed on Arnoldian lines by Arnold's own disciple Cotton: at Rossall subsequent headmasters cut down the powers of the prefects within Arnold's limits: and Cheltenham, under Barry, abandoned its alternative experiment, which had proved unworkable.

It is, we believe, its very universality and its success in driving out all rivals which have made the Arnoldian system appear to many to be so obvious a development as to have needed no master mind for its origination. The decade before its acceptance should dispel this feeling of inevitableness. When Cheltenham was founded by zealous Evangelicals, Evangelicals had not yet reconciled themselves to the public school system. It was primarily a day school. But its chief peculiarity was that the headmaster was responsible only for his pupils' intellects; their conduct was supervised by a committee, which dealt with schoolboy offences like a board of magistrates. A third difference, the existence of a Military and Civil Service side, to which Woolwich and Sandhurst stand in the same

---

[1] This is the line on which Dr Montagu Butler in Roberts's *Education in the Nineteenth Century* argues against the myth theory.

relation as do Oxford and Cambridge to the classical side, became the parent of all modern sides, though most of them fell short of their model and became mere dumping-grounds for the inefficient. The continuance of day-boys at Cheltenham—in this respect imitated by Clifton—and the general adoption of modern sides, show that the peculiar disciplinary system was not swamped by a mere desire for assimilation. The reputation of Cheltenham under Dobson (1845–1859) stood high; its practice is often quoted by the Public School Commissioners on doubtful points in connection with the intellectual *régime* of the schools which were within their purview. Dobson was a fine teacher and organiser of teaching; probably more intellectual work was done than at the public schools. There was never, as at Marlborough, a danger of a collapse. The disciplinary system merely gave way to the rival system because the latter was seen to be successful elsewhere while the former proved to be simply unworkable. The failure of a rival system at a school which in many ways was a pioneer brings into relief the success of Arnold's system as it was consciously transplanted to Marlborough by Cotton.

Marlborough was founded by local enterprise, aided by a host of prominent supporters, especially to afford education to sons of the clergy. The advent of the railway had ruined coaching; and a historic mansion, which for many years had served as a coaching hostelry, was secured as a home for the new school. The appearance of two hundred boys proved that it met an effective demand. Most of them were under sixteen; some came from home, some from private schools, some from local grammar schools. It was thus an illuminating experiment. It was free from traditions, good or bad. All that was brought was boy nature. The masters could feel that they had a free hand to suit their system to their material; if they failed, they could not blame preceding generations; if they succeeded, the credit was their own. Fame did her best for the new enterprise; within a short time the numbers stood at five hundred. But the first builders did not erect a lasting structure. Something was amiss. The boys exhibited the sporting instincts of all English country lads: their poaching exploits threw the feats of Tom Brown's schoolfellows into the shade. "The general feeling between the masters and the boys was one of distrust and enmity[1]." The school got out of hand; in 1851 there was a rebellion of the same type as had occurred so often in the older schools. The headmaster knew that the boys had ground for their complaints; he compromised; things were patched up for the moment; the mutiny broke out again; books were burned; boys were expelled; finally the headmaster resigned. The first stage in the experiment was completed, and the result could be written up. The old *laissez-faire* methods of public schools were a failure, not through bad traditions, but through an inherent defect of their own. They had been tried on new material, and had produced the old results.

Here was an opportunity for a crucial experiment on the part of Arnold's disciples. The governors elected Cotton, the "young master" of Tom Brown. He made the prefect system a reality. A crusade was proclaimed on drinking and breaking bounds. The prefects spent most of their half-holidays in "drawing" public-houses. There was opposition. Cotton assembled the school and addressed them thus: "The Council informed me on my appointment that the school was in a bad state of discipline, and they hoped that I would allow no boy to go out except in pairs under a master. I told them I could not accept office on such terms, that the school I hoped to govern was a public school, not a private one, and I would try to govern it by means of prefects. The school knows now how matters stand. They must either submit to the prefects or be reduced to the level of a private school and have their freedom ignominiously curtailed. The prefects are and shall be, as long as I am head, the governors of the school. As soon as I see that this is impracticable, I shall resign[2]."

---

[1] E. Lockwood, *The Early Days of Marlborough College*, 1893, p. 89. This book gives a vivid account both of the life and of the mutiny.

[2] A. G. Bradley, *History of Marlborough College*, p. 138.

Cotton was victorious. He and his assistants wisely saw that some outlet for the boys' physical energies was necessary, and they wrote circulars to the parents in support of games. Football had for some time been the chief winter pastime in public schools; but Marlborough had much to do with making it a regular institution. Cotton and many of his staff came from Rugby; hence the Rugby variety of the game was introduced. Old Marlburians were responsible even more than old Rugbeians for creating university Rugby football. From the universities it spread to the nation. Well may we wonder what the devoted bishop of Calcutta, if he could revisit this earth on a Saturday afternoon, would think of the later developments of his device for preventing Marlborough boys from poaching. Critics of Arnold sometimes hold him responsible for the subordination of work to games in public schools. Arnold's whole direct contribution was that he sometimes stood on the touch-line and looked pleased. Indirectly he dammed various undesirable outlets for boys' vitality, which in consequence flowed the more vigorously within permitted channels. Cotton saw how games had proved a counter-attraction and deliberately encouraged them. He can scarcely be blamed because others have carried them to excess. Nor was he a Prometheus who slipped a dose of animal spirits into little men and produced the race of boys, as any reader of accounts of school life in the thirties and forties will admit. It is less easy to say when Marlborough masters ceased to be the "natural enemies" of their pupils; but it is not an unlikely hypothesis that games contributed to this result. Cotton was succeeded by another Rugbeian, Bradley (1858–1870), and for a time it won a pre-eminence in scholarship and sport almost without a parallel. Arnold's system had been justified by one at least of her children.

Rossall brings to our notice an over-development of Arnold's system. Woolley, the first headmaster, had been a great friend of A. P. Stanley at Oxford, had been greatly impressed by his account of Arnold's work, and doubtless believed that he was copying its main feature. He had

not, however, seen the system at work, and the turn which
he gave to it overstrained its possibilities. His prefects
practically ruled; he was little more than a constitutional
monarch. His successor Osborne (1849–1870) was surprised to discover that, when his prefects "advised" him
to give a half-holiday, he was expected to take their advice
as that of a cabinet. He at once pruned down the system
within Rugby limits, though there is no evidence of any
direct contact with Arnold or his disciples. When the
monitors tendered their resignation, he merely remarked,
"Gentlemen, you are monitors and will continue to be
monitors." An exaggerated imitation is distinct evidence
that Arnold's contemporaries recognised that he had added
something individual to the previously prevailing practice.
It may be significant that the "natural enemy theory" is
recorded to have come to an end under James, because
James came from Marlborough, and Marlborough was
made by Cotton, the very man in whose favour Tom
Brown relaxed the theory!

Space forbids a detailed account of the rise of subsequent
new schools; but Arnold's spiritual descendants were
carrying his system everywhere. Wellington won its
position under Benson (1859–1868), a pupil of Prince Lee,
one of Arnold's masters, at Birmingham, and himself a
master at Rugby; Haileybury under A. G. Butler (1861–
1867), a pupil at Rugby under Tait and a master under
Temple; Clifton under Percival (1862–1878), another Rugby
master. Of the older schools which developed on the same
lines, Repton owes its position to Pears (1854–1874), a
house-master at Harrow under Vaughan, who raised the
numbers from fifty to 250. Malvern was founded "on the
system of Winchester," which we take to be the first
attempt, while adopting Arnold's system, to dissociate it
from Rugby. It is interesting in this connection to notice
which schools play Rugby and which Association football.
If a school plays Rugby, it is almost always possible to
prove that it consciously followed Arnold's traditions and
acknowledged it; such is the case with the majority of
great schools outside the seven. The converse is not so

universal; Repton, for instance, plays Association because the Rugby influence came by way of Harrow. As time went on, there was a tendency, especially in the case of High Church schools, which could not forget Arnold's theological views, to look to Winchester as the fountain of the system[1]. Was not Winchester the oldest of our public schools? Did not Arnold, in his defence of the prefect system, sign himself "A Wykehamist"? The mediaeval associations appealed to the High Church clergy, who were fast becoming the prevailing party; and perhaps it was well, in the interests of the system, that they should believe that it was under Arnold exactly what it had been in the days of William of Wykeham. Undoubtedly the schools with a High Church bias tended to get their masters from Winchester, where Moberley was supposed to have suffered in loss of numbers from his religious views. Bradfield, Lancing, and Radley represent this tendency. Sherborne is also a school where no direct Arnoldian influence can be traced. But even when full account has been taken of all the schools where no such influence is evident, it is clear that it was the others which led the way, attained the more commanding numbers, impressed the public mind, and carried the rest along with them.

Arnold's influence was by no means confined to the twenty or more schools which became large boarding-schools and rivals of the seven. Four examples may be taken from the great day-schools. Prince Lee, afterwards bishop of Manchester, left Rugby to become headmaster of King Edward's School, Birmingham (1837–1848). Among his pupils were three great bishops, Benson, Lightfoot, and Westcott. Walker, a pupil of Rugby under Tait and a master under Temple, spread Arnold's influence, first to Manchester, where his work was warmly commended by the Schools Inquiry Commission, and afterwards to St Paul's (1876). Mr McDonnell, in his *History of St Paul's School*[2], describes him as "the one headmaster of his time

---

[1] The late Mr Leach, whom no one would suspect of clericalist sympathies, was undoubtedly led astray by his Wykehamist loyalty.

[2] p. 451.

who attempted to show that education of the best possible kind, both moral and intellectual, could be given in surroundings different from those of the stereotyped boarding-schools." Finally, J. S. Phillpotts, a Rugby master, initiated the growth of Bedford (1862–1874) from a curse to the town under guise of a charity[1] into its present position as a school which has attracted residents to Bedford on such a scale as to double the population of the town in twenty-five years.

Arnold was evidently not without honour in his own country, as in addition to Lee at Birmingham we find one of his assistants, Hill, headmaster of Warwick from 1843 to 1878, and one of his pupils, J. P. Collis, raising the old foundation school at Bromsgrove[2] into a really good first-grade school, though smaller in numbers than most of those which we have mentioned. Still more interesting is it to find Arnold influencing Nonconformist schools. Mill Hill was founded in 1807 and was intended from the first to follow public school lines; but, apart from the classical curriculum, the founders had evidently no clear idea what were the points to be imitated in a public school of their day, and we hardly wonder at it. But Priestly (1834–1853) considered the problem solved by the appearance of Arnold; for he corresponded with him[3], tried to imitate his confidence in boys, and occasionally despaired. "This is what Arnold calls 'boy nature,'" he exclaimed when some boys had committed an act of meanness, "but what am I to do with the eleven boys[4]?" Here is an instance of a headmaster of another denomination treating Arnold during his life-time as the accepted ideal of a head. When Arnold's *Life* was published, a member of the committee suggested that many of his customs might be introduced at Mill Hill, but Mr James considers[5] that the imitation

---

[1] *Report of Schools Inquiry Commission*, p. 531.

[2] Later Millington, a disciple of Thring, left a lasting name here. We wonder if there is any other instance of a school which came under the double influence of Thring and of Arnold.

[3] N. G. B. James, *History of Mill Hill*, p. 129.

[4] p. 141.   [5] p. 174.

"was too close and detailed" and lacked the spirit of true confidence in the boys and reliance on the monitors.

It must be admitted that Arnold's influence was helped on by the fact that he was a Liberal and a Broad Churchman. Conservatives and High Churchmen were, so to speak, the natural allies of the public schools and might be suspected of more anxiety to defend than to reform them. Arnold largely won over those who would support them only if they were reformed. He defended them more for what they might become than for what they were. His type of churchmanship, which sought union between the Church of England and Nonconformists, not from indifference to distinctive tenets, but from his profound sense of the importance of what they had in common, was the only type which could have led Nonconformists to send their boys with perfect confidence to schools staffed for the most part by clergy of the Church of England. Whatever be our views on the question of the "schoolmaster-parson" at the present day, it is indisputable that, almost up to the close of the nineteenth century, parents had more confidence in clergymen as headmasters than in laymen. Even Nonconformist members of governing bodies hardly trusted a layman to exercise the same influence on his pupils' characters, even if they were able to escape a suspicion that his reluctance to take orders was due to a feeling of unfitness. Indeed Arnold is sometimes blamed for perpetuating the clerical headmaster by being so unconscionably good a specimen of a bad class!

If we are satisfied that Arnold really exercised the influence which is attributed to him, it hardly matters to discuss whether his reputation is deserved. It is always easy to show that a great man was the product of his time, but this does not prove that he was *merely* its product. Arnold knew what other schools were doing, he read current educational literature, he bore the impress of Corpus and Oriel. He could not have succeeded had the time not been ripe; there was need of parents who demanded an improvement in the moral and intellectual tone of schools before schools could be created to satisfy their demands. Nor could he have succeeded in "mending" the public schools among a people who had not the English preference for "mending" to "ending." But, when it is urged that his reputation is due only to the lucky accident of his possessing two such biographers as Dean Stanley and Thomas Hughes, we have to ask whether it was not precisely this power of influencing pupils so unlike as Arthur Stanley and Tom Hughes which was the secret of his greatness. All his life he was getting other people to transmit his enthusiasm. That was how it spread. That is how the influence of all great moral reformers spreads and is the proof that a man is a great moral reformer.

More serious than such arguments is Mr Lytton Strachey's line of criticism in *Eminent Victorians*. He recognises fully as a historical fact that Arnold set the type for public schools in the nineteenth century; he indulges in no stock argument by which a great man is explained as a mere link in a chain of causes; he does not even labour the point that some of his contemporaries labelled his products as prigs. Had no one described them by some unpleasant epithet, the probability would be that there was nothing new in the type. In reading Mr Strachey, however, we must carefully distinguish the definite arguments from the general impression produced by his masterly power of grouping his material. We believe that Mr Strachey could tell the truth, the whole truth, and nothing but the truth, and yet so group the truth that he would make St Francis appear as a super-tramp and Caesar as an arch-gambler who won the world by "going double or quits" over his gaming debts. The serious educational criticism is contained in his account of the manner in which a reforming headmaster would proceed to-day. He would try the effect of civilising his pupils. He would invite his sixth to his wife's drawing-room; he would introduce them to modern literature, art, and music; he would make them realise what counted to men. We suspect that, allowing for the difference of the age, this was what Vittorino da Feltre and the other great Italian teachers of the Renaissance did. Thring is certainly far nearer to this ideal than Arnold.

Arnold was something of a Puritan; he thought it waste of time for boys to read *Nicholas Nickleby*. Yet, if Arnold had been a century ahead of his time, he would very likely have failed. The father of Matthew Arnold must surely have had something of the spirit of sweetness and light in him, but the age was not congenial to it. The young barbarian of the thirties was not prepared to be moralised by aesthetic. The bullies of Tom Brown were very different raw material from the athleticised products of the preparatory school who are depicted in the *Loom of Youth*. Mr Strachey's error is the same as that of certain contemporaries who think of Russian Bolsheviks as British working men who happen to speak a foreign language. Bolsheviks are the brutalised products of brutality; so were the fag-roasting bullies of Rugby. British working men are good-hearted folk who from time to time get a wrong sense of values into their heads; so are Alec Waugh's athletic-crazy public school boys. Mr Strachey makes good sport with Arnold's references to the Old Dispensation; but, to brace himself for his task, Arnold, like Luther, had to think he was fighting the devil in hand to hand conflict. Nowadays the devil lays mines and disappears, and headmasters need wile rather than hard hitting to defeat him.

The mention of the *Loom of Youth* brings us to our last point. There must be readers who have exclaimed, "Why discuss whether Arnold was the father of the public school system, when the progeny is so little one to be proud of?" The public schools have certainly run off Arnold's main track on to the siding of athleticism. A means has become an end. Alec Waugh's picture is incomplete, but it is probably true. Very bad things happen in public schools; they probably happened far more frequently a hundred years ago. There are many good things which public schools fail to do; in particular, they fail to make the majority of their pupils into really educated men; we believe the same to be true of every single kind of educational institution in the country. Unfortunately it is very difficult to see any man or any institution as it really is and not to condemn it; because we unconsciously make comparisons with other men or other institutions, which we have never seen without a halo. Still more difficult is it to see the seamy side of anything and to supply the good side. Moreover to know a man or to be a member of an institution is a very different thing from seeing it as it really is. Alec Waugh's description of his old school may contain nothing but truth; yet those who are led by its perusal to a wholesale condemnation of modern public schools, had they happened to be pupils at that school, might not have recognised the picture. If a full picture were painted of any educational institution, old university or new, municipal school or elementary school, its admirers would be aghast. The failures it turned out, the chances it missed, the worst acts any of its members committed—in most cases only the recording angel chronicles them. May it not be that Alec Waugh's school was superior in this, that it made him long for what it appeared not to supply—which is half-way to supplying it—while the majority of institutions send forth their alumni unconscious of what they lack?

In any case Arnold is no more responsible for the development of public schools for all time than was St Francis for the friars of Chaucer's day or Aristotle for a fourteenth century disputation. His prefects were the sixth form chosen for their brains, not athletes chosen for their bodily prowess. Games were to him merely a particular way of spending leisure, preferable to poaching, window-smashing, or drinking, not the serious purpose of life. Arnold routed the army which the devil brought up against him in his own day, so that few of his Old Regulars are fighting now; he is not to blame that the devil has raised new levies. Bullying is dead; fear of "bad form" has taken its place. Hostility to religion has been replaced by indifference, intentional blasphemy by meaningless oaths, lawlessness by over-obedience to the "bloods," idleness by turning play into work. To put the matter to a practical test: would a parent nowadays send his son to a public school if he had only the schools of 1820 to choose from? And are there not plenty of schools, large and small, to which he can safely send him to-day? The devil's reserves are not equal to his shock troops. A few of the latter remain, and some of Alec Waugh's readers may mistake them for new recruits: they are only the hardest to kill of the original force. If anyone under estimates Arnold because he did not anticipate the devil's moves a hundred years ahead, that man does not know the devil.

REFERENCES

A. P. Stanley, *Life and Correspondence of Thomas Arnold*, 1844.

J. J. Findlay, *Arnold of Rugby*, 1898 (includes articles and sermons by Arnold himself).

Thomas Hughes, *Tom Brown's Schooldays*, 1857.

Sir H. C. Maxwell Lyte, *History of Eton College*, 1877.

A. F. Leach, *History of Winchester College*, 1899.

S. Butler, *Life and Letters of Dr Samuel Butler*, 1896.

W. H. D. Rouse, *History of Rugby School*, 1909.

Alexander Hay Tod, *Charterhouse*, 1905.

E. W. Howson and G. T. Warner, *Harrow School*, 1898.

F. D. How, *Six Great Headmasters*, 1904.

John Sargeaunt, *Annals of Westminster School*, 1898.

A. G. Bradley, A. C. Champneys and J. W. Baines, *History of Marlborough College*, 1893.

Edward Lockwood, *The Early Days of Marlborough College*, 1893.

J. F. Rowbothom, *History of Rossall School*, 1894.

A. F. Leach, *History of Bradfield College*, 1900.

M. F. J. McDonnell, *History of St Paul's School*, 1909.

Rev. the Hon. W. E. Bowen, *Edward Bowen, a Memoir*, 1902.

Schools Inquiry Commission, *Report*, vol. III (Bedford, Manchester, Birmingham, etc.).

Lytton Strachey, *Eminent Victorians*, 1918.

CHAPTER IV

NEW TYPES OF EDUCATION

ENGLISH education has developed from its two poles. It began, at the one end with the two universities and a few public schools, at the other with the monitorial schools of Bell and Lancaster. The middle was filled in last. The age of leaving the elementary school was gradually raised, "ex-VII standards" were added, evening continuation schools were attempted, till the Fisher Act of 1918 finally completed the growth that came from the bottom upwards. Concurrently there was taking place another development from the top downwards. The reform of public schools was followed by a revival of the smaller grammar schools along similar lines in the seventies. The success of this experiment led to a further demand for secondary education, and the beginning of the twentieth century saw the creation of municipal and county schools. The two growths thus met in the middle. When the continuation school clauses of the Fisher Act come into full force, it will be possible to say that all English boys and girls between five and eighteen are being educated. The period from 1815 to 1918 has secured the quantity of schooling; future improvements must be in its quality.

For thirty years after 1815 the universities, the public schools, and the monitorial schools were almost the only ancestors of our present educational institution which had any vitality. It is obvious, however, that two universities and less than a dozen public schools were educating only a fraction of the population which was over the very low elementary school age of that time; and we must consider how the rest were provided for, so far as they were provided for at all.

The *Report* of the Schools Inquiry Commission in 1868 is a mine of information concerning the old grammar schools. There were no less than 782 endowments for secondary education, though in fifty cases the schools had ceased to exist at the time of the Commission. Of these schools, 209 or 27 per cent. were nominally classical, though 132 of them sent no boys to the universities; 183 or 23 per cent. taught Latin but no Greek, and 340 or 43 per cent. were non-classical. They taught 9279 boarders and 27,595 day boys. The classical schools mostly dated from the Middle Ages or from the reign of Queen Elizabeth; the non-classical foundations were later. The early foundations almost invariably provided for the work being carried on by "one schoolmaster and one usher." Such an arrangement was almost unworkable, however small the number of pupils; yet the numbers were rarely sufficient to permit of more, and sometimes the funds were barely adequate for that. The Leeds judgment (1805) had forbidden a grammar school to be turned into a non-classical school, even where there was no demand for a classical education. It became, however, more and more difficult to enforce this decision, and in 1840 an act was passed allowing the Court of Chancery to relax it. The Commission found great variations both in curriculum and in efficiency according to locality; but whatever improvements had taken place were much more recent than 1815. The classical teaching was generally poor. The decadence was most noteworthy in Cumberland, Westmorland, and Cornwall, where the main function of classics seemed to be "to furnish the pretext for the neglect of all other useful learning[1]." In Staffordshire and Warwickshire there were only 97 boys who with unlimited time and with the help of dictionaries "would be able to make out an ordinary passage of Cicero or Vergil[2]." In Lancashire, however, many had recently adopted a "commercial" curriculum, not without improvement. Generally speaking, the non-classical schools were even worse than the classical; science was not taught at all, and French and mathematics were badly taught. In fact no one had a clear idea what a non-classical school should do. In many cases the state of things amounted to

[1] *Report*, p. 133.   [2] p. 137.

a positive scandal. At Whitgift School, Croydon, now a first-grade school of over 300 boys, the headmaster had held office for thirty years but there were no pupils! Sedbergh, which earlier in the century a headmaster named Evans had conducted with great success, and which has risen again to a prominent position, had dropped to thirteen boys, but the governors had no remedy against the headmaster. Much the same happened at Wakefield, the head having discovered that his tenure was a freehold. At Kingston the dormitory had been turned into a billiard-room, and the headmaster complacently assured the investigators that "it was not worth while with £200 a year." At Skipton the head employed his son and nephew as assistants and the teaching was hopelessly bad. At Bingley the headmaster taught his own son and the vicar's and neglected the rest. Since the Restoration, governors had far too often been guilty of neglect and sometimes of actual jobbery and misappropriation. Probably at any given time, however, there were a few schools, though not always the same schools, in which a good scholar was giving a sound classical foundation to a few boys who would proceed to the universities, as was the case with Dr Johnson. And in such cases the boys may have had other advantages. Charles Kingsley, for instance, though he laments that he was not sent to a public school, from a notion, probably mistaken, that it would have cured his shyness, would probably never have had the same opportunities for pursuing his botanical and geological hobbies as he had at Helston Grammar School[1]; and Kingsley did not miss his first in classics through his scientific pursuits.

Besides the endowed schools there were about 10,000 private schools. These no commission ever investigated, and nothing like an adequate history of them will ever be told. They were of every variety of kind and quality. Their pupils would now be found in public schools, in municipal and county schools, in technical schools, in elementary schools. Wealthy parents might send their sons to a

[1] *Charles Kingsley*, by his wife, pp. 7–9.

private school from fear of bad tone or bullying in a public school or to secure their own form of religious influence. Country clergymen, lawyers, and doctors had no fixed tradition in the matter; it depended on such accidental factors as acquaintance with the headmaster where a boy was sent. Farmers and shopkeepers had no other provision than private schools in districts which had no neighbouring grammar school or where it was totally inefficient. Social distinctions operated more powerfully to prevent parents from sending their children to elementary schools when elementary schools where charitable and not public institutions. Cheapness or dearness, the efficiency of the headmaster or the inefficiency of his grammar school rival, the success with which Latin was taught or the fact that Latin was not taught at all, the desire to keep a boy at home or the desire to get rid of him from home, might any of them be reasons for choosing for him a private school. Quite a substantial proportion of boys reached the universities who had never been to any endowed school.

One characteristic only did private schools possess in common, that the boys were much more closely supervised. This was what Cotton referred to when he told his Marlborough boys that he would not govern them as a private school. The words would call up to his youthful hearers a vision of boys marching two by two and watched every moment of day and night. There had been a time when this was a deliberate ideal in England, as it has always been in France. Public school liberty arose because it was accepted as good for the boys. The really devoted parent and the really devoted teacher believed in supervision. Locke was an Englishman to the core; but he believed in the private tutor. This older attitude was by no means dead. With the aristocracy Eton, Harrow, or Winchester had undoubtedly become the fashion, but it was not *de rigueur*; the professional classes still halted between two opinions.

The methods of teaching both in classical and in non-classical schools would be inconceivable to-day. Outside the public schools, the text-books which were in use are

our main source of evidence; but they are amply sufficient.
A modern teacher would fling them away and dictate his
own. In classical schools the *Eton Grammar*, a descendant
of Lily's, was in common use. Garretson's *Exercises* chiefly
astonish us by assuming that the whole of the accidence is
learned before the pupil attempts to write the simplest
Latin sentence. On the very first page words of all declensions and all conjugations are showered on the learner,
who apparently writes Latin by rule before he has seen it
written. The exercises follow the order of the rules in the
Eton syntax, but assume a rate of progress which we know
to be impossible. The dictionary confuses its user by giving
from half-a-dozen to a score of English equivalents for
a Latin word and *vice versa*, with no examples to show their
meaning. When the pupil reached the stage of reading
authors, no edition with vocabulary and notes welcomed
him. The Eton books of extracts were indeed editions, but
they were intended for the upper forms only, and they
perplexed more than they elucidated. Plain texts of Vergil,
Caesar, and Nepos were the rule. To make beginners look
out every word in the dictionary and hammer out the sense
for themselves was regarded as part of the mental discipline.
It rarely occurred to anyone that the method by which the
learner starts should bear some relation to the methods by
which his mind must work if he is to become expert.
A method which eliminated *Sprachgefühl* and unconscious
use of analogy could not lead up to a sense of style or a
power of translation at sight. It created the habit of
regarding Latin sentences as brick puzzles—the idea that
Latin translation consists in forcing the words by rule into
grammatical but nonsensical English. The *Gradus* created
the same brick-puzzle conception of the way to piece
together Latin hexameters and pentameters. It may be
safely assumed that Butler's improvements in the teaching
of classics were long in reaching the grammar and private
schools, save in occasional instances such as that of Don-
caster (1808–1846) at Oakham, who practised them with
success. A few teachers like the Hills[1] may have freed

---

[1] See below, p. 92.

themselves from the incubus of the text-book by oral teaching on their own lines.

The non-classical schools provided a curriculum hardly as wide as that of elementary schools at the present day. Outside the "three R's" the text-books indicate cram of the worst kind. Most of them were set out in the form of a catechism, and were clearly intended to be learned by heart, the teacher's sole function being to ask the questions prescribed in the book. Among the opponents of the traditional classical course had arisen a passion for "useful" knowledge such as excited F. D. Maurice's query, "Useful for what?". The seventeenth century might be thought to have exhausted the possibilities of abstracts and epitomes; but the sum of human knowledge was greater now than in the age of Comenius, and closer packing was needed to get it into the required space. Here are the contents of a little text-book of 340 pages bearing the date 1821, which was presumably popular, since this is the eighteenth edition. It is styled *An Easy Introduction to the Arts and Sciences.* It deals in catechetical form with religion, logic, morality, atmospheric phenomena, sound, earthquakes and volcanoes, the tides, metaphysics, jurisprudence, medicine, chemistry, botany, grammar, rhetoric, metre, mathematics, architecture, painting, sculpture, mechanics, chronology, astronomy, geography, history, mythology, natural history, mineralogy, pneumatics, hydrostatics, electricity, galvanism, artificial memory, and the drama. The reasons for the sequence are not indicated. Only when he reaches mythology does the writer really launch out, this section occupying thirty pages, an amount beaten only by natural history with thirty-six. A small amount of mind-building material could possibly be extracted from this book, but Mangnall's *Questions* probably accomplished, more completely and more distastefully than any book ever written, the task of conveying to the learner an impression of familiarity with every classical, historical, political, or legal allusion, without giving a grain of real knowledge.

Even the text-books which limited themselves to one subject were in other respects no better. Guy's *Geography* a standard class-book in the middle of the century, boasts eloquently of a "new plan" "which was pursued by the compiler for years in the Royal Military College, and in no place of Education is this branch of Knowledge taught more expeditiously or more thoroughly." The "plan" is nothing else than this:—"Only the pages printed in the larger Roman type [fifteen pages entirely composed of strings of names of the features of each continent] should first be learned by heart. The divisions printed in Italics at the head of each country may form a second course [mainly provinces and chief towns]. And, if the pupil's time will permit, a third course of very careful reading through the smaller type (so as to enable him to answer the General Questions subjoined, page 163) will communicate a much greater body of valuable information than can be derived from any other school treatise." These questions are, "Is the country divided into provinces, governments, departments, states or counties, etc.? and how many? Have their names changed? If so what are they? Repeat the chief cities and say for what noted," etc., etc. Some history text-books were in catechetical form, but the best at least gave a continuous narrative. Though modern text-books of history do not inform their readers that Homer was the most famous of Greek historians, they have not made so great an advance on the pedagogic side as have the best geographical text-books. Popular astronomy benefited more than any other scientific subject from the love of presenting the results of modern science to schoolboys and schoolgirls; and, the present writer, having as a boy of eight lighted on an old school-book used by his aunt, is able to affirm that much of it was intelligible[1]. The same, however, cannot be confidently asserted of the teaching which had been given from it, as his aunt could scarcely have been trusted to recognise Jupiter with certainty. With what success the "Use of the Globes," which properly handled would have been a fine exercise

---

[1] There is no date in the book but it must have been published before the discovery of Neptune but after that of the first four asteroids.

for the intelligence, was taught must, we fear, be left a matter of conjecture. Would that we had as clear an idea how an early nineteenth century teacher proceeded with the following problem as we have of the way in which Brinsley taught Latin in the early seventeenth century!

To find at what time any star rises, culminates, and sets at any given latitude and day.

Adjust the globe to the state of the heavens for that day and place at noon, bring the star to the eastern verge of the horizon, the horary circle will then show the hour of its rising; bring the star to the meridian, the circle will then show the time of its culminating; and the time of its setting will be shewn by bringing the star to the western verge.

What is the time of Aldebaran's rising, culminating, and setting June 16 at London? *Ans.* About $\frac{1}{2}$ past 3 in the morning; culminates at 11 A.M., and sets at $\frac{1}{4}$ past 6 P.M.

The more enlightened text-books of popular science, dealing with light, mechanics, hydrostatics, etc., in a non-mathematical way, bear a strong impress of Rousseau, both in subject-matter and in the idea of experimenting with improvised apparatus. The omniscient tutor who appears in this class of book is clearly cousin german to Mr Barlow of *Sandford and Merton*. They were presumably meant for tutors and parents of Edgeworth type rather than for schools.

We can hardly condemn the schools or the parents of the period for clinging to their classics. The weapons of the "reformers" were hardly of a kind to drive classics from the fortress in which it had been ensconced for centuries. Before new subjects could demand admittance, their supporters must show that they could be taught as intelligently as Butler and Arnold were teaching classics.

Contemporary literature preserves for us some recollections of the private school. Dickens, in Mr Squeers's Dotheboys Hall, has created one immortal picture of the worst type. It may be well therefore to give a short account of one of the best.

Private schools have at least the liberty to experiment.

A remarkable experiment was made in the early years of the century in a private school near Birmingham by two brothers who afterwards became famous in other spheres, Rowland Hill, the author of penny postage, and Matthew Davenport Hill, the criminal law reformer. Not only so, but their experiment was an application to school conditions of the very principles which they afterwards so successfully applied to the body politic, that punishment should be reformatory, and that up to a certain point by demanding less you get more. The Hazelwood scheme gave far more self-government to the boys than any form of the prefect system. The closest modern parallel is the George Junior Republic. It is thought to have had some influence on Thomas Arnold.

The brothers Hill took over their father's school in Birmingham. He was so poor a financier that Rowland managed his business affairs from the age of seventeen. The boys had been brought up in the school atmosphere; Rowland had begun to teach at twelve. They were therefore largely self-educated, but this was not without advantage both to the scope of their interests and to their pedagogic attitude. A formal schooling might have confined them to classics; as it was, their interests covered not only mathematics but subjects so unusual in those days as surveying and various manual crafts. They avoided, however, the growing craze among educational modernists for the mere pouring forth of knowledge; indeed the most striking feature in their teaching was their constant use of the pupils' activity. Classics, mathematics, French, and English constituted the class syllabus; but rarely has a system of options been so well devised to encourage the pupils to devote serious attention to hobbies of their own choice. It is, nevertheless, sad to think that it was the lack of that prestige which comes from university distinctions which prevented their experiment from having a wider influence and left them without successors.

Their methods of government and teaching were so interdependent that neither would retain its identity without the other. Both depended on two premises, the first that the motives which influence adults are among those which influence boys, though they never regarded them as the sole motives; the second that a right training for life should therefore embrace the direction of these motives which commonly guide life. The second of these propositions would commend itself to modern educationalists if they could convince themselves of the truth of the first. But the first is truer than is often thought. The old mistake was for scholarly men to picture all boys as budding scholars; the new mistake is to forget that the majority of *men* have never grown up either intellectually or morally, but remain big schoolboys—good-hearted, energetic, impulsive, short-sighted, changeable, tireless over a self-imposed task but ready to use any device to shirk a task imposed by others, straight in their dealings with their own companions but inclined to regard all other types of mankind as unreasonable. Personally we are convinced that the minority of men who think ahead and regulate their conduct by logical principles begin to do so at school and that the rest remain such as we have described.

The Hills' experiment then was an attempt to readjust the balance between the motives for study which might be brought to bear on boys. Of these, love of the subject, joy in successful activity, competition, reward, and punishment have at different times been in favour. The Hills took a very sensible view concerning the scope of the first motive. In few cases will boys really prefer classics or mathematics to lighter pursuits. Hence this motive was restricted to choice of options—general reading, composition, and various manual subjects, such as drawing, modelling, and surveying. Even in these congenial subjects they saw that interest alone will not make a boy wish to continue when difficulties become rife and steady application is needed: so in every case they required the definite completion of some piece of work before any account was taken of it. The same principle was applied in the regular class subjects: as soon as the pupil had done his work *without a mistake*, he could leave the class. In no subject was passive receptivity allowed except in the early stages of learning languages, which they reasonably regarded as an essentially imitative process. The use of the dictionary was therefore postponed and very careful class work took its place. The Hills had hit on the right principle, though it has been left to recent times to work it out in the direct method. But for subjects like history, descriptive geography, and popular science, the bold plan was adopted of letting the pupils read what they liked so long as they were willing to stand an oral test on it, a method which would win the approval of Miss Charlotte Mason at the present day. Joy in successful activity was therefore well recognised; and this joy is identical with the play motive, which was at one time thought to be peculiar to childhood, but is now recognised as the spring of energy not only in the artist but in every worker who approaches his work in the artist's spirit.

The three motives of competition, reward, and punishment were rolled into one. The Hills had no false illusions about the sense of duty, which they recognised to be the goal of education rather than its spring. Schoolboys have a sense of duty just as soldiers have. Soldiers will face death, but they will not dig trenches, from a sense of duty. Adult work, save when it is done in the spirit of the artist—and preliminary spade-work can hardly be done in that spirit—is mainly based on one of these three motives. To the Englishman or American competition means "beating the other fellow," not, as with the Latin races, hoping for a statue to record your victory. He neither brags over his success nor, like the old Assyrian kings, wishes to engage inferior rivals in order to secure a soft victory. Competition was accepted at Hazelwood as an honourable motive. The shape, however, which it assumed was peculiar. A foreigner might say that it was the natural shape for it to assume among a "nation of shopkeepers." Among adults in a mercantile community money is the usual reward of industry, and want of it the usual punishment for idleness. If, as Spencer afterwards asserted, the consequences of action in childhood ought to be made as like as possible to those of mature life, the corollary seems to be obvious, and the Hills did not shrink from it. But the Hills were acquainted with political economy, and knew that money is only a symbol of value and a medium of exchange, the true value residing in the commodities which it will purchase. They therefore invented a school coinage which would purchase those commodities which schoolboys desire, holidays, privileges, and the like. Punishments consisted in the loss of these counters or "marks." Marks, *i.e.* dummy coins, were won for place in class, but mainly for the performance of options, while they were lost wholesale for even a single mistake in set work. Punishments for work, in the strict sense, only began with bankruptcy, when detentions were imposed until enough optional work had been done to render the defaulter once more solvent.

Ardent supporters of the Liberal movement, the Hills introduced the methods of constitutional government into their school. The masters regulated the curriculum, but the boys, through elected committees, controlled the discipline. The constituencies were so arranged as to give great weight to position in the school. The criminal code was the work of the boys, though masters were, so to speak, *ex officio* magistrates in class. In cases of doubt the boys themselves furnished judge and jury. The authors of this system, which reads at first like a Gilbert and Sullivan opera, claimed that it worked so well that justice rarely miscarried. Corporal punishment was abolished; fines, loss of privileges, temporary interdiction of social intercourse and, in the last resort, confinement in the dark being the recognised penalties.

Fortunately we have the impressions of an old pupil, who seems to be a man of common sense, on the effects of the system. W. L. Sargant, in his *Essays by a Birmingham Manufacturer*[1], writes: "By juries and committees, by marks, and by appeals to a sense of honour, discipline was maintained. But this was done, I think, at too great a sacrifice: the thoughtlessness, the spring, the elation of childhood were taken from us; we were premature men:

[1] Vol. II, Essay 3, pp. 186–192.

one of my younger schoolfellows told me that as an elder boy, being appointed after I left a guardian over his juniors"—this was the way in which the happy-go-lucky juniors were by a kindly but steady pressure broken in to the system—"the responsibility weighed on him so heavily that he meditated suicide; and yet there was not a tinge of morbidness in his temperament. The school was in truth a moral hotbed, which forced us into a precocious imitation of maturity. I have heard an Oxford friend say that Arnold's men had a little of the prig about them: I know too well that some of us had a great deal of the prig about us: I have often wished that I had the 'giftie to see ourselves as others see us'; but I have comforted myself with observing that in later life my schoolfellows (perhaps therefore I myself) outgrew this unamiable character."

With this verdict that it was a hotbed of prigs some readers may be content to leave it. Clearly it was not an aggregate of units struggling each against like the world of the Manchester School. It did not produce an "economic boy": there was no "de'il tak' the hindmost." The smaller and weaker, who were slaves at the public school, were treated as colts to be trained at Hazelwood. And is not this the only judicious relation which can subsist between older and younger boys? The system clearly escapes the Scylla of encouraging a "mercantile spirit," if indeed it was not a moralising of that spirit: what of the Charybdis of training prigs? A prig, we take it is one who does by rule good actions which other people, if they do them at all, do automatically. Consequently, every time he does a good action, he is aware of the fact. He is therefore in risk of being conceited, and he may also become a casuist. He is inclined to become self-centred, in which case his separate virtues become an aggregate vice. He may be suspected of being censorious; for his habit of finely weighing his own motives may be transferred to those of others. If priggishness be accompanied by none of these derivative qualities, it annoys us only mildly, in the same way as a halting speech, a clumsy stroke at cricket, or any other action in which the effort seems disproportionate to the achievement. A prig is like a man who has learned etiquette from a book: he does not know how to be good neatly or naturally. Most boys pass through a hobbledehoy stage of awkwardness before their manners become automatic; may it not be that they have to pass through a stage of mild priggishness before their morals become so? If so, our aim is to keep this priggishness within its proper limits; and unfortunately a system, whatever it is, which suits the average boy, may over-develop it in a specially susceptible boy. It is extremely probable that the Hills' system did make for overmuch introspection and for an over-developed sense of responsibility. But it was an experiment, and a slight modification may be all that was needed to achieve success. Possibly the absence of group games, for which running, jumping, swimming, and gymnastics were not a complete substitute, and the number of hours spent indoors, even though many of them were spent on music and hobbies, were the factors which needed to be changed. To feel responsibility all day long is enough to drive any man, much more any boy, mad; but a system which encourages a sense of responsibility is good, as long as a time limit is set.

Even the curious system of self-government must not be dismissed too lightly. Introduced into an old-established institution in which "schoolboy trade unionism" had long prevailed, it would doubtless lead to anarchy as surely as the change from autocracy to Soviet government did in Russia. But it is conceivable that, once firmly established, a system by which boys devise the scale of penalties might work at least as easily as the prefect system by which the senior boys administer them. The danger of a boy State is more likely to be ultra-conservatism than ultra-radicalism. The Hills argued that public opinion alone is really effective in enforcing rules and that a slight inferiority in the rules is amply compensated for by a real enforcement. The insuperable difficulty in rejecting it is that it worked; and, till it is given a fair trial again by a believer in it and found not to work, that is a powerful argument. The history of the experiment is a further caution against a belief that the internal management of schools could only have developed on one set of lines. Here, slightly before Arnold's time, was an experiment different from his; but Arnold was a man of known attainments, working in a famous school, who found imitators, while the Hills were men of moderate education, working in a private school, who found none.

Having glanced at various types of secondary schools, we naturally ask next what part was played by private tutors or parents. Private tuition was not popular among the wealthy class in England, the only class which could afford it, as it had been in Renaissance times, or as it was in France to a much later date. Except those who entered the navy or army at an early age, the bulk of persons sufficiently distinguished to have found their way into the *Dictionary of National Biography* seem to have been at a school. Rousseau's writings initiated a real movement in connection with home education, but it mainly concerned children below school age. It was probably one factor which contributed to the raising of the usual age for entry to a secondary school. At the Renaissance the usual age was six; Fox entered Eton at nine, Salisbury at ten, Gladstone at eleven: in the forties twelve was a usual age; by the sixties entrance was deferred till fourteen, and a preparatory school course preceded. In the case of day schools, eight or nine was a common age for entry in the first half of the century. Before preparatory schools became standardised it is not always easy to distinguish between a school and a tutor who took a number of pupils, as Arnold did at Laleham.

The Edgeworths were, in the British Isles, the pioneers of reform in the home education of children. Their work does not fall within our period, but its effects lasted into it. R. L. Edgeworth's *Practical Education* defended private education as ideally the best, but, where expense forbade, urged the postponement of schooling as late as possible. But, more than this, it suggested a reasonable scheme of home education to occupy these years of childhood. Home education in fact was reformed before the reform of school education had begun. The modern parental tradition dates from this period. Toys became a recognised educational agency; games began to come into their rights; hobbies were encouraged. This civilising of children before they were sent to school has been of inestimable value. So long as boys were thought to have no inclinations except towards the exercise of their muscles and no opportunity was given for the development of other parts of their nature, the results naturally seemed to justify the belief. As soon as they were offered playful exercises which involved a use of their senses, of dexterity, of resource, of inventiveness, and of imagination, they responded with alacrity. The mere winning of parents' interest in such matters was itself a gain; for, the more parents came to take part in the life of their children, the more influence did they come to exercise over their characters. The days when a father was regarded as properly an object of "awe" to his children—Locke's ideal—were over. "Sir" was exchanged for "papa," and "papa," in the less affected days that followed, for "dad."

These results have extended to multitudes who never heard the names of Rousseau or of the Edgeworths. The effects on definite instruction, such as playful methods of teaching reading, arithmetic, geometry, and drawing, and especially the attempt to teach elementary popular science, were more the mark of their conscious followers. The reason is not far to seek. The mother has inherited the tradition more than the father. Untrained maternal instinct was able to execute the programme in the one case, whereas considerable knowledge and thought are required in the other. It is, however, marvellous how a little judicious encouragement by parents who are without any special equipment will conduce to forming in a child a permanent taste for such subjects as history, geography, or popular science, even if the help be no more than assistance in reading a book. Till the spread of Kindergartens, it is doubtful whether professional teaching ever succeeded as well as such encouragement by parents and other relatives.

On the whole, however, formal education fell into the hands of governesses and small preparatory schools rather than of parents. As private schools lost ground with older boys, they gained it with younger children. The earlier stages of the rise in the age of entering school gave scope to the type of small preparatory school kept by elderly spinsters, while the later rise in the age of admission to large boarding schools introduced the more ambitious preparatory school of recent times. The latter may have to fight hard against preparatory departments instituted by the bigger schools: the former have already had to yield to a considerable extent to the Kindergartens which have become popular since the eighties. Doubtless they shone in part with a lustre borrowed from a few "teachers by the grace of God" such as Mrs Barbauld; but the majority taught the three R's, the counties of England, the dates of the English monarchs, and the Latin declensions to children from seven to eleven, unaffected by modern views as to the use of play, or constructive work, or experiment.

The Rousseau-Edgeworth movement differed in many ways from that of the Froebelians. It often forgot that children are children; it believed that character could be formed by an incessant iteration of moral saws; and it exalted the importance of "useful information." The spirit of Dr Watts and Dr Watts's prose imitators was everywhere. But home education is less liable than school education to be spoiled by a craze: almost any movement which stimulates parents is good; for the parent, watching more closely than the teacher the progress of his child's mind and supplied by Nature with the gift of understanding it, will usually know when a theory is being ridden to death. Hence the Edgeworth movement exhibited little of that too close adherence to the methods of its founder which, in the case of Pestalozzi's followers in elementary education, spoiled most of the good which might have come from following his spirit.

Hitherto we have been speaking only of the education of the upper and middle classes. At a time when the community as a whole was hardly yet convinced of the desirability of elementary education for the working classes it was hardly likely that it should contemplate their further education. Higher education had always been a possession of the minority. The Middle Ages, in one sense, had been more democratic than subsequent periods; poor boys were not altogether debarred from a clerical education; but the clergy were a class by themselves, outside social distinctions, and the boy who entered their ranks ceased to be a member of any secular class. A manual calling had always been considered incompatible with a knowledge of more than the three R's. From the strictly utilitarian standpoint of the Middle Ages, there was no unfairness in this; book-learning was merely one form of technical training, and King John, not being a priest, could no more sign his name than the humblest villein. But the Renaissance treated education as having some other end than utilitarian; it made for complete living, and was therefore sought by all who could afford it. Its restriction was therefore an injustice, based on notions which are now passing away.

Sooner or later the doctrines of the French Revolution were bound to lead to a demand by the workers for levelling up or levelling down—for education or bolshevism. The years following 1789 were a time of party bitterness such as it is hard to realise to-day. The High Tories were under no illusions. The "stupid party" they were in one sense, that they had not the imagination to conceive that a more equal world would be a happier world. But they were not stupid, if stupidity means wrong judgment as to cause and effect. They were quite right in recognising that the Reform Bill was the first step towards political and social democracy, and therefore in treating the aristocratic Whigs as conscious or unconscious revolutionaries. After 1832 they saw that the battle was lost, and were content to be a brake on the democratic wheel—a function indispensable at times, though only intermittently needed. Till 1832, however, they were powerful enough, had they pleased, to suppress, and even after 1832 to hinder, any attempt at the adult education of working men.

It was therefore fortunate that the initial attempts came in a form which they did not recognise as the thin edge of the wedge. They held that workmen should not be educated "above their class," lest they should be unwilling to follow the drudgery of manual labour. This principle did not seem to apply to teaching them how to perform that labour. Here was a gap through which education could creep. The gap was quite recent. Fifty years earlier little which could stimulate the mind could have been taught in connection with the technical equipment of any manual craft. But natural science was just reaching the stage when it could be applied to industry. It was after all perhaps fortunate that the educated classes of those days—who were included in the middle and upper classes, though not identical with them—did not generally recognise experimental science as a branch of liberal education, otherwise they might have annexed it. As it was, owing to its technical character, they gave the working classes access to this branch of liberal education; for such we must call any knowledge which enlarges the horizon, stimulates thought, and creates a sense of proof and of the relation between cause and effect.

Though school science rarely did any of these things in its early days, very elementary science in the hands of men like Birkbeck certainly did. It was almost an accident which led to the beginnings of artisans' education. Anderson, a professor at Glasgow, had begun to hold systematic evening classes in 1760 and encouraged the attendance of working men. He was an early pioneer of science and foresaw its industrial bearings. He left all his money by will to found a new type of university in which science should have priority; but, as his property only amounted to £1000, his trustees had to be content with establishing one chair of physics. Birkbeck, a Lancashire boy, educated at Edinburgh University, where he became acquainted with Scott, Jeffrey, Sydney Smith, and others of the galaxy of Edinburgh notables, was appointed to this chair. He needed apparatus and he had to instruct workmen how to make it. He was surprised at the zeal with which they listened to his directions, and he invited some of them to his lectures. Lack of space led him to propose lecturing to them separately. His committee opposed. "If invited, the mechanics would not come; if they came, they would not listen; if they listened, they would not comprehend." Birkbeck insisted; they came, listened, and comprehended. Birkbeck had grasped the art of explaining technical matters in non-technical language—an art needed for other audiences besides mechanics. His topic was the mechanical properties of solid and fluid bodies, and his audience soon rose to five hundred. In a few years Birkbeck left Glasgow to start a medical practice in London, but the classes at "Anderson's Institution" continued till 1823, when, owing to a dispute with the management about the use of the library, the mechanics seceded and formed their own organisation. They copied the name of the parent body and so arose the name of Mechanics' "Institutions" or "Institutes." In two years there were 1300 students and a library of 1639 volumes. The students appointed the lecturers and re-elected them annually. In one case five candidates were subjected to a lecturing competition! The sequel is instructive; the selected candidate proved a complete failure. In course of time a more normal type of organisation was adopted, and appointments were made by a committee. Though the first enthusiasm died out, the Institution continued to do sound work, attracting to its classes even students of the University such as the future Lord Kelvin. Professors from Anderson's, which was developing into something more like a university, often lectured there. In 1879 it was swallowed up by the more modern organisation of technical instruction and its old democratic government passed away. Since 1881 it has been known as the Glasgow College of Science and Arts, and forms with Anderson's and two other colleges a part of the Glasgow and West of Scotland Technical College, whose diploma qualifies for all but the final year of the degree of Glasgow University.

The London *Mechanics' Magazine* now proposed the establishment of a similar institution in the metropolis, which was supported by Francis Place, "the radical tailor," who exercised a great political influence over artisans. He and Birkbeck collaborated and, after considerable difficulty due to personal matters, the Institute was started. The scheme was advertised by the radical newspaper the *Morning Chronicle*, and £2000 was raised by Lord Brougham, always a friend to popular education, and others. Birkbeck had to lend a large sum to make up the deficiency. In 1826 the Institute was opened by the Duke of Sussex, one of George III's sons, who had previously helped Lancaster. The apparatus cost 250 guineas, and there was a museum and a chemical laboratory. The movement met with some opposition, in which unfortunately the clergy took no inconsiderable share, but a swarm of similar institutions followed, the movement spreading to many foreign countries. By 1850 there were 610 institutions with 102,050 members[1]; and 1837 Unions of Institutes were formed to engage common itinerant lecturers, though these unions were for the most part short-lived.

Perhaps the most elaborate example was that at Liverpool, to which William Ballantyne Hodgson was appointed secretary in 1838 at the age of twenty-three. Hodgson was one of the many men filled with a thirst for knowledge and a desire to convey it to his fellow-men whom Scotland produced in the first half of the nineteenth century. The son of strict Calvinist parents, he would in any case have known little of the joys of childhood; but he allowed himself less. He never slept more than six hours and spent the rest in omnivorous reading. From Edinburgh University he went to Liverpool. There he had no easy time. Lectures of one kind or another went on from 8.30 in the morning till nine o'clock at night. Forty-eight lecturers contributed. But Hodgson proved himself even at this early age a consummate manager of men; he smoothed away all difficulties, and proved a regular master of method to elderly and distinguished lecturers who were unskilled in adapting their subject-matter to their audience. He spent his holidays in going round Scottish high schools to pick up

[1] J. W. Hudson, *History of Adult Education*, 1851, preface.

hints, and was one of the first vigorous critics of the pre-valent catechetical teaching. From 1847 to 1851 he was headmaster of a school in Manchester, but was then seized with a travel mania. The experience which he thus acquired made him a valuable member of the Newcastle Commission. From 1871 to his death he was the first occupant of the chair of political economy in Edinburgh.

Mechanics' Institutes, however, did not long fulfil their original object. Two changes became noticeable. By 1850 the membership had largely ceased to be composed of working-men, who were replaced by clerks and ap-prentices. At the same time the educational side was subordinated to the recreational, and definite courses of instruction gave way to occasional popular lectures. Henceforth their history belongs less to that of education in its more restricted sense[1] than to that of clubs, libraries, Athenaeums, mutual improvement societies, village reading rooms, and the like, which form an honour-able chapter in the history of mid-Victorian endeavour. J. W. Hudson, writing in 1851[2], says that the Watt Institute in Edinburgh was then the only establishment in Great Britain which deserved the title of a "People's College."

The interaction of English and Scottish education has been of immense advantage. Two substances are necessary before chemical action can take place; and the meeting of English and Scottish ideas set up a ferment in educational thought. The English system was aristocratic. When the awakening came, it was therefore bound in England to take the form of an improvement in the *quality* of education, for aristocracies like things good of their kind: not in its distribution, for aristocracies are exclusive; nor in its character, for aristocracies are conservative. It was also likely to concern itself with the humanities rather than with the physical world; for statesmanship is the hereditary

[1] An account of their spread and decline is given in an article by Sir Philip Magnus in R. D. Roberts's *Education in the Nineteenth Century*, pp. 148–156.

[2] *History of Adult Education*, p. 75.

occupation of aristocracies. Probably the reason why English education was aristocratic was that the English Church was aristocratic, which in its turn was because Henry VIII and Elizabeth had secured that the bishops should be virtually state-appointed officials. What the State was, the Church became; what the Church was, the universities became; and what the universities were, education became. In Scotland the Church was presbyterian, that is, as democratic as the state of popular education permitted. And so strong was theology in Scotland that, what the Church was, both State and education tended to become. The parish school was the citadel of Scottish education. The four universities taught boys of the same age as those in the English public schools; but they drew from the parish schools and therefore from all classes. When the awakening came in Scotland, it consequently took the form of a demand for a wider extension of education, for democracy stands for equal opportunities; and for a change in its subject-matter, because the plain citizen was not looking forward to becoming a member of parliament or an ambassador. An uncongenial climate had made the Scotsman a keen man of business and, after the Industrial Revolution, a keen manufacturer. His interest was in political economy, in natural science, and in whatever else "paid."

Both tendencies were needed. The community needs a select body of carefully educated persons, in the interests alike of capable administration, of increase in the national wealth, of discoveries which promote the general happiness, and of the diffusion of ideals of culture which make for the fuller life of all. But it is likewise necessary that the area of choice should be as wide as possible, so that all who are born with the requisite ability should find their way into the select circle. Further, the whole community should be educated in the manner and up to the point which makes for fulness of living. Lastly, the highest education must be specialised along all the paths which lead the community to wealth, happiness, good government, and intellectual, aesthetic, and moral excellence.

The English striving for the higher education of the few in certain limited directions needed supplementing by the Scottish demand for a wider diffusion and a wider range of education.

That these tendencies were really inspired from Scotland there can be little doubt. Lancashire and Yorkshire were industrially in advance of the northern kingdom, but it was only after they had been stirred from Scotland that educational need created an educational demand. In elementary education Bell and Lancaster were English, for Scotland already had a school in every parish, but its great reformers, Robert Owen, Wilderspin, and Stow, all worked in Scotland. The *Edinburgh Review* was the main critic of the English universities and public schools. The early advocates of science—George Combe, Birkbeck, Hodgson, and William Ellis—were all either Scots or educated in Scotland. Adult working-class education started there. The new subjects were welcomed in the Scottish universities.

The democratic tendency had close relations with the scientific and the secularist movements. The reasons are not far to seek. The English Church, being aristocratic and conservative, sided with the old classics against the new science. Nonconformity was therefore drawn to democracy, innovation, and science. On the other hand, the French Revolution had been at once anti-Christian and anti-monarchical; hence there tended to be an alliance between Radicalism (a very different thing from Whiggism) and unorthodoxy, whether unitarian, agnostic, or atheistic. The Church and aristocracy being in possession, the two oppositions tended to act together and to be regarded as the right and left wings of one party. The practical question was the exclusion of non-Churchmen from the universities and from opportunities of higher education. The Nonconformist Academies, which met the need in the eighteenth century, had strangely decayed. They would not, even if they had survived, have met the needs of the secularists. An opposition composed of so many elements could adopt only one solution, the exclusion of theology altogether from the university which they desired. This was a peculiarly British solution. Elsewhere, save where secularists are in the majority, there are either separate universities for different persuasions, or two denominational faculties of theology in the same university, or faculties in which two or more denominations consent to sink their differences. The last solution is now-a-days becoming popular in Great Britain; but, whereas now our tendency is to harmonise differences, then it was to emphasise them. The opposition were anxious therefore to found a university in London from which theology should be excluded, and in which of course there should be complete equality as regards appointment to the secular chairs. To-day the second point would be taken for granted; and the opposition to the exclusion of theology would be based on the very opposite grounds, namely, that it is desirable that the future clergy should mix with men destined for other professions and with men holding other beliefs. In those days isolation was regarded as essential for the tender plant of orthodoxy. The new University College was opened in 1827 by the Duke of Sussex, ever a liberal in educational matters; but even Arnold denounced "that godless institution in Gower Street," and some of the Nonconformists, including the headmaster of Mill Hill, shared his opinion.

But the Church soon saw that the new college fulfilled other purposes than disseminating unorthodox views. It taught subjects which could not be found in the curriculum of the universities and public schools; it was incomparably cheaper and brought education to the student's very doors. In self-defence these attractions must not be allowed to lure the sheep from the fold. King's College was founded in 1828, and was soon housed in the Strand. University College had, however, been intended to become a university. A compromise was reached, and a charter was given in 1836 to a federal university, which should consist of University and King's Colleges and of any other institutions which should be founded to provide education of a university type.

At its institution London was meant to be a real teaching university. Events, however, took a different turn. Institutions were admitted which were hardly of university calibre, and the certificates of study required for presentation of students for examination lost their value. Colleges sprang up in different parts of the country which were anxious to prepare for a university degree, and in 1858 the reactionary step was taken of awarding the degrees solely on examination. This lapse must not make us forget that the two original colleges were all the time doing real university work, and that the ideal of scientific research probably won earlier recognition in University College than in any British institution. We have now reached a point where a more detailed examination of the scientific influence on education is needed.

REFERENCES

Schools Inquiry Commission, *Report*, 1869.

M. D. and R. Hill, *Plans for the Government and Liberal Education of Boys in Large Numbers*, 1822.

—— *The Laws of Hazelwood School*, 1827.

W. L. Sargant, *Essays by a Birmingham Manufacturer*, vol. II, Essay 3.

Various text-books referred to in the text.

Charles Dickens, *Nicholas Nickleby*, 1839.

A. Paterson, *The Edgeworths*, 1917.

Thomas Day, *Sandford and Merton*, in 3 vols, 1783, 1787, 1789.

J. W. Hudson, *History of Adult Education*, 1851.

A. Humboldt Sexton, *The first Technical College*, 1894.

J. G. Godard, *George Birkbeck*, 1884.

J. M. D. Meiklejohn, *Life and Letters of W. B. Hodgson*.

CHAPTER V

THE SCIENTIFIC MOVEMENT

THE first movement for the recognition of the importance of scientific research had taken place at the beginning of the seventeenth century. Its herald was Bacon. It was followed by efforts to introduce teaching about natural phenomena into schools. The movement proved abortive, and a century and a half passed before it was renewed with any serious prospect of success. It is important to examine the reasons for the failure of the earlier movement if we are to understand why it was that the teaching of natural science first became possible at the period which we have now reached.

Let us take our stand for a moment in the year 1648. We might well have thought that the knowledge of the natural world had made great strides. In mathematics the spread of the Arabic notation had made arithmetical computation comparatively easy, algebra had become known to Western Europe, trigonometry had been established a century before by Müller's table of sines, decimals had been invented in 1586 and logarithms in 1614. In astronomy, the science most dependent on mathematics, Kepler's results published in 1609 and 1619 had made for the acceptance of the theory of the Solar system which Copernicus had put forward in 1543. In the more observational sciences, the blind following of Aristotle was yielding to observation and experiment. All Europe knew how large and small stones had been dropped from the leaning tower of Pisa to settle the question whether the larger and heavier would fall more quickly. Scientific instruments were constantly being invented—the telescope, microscope (1608), thermometer (1620), and barometer (1643). Mechanics, hydrostatics, pneumatics, and light had become established branches of knowledge. The force of magnetism had been discovered by Gilbert (1600), and in a different domain Harvey's discovery of the circulation of the blood (1628) had laid the foundation of modern physiology.

Yet the possibilities of making natural science a branch of school education were by no means as rosy as this list might suggest. There were no scientific societies or scientific periodicals. It was hard even for one investigator to learn what another was doing, and almost impossible for the general public to know that anything was being done at all; and there was no body of expert opinion to discriminate between the discoverer and the quack. Books on the possibility of reaching the moon were taken seriously, while Gilbert was set aside even by Bacon as an impostor. Bacon was almost the only man who had a clear idea as to the methods by which scientific research would progress in the future, and even he held a very mechanical view of the inductive process. He regarded it as a method almost as easily reducible to rule as the syllogistic method which preceded it. The educational innovators who believed themselves to be his followers—Hartlib, Petty, Dury, Comenius, and the like—did indeed realise the need of research, but as a body they seem to have thought that they had lighted on an instrument which would have done its work in some fifty or a hundred years' time and that, even before it had made all dark places bright, they could forthwith proceed to teach a systematic exposition of the universe. "Pansophia" was but a new scholasticism. We have merely to read the headings of the chapters in Comenius's text-book of *Physics* to see that the teaching of "natural philosophy" in the schools of the seventeenth century would have been radically unscientific. It would have taught nothing of method, it would have given more false information than true, and it would have annexed to the sphere of authority the one domain which, by its neglect in schools, was left free from its domination.

Mathematics, however, was ripe for inclusion in the school curriculum; it found a definitely organised body of principles capable of being so taught that the pupil had full scope for the use of his intelligence. Whereas natural philosophy would at that date have tended to produce an attitude of passive receptivity, mathematics would have promoted active thought. For no single branch of experimental and non-mathematical science had advanced beyond its beginnings, and the teaching of such science would have been the teaching of smatterings. The text-books would probably have been Pliny and the other ancient writers enumerated by Vives and Milton, and what little recent research there was could easily be taught to the sixth standard of an elementary school.

When we pass on to 1830, what a change do we find! Chemistry, in the seventeenth century still associated with the black art, has entered on a new career with Priestley's discovery of oxygen in 1784. Geology has sprung into being; the order in which the sedimentary rocks were deposited has been determined; the classificatory stage is making way for the explanatory as it is realised what immense effects can be produced by the steady operation of minute processes over enormous periods. Botany and zoology indeed cannot be said to have entered on the explanatory stage till the publication of Darwin's *Origin of Species* in 1859, but there was a vast difference between the work of Jussieu and Cuvier and the fairy tales which were told in the name of "natural history" at the time of the Renaissance. The progress of physiology had made medicine something more than a dangerous double-edged tool. Electricity had been discovered. Still, it must be confessed that even in 1830 mathematics and its astronomical and physical applications were still far ahead of the non-mathematical branches of science.

While the sequence of actual discoveries is fairly well known, it is less commonly recognised that the advent of each new science meant an addition to our ideas of scientific method. Though existing sciences might have worked out their methods so well that their students could in six months pass through centuries of scientific discovery, yet the best exponents of a new science would still for several generations be groping for a method. So long as mathematics had the field almost to itself, men's ideas of scientific method were almost entirely deductive. For, though astronomy involved observation and physics experiment, the work which tried the investigator's mettle consisted in the mathematical and deductive calculations involved in verifying the hypothesis. Kepler, Descartes and Newton are the scientific men of genius in the seventeenth century. But the rise of chemistry involved an emphasis on an entirely different attitude of mind; initiative was now displayed in devising experiments which would isolate a particular phenomenon not merely in thought but in the physical world of things. Geology was different again. Here genius was shown in the invention of hypotheses; the hypotheses occurred only to the investigator who could hold vast bodies of evidence in one grasp of his mind; and they were tested by seeing how far they explained all the known facts. For the time being the biological sciences called mainly for a perfection of the power of punctilious observation. The truth of the doctrine of the relativity of scientific method is perhaps best realised if we think of the sciences which are hardly yet out of the groping stage, such as anthropology and meteorology. The sciences which deal with the past history of man, as geology deals with the past history of the surface of the Earth, illustrate it particularly well. Attempts to explain the growth of languages, mythology, religious and social institutions, were in the second half of the nineteenth century almost in the same tentative condition as many of the physical sciences in the first half of the seventeenth, and it was possible in this sphere for such speculations as the sun-myth theory to obtain general recognition. It is true that, as a science advances, it may lose some of its peculiarities of method; there is now a physical chemistry and a chemical biology, and, since the discovery of radium emanations, there is beginning to be an evolutionary chemistry; but the approximation is never complete.

There is of course a sense in which all scientific reasoning is of one general type. There are certain tools which every science applies more or less—observation, experiment, statistics, mathematical processes, hypothesis and verification. These tools are used to do two main types of work, deductive and inductive reasoning. But in the case of each separate science researchers have to learn how much of the work each tool will do, at what stage in the collection of evidence hypotheses may profitably be formed, what scope is afforded for experiment, how the complexity of causes and effects is to be disentangled. No man could by the study of Mill's or any other canons of induction develop the chemical or the geological or the biological sense. Sometimes perhaps a guiding principle in the technique of a particular science is run to death. The layman has a suspicion that this has occasionally happened with the geological principle of never explaining by crustal movements anything which can be conceivably due to the action of water or ice. But the exceptions only prove the rule that the expert in any science has acquired an added sense which tells him how to use his own tools.

Perhaps the very diversity of the subjects discovered by the general term "natural science" was one of the chief obstacles to the demand for the inclusion of science in the school curriculum. The different branches involved so many different methods, gave such a very different training, and based their claims to inclusion on such very different grounds that the general public was perplexed. The story of the struggle of science for admission to places of higher education is generally told in the form of a record of a campaign between scientific enlightenment and classical obscurantism. This method of writing certainly gives the actual incidents of the struggle, in much the same way as the despatches of war correspondents give the separate incidents of a battle. It is probably more picturesque; the account of a hand to hand combat between Huxley and the bishop of Oxford gives scope for descriptive power. But it is possible that, as in the case of a war, the real explanation of the success or failure of the combatants is only to be discovered by examining how far there existed unity of command among their respective general staffs. And we think that such an examination would show that from 1830 to 1870 the cause of science was represented by a number of distinct armies whose leaders were in no agreement as to the reasons why they thought science should be taught, what should be included under the term, to whom it should be taught, or what were the right methods of teaching it.

At the beginning of the century the only representatives of the scientific as distinct from the humanistic side of studies at the universities were the mathematicians; they alone represented the only side of scientific knowledge which had a long tradition behind it; and we might have expected them to have been the first to attack the classical monopoly in the schools. Indeed the neglect of mathematics was a much more striking evidence of the extent to which the schools had lagged behind the progress of modern thought than the total absence of such a new subject as chemistry. At Cambridge mathematics was in so dominant a position that no candidate could take the classical tripos till he had obtained mathematical honours. The interest of the intellectual world in mathematical studies is shown by the number of articles on them in the *Edinburgh Review*, which astonishes the reader of the present day who is not accustomed to see such topics treated outside the pages of distinctly scientific journals. We may well begin therefore by noting the attacks on the university mathematicians and the position which they themselves took up.

In 1805 and again in 1830, the Edinburgh Reviewers, who were loth to miss an opportunity of criticising the English universities, took up the question of their treatment of mathematics. The charges against the two universities were different; the fault of Oxford was that it neglected mathematics altogether, that of Cambridge that it clung to old-fashioned geometrical methods in preference to more modern analytic methods; but in both cases the result was a failure to produce original mathematicians whose work would compare with their continental contemporaries. Copleston's reply on behalf of Oxford to the earlier attack, and still more the fact that it was regarded by his fellow Oxonians as a masterly vindication of the University, is a striking evidence how profoundly the Oxford tutor of those days was out of touch with the intellectual progress of his age. Whewell's line of defence on behalf of Cambridge at the time of the second attack was of a very different character. Many of his views appear old-fashioned at the present day, but he has at least a coherent theory of university education and is not averse from change as such.

Whewell wrote at a time when murmurs of the coming storm were beginning to be heard but no eminent exponent of the scientific demand had arisen. There was a vague desire to make education more "practical." Liebig had introduced chemistry into the German university of Giessen in 1825. The British Association had been founded in 1831. Men were working hard to found the new sciences. The connection of science with industry was for the first time being recognised. Working men were crying out even more than the leaders of industry for instruction in the new learning. Articles, letters, and speeches were suggesting that the material of education should be changed, though no book had yet been written to set forth the new ideas, nor had anyone really thought out what form the new education should take.

Whewell, however, the champion of the mathematicians, goes a very small way in support of changes in the curriculum. Like all educationalists of his day he approaches the question from the point of view of giving a logical training to the mind. He is quite ready to admit that the universities should prepare certain of their students to be the future researchers in chemistry, geology, and biology. But he declares that "habits of thought must be *formed* among other subjects," though, when formed, "they may well be employed on these[1]." He believes, in short, that persons who are to build up the new sciences on sound lines must be prepared by studying those which have already reached a high degree of organisation. The value of the older mathematical sciences in giving this training depends, he holds, on the methods employed in studying them.

[1] *Principles of English University Education*, p. 42.

Analytic mathematics only makes mathematicians, the study of geometrical mathematics makes reasoners. Analytic methods are mechanical: a result comes out, but you have not thought it out; "we dismiss from our minds altogether the conceptions of the things which the symbols represent," "the steps of the process are not acts of thought," "we are carried along as in a railroad carriage[1]." They afford no training—or a bad training—for the ordinary affairs of life[2]. "If we can only have analytic mathematics in our system of education, we have little reason to wish to have in it any mathematics at all[3]." The following is his description of what mathematics, studied along the right lines should do. "We are in that study concerned with long trains of reasoning in which each link hangs from all the preceding. The language contains a constant succession of short and rapid references to what has been proved already; and it is justly assumed that each of these brief movements helps the reasoner forwards in a course of infallible certainty and security. Each of these hasty glances must possess the clearness of intuitive evidence and the certainty of mature reflection; and yet must leave the reasoner's mind entirely free to turn instantly to the next point of his progress": hence, he argues, comes the success of mathematics in having trained so many eminent lawyers."[4] He interprets the whole history of the development of human thought from Thales onwards as showing that, where the exact sciences were honoured, there progress was made; but, whenever they were subordinated to speculative systems, there followed stagnation. Looking around the Europe of his own day, he sees the greatest cause for alarm in the fact that Germany seems to be dominated by metaphysicians. "Those who are universally allowed to be the greatest philosophers of our own day in the German universities, Hegel and Schelling, cannot understand that Newton went further than Kepler had gone in physical astronomy and despise

[1] *Of a Liberal Education*, p. 41.
[2] *Op. cit.* p. 45.   [3] *Op. cit.* p. 50.
[4] *Principles of English University Education*, p. 13.

Newton's optical doctrines in comparison with the vague
Aristotelian dogmas of Göthe respecting colours[1]." Sometimes Whewell's language might be interpreted by modern
educationalists as inculcating a belief in authority. "The
critical system seems to me to be properly addressed, not
to students who are undergoing education, but to philosophers who have been already completely educated";
"nor can I believe that to put young men in such a position
at the period of their lives when they ought to be quietly
forming their minds for future action can have any other
result than to fill them with a shallow conceit of their own
importance[2]." But it is not to authority in any bad sense
that he wishes the learner to yield, but to the force of
proof. He wishes to train the mind in subjects where
conclusions can be subjected to undeniable tests, in order
that he may really feel the nature of truth and may know
that facts cannot be argued into being other than they
really are. Had not Whewell an intuition of the danger
into which Germany has been led by prematurely committing research in subjects where conclusions are not
easily tested to persons in whose minds the feeling of truth
has not been firmly planted? And had the new sciences
yet reached a stage where by themselves and without a
preliminary gymnastic of mathematics and physics they
could plant this feeling? Would a man whose studies had
consisted in learning and accepting the recent discoveries
of elementary chemistry and classificatory biology, in
observing and memorising the parts of the human frame,
and in hearing lectures on the contending hypotheses of
opposing geological schools, have been a competent judge
whether a hypothesis was or was not proved? And, till a
man can judge of the hypotheses of others, is he fit to form
hypotheses of his own? If it be replied that it is only by forming hypotheses of your own that you can learn to pronounce
judgment on those of others, there is much force in the
contention; but, if you try to form them upon a subject-
matter where experts differ, how can you tell whether
you are learning how to form them rightly? It would

[1] *Op. cit.* p. 25.   [2] *Op. cit.* pp. 46–53.

appear that, so long as any subject is in its infancy, its exponents must begin by studying more advanced subjects and as wide a range as possible of these subjects, so that they do not confuse the special methods of each subject with the general principles which determine whether a proposition is proved or not.

Whewell's programme consisted (1) in teaching mathematics at school by practical methods[1]—he suggests a syllabus in mensuration; (2) in making mechanics and hydrostatics compulsory in the early stages of the university course[2]; (3) in restricting the growth in the number of university examinations which were beginning to crush out the voluntary pursuit of side-tracks, and in restoring the importance of college tutorial work[3]; (4) in studying the older branches of science historically and reading accounts of discoveries by the original discoverers, such as Newton[4], and in asking questions in the tripos on the difficulties which those discoverers had met in the course of their researches and the ways in which they had overcome them[5]; (5) in introducing some way through the course optional college lectures on what he calls the "progressive" sciences, in order to stimulate the mature student of real intellectual tastes by the sight of little-explored regions in which he could exercise his talents[6]; and (6) in establishing a post-graduate tripos in these sciences for those who wished to continue the study of them[7].

Reform is often brought about not by men with the widest views who see many sides of a question, but by enthusiasts who see one side only—the side which preceding generations have neglected—and work for it heart and soul; as, for instance, Rousseau, the most unbalanced of educational writers, was also the most effective. Now Whewell was a better judge of a good education, of the possibilities which various subjects possessed for giving it,

---

[1] *Op. cit.* p. 161.
[2] *Op. cit.* p. 17.
[3] *Op. cit.* pp. 54–67; *Of a Liberal Education*, pp. 169–215
[4] *Of a Liberal Education*, p. 25.   [5] *Op. cit.* p. 206
[6] *Op. cit.* p. 213.   [7] *Op. cit.* p. 224.

and of the methods of teaching which would bring out those possibilities, than many later scientific partisans; but it is doubtful whether such discriminating moderation would have advanced the cause of science far, even though the establishment of the Natural Sciences Tripos at Cambridge in 1851 and of the honours school at Oxford in 1853 preceded the main period of agitation. But the fact that science had to enlist less thoughtful partisans in order to win success was partly responsible for the uneducational methods by which it was at first taught.

George Combe, the earliest of these partisans, was not really a scientific man at all. Self-educated, he was attracted by the phrenological ideas of the German Spurzheim. Phrenology at this period had a great attraction for a certain type of mind, because it appeared to offer a clear and simple materialistic explanation of human action and to bring it within the operation of laws which physical science could readily investigate. On the basis of phrenology as a physiology of the mind a scheme of education was to be constructed as the mind's diet. The idea harmonised well with the prevalent educational theory which regarded the mind as divided into a number of faculties; for it was these faculties which the phrenologists believed that they had located in particular parts of the brain. Psychology was in those days in the pre-scientific stage through which all sciences have passed, and attempts to build education upon it were like building upon the sand. The present prejudice of old-fashioned teachers against it is a survival from those days. All writers of that period repeated Pestalozzi's dictum that education consisted in the "harmonious development of all the faculties," which to the phrenologist meant all parts of the brain. But Combe was no clear thinker and from an ultra-disciplinarian theory he somehow reached an informational system of practice. His *theory* was expressed in the sentence, "We should train to *do* more than to *know*. In framing books for schools it would be well to ask ourselves, 'What does this book teach people to do?'"[1] Theoretically then he

[1] William Jolly, *Education as developed by George Combe*, p. 13.

condemns the mere receiving of information; indeed his ground of attack on language teaching is that this is all it is. "Language, apart from its applications, is a collection of mere unmeaning arbitrary sounds[1]." But like the realists of the seventeenth century, whose educational axioms are excellent, he does not seem to see their bearing on problems of curriculum. Logically he should have admitted no subject without facing the question, Can school children manipulate this subject? Practically he seems only concerned with the value of the knowledge which is conveyed by a subject on the tacit assumption that it is mastered. He therefore demands the subordination of the "instrumental" subjects, by which he means those which teach us how to use the tools of thought, to those which give "positive" knowledge. As with the German Philanthropinists, physiology is to be taught because bodily health is desirable, phrenology because mental health is desirable, ethics to make us good individuals, sociology to make us good citizens (not history, because it is a record of cruelty[2]), and various branches of science to make us good workpeople. A smattering of everything is of course a logical outcome of the theory of a harmonious (interpreted as equal) development of all the faculties; but the idea of developing them by practice seems to have been lost in the attempt to secure their equality, since in no one of them would the pupil ever reach the stage at which he would be anything but a recipient.

After adumbrating his views in the *Phrenological Journal* in 1827 and amplifying them in lectures to the Edinburgh Philosophical Society from 1830 to 1840, he was able in 1848 to establish Williams's Secular School in Edinburgh with an encyclopaedic curriculum; but, though it started with *éclat*, it collapsed in 1854. It was, however, imitated by other "secular schools" in various towns, as was not unnatural at a time when facilities for higher elementary education were almost non-existent and when those for lower secondary education were miserably poor; but the schools were mostly ephemeral. Combe's strong point was

---

[1] *Op. cit.* p. 25. [2] *Op. cit.* p. 109.

what we may call the political side of education. He did
good work in emphasising that the extension of the
franchise in Great Britain would be a blessing or a curse
according as the masses were educated or not, and that
an illiterate proletariat might ruin the rising democracy
of America. His aims—the inculcation of the social sense
and a feeling of responsibility, the attraction of thoughtful
men into political life[1], and the recognition that some
subjects which give the idea of causation must be included
in the curriculum[2]—were excellent. The speeches and
articles which he continued to produce all his life had
a stirring effect; but he had not sufficient practical
acquaintance with the process of education to be a
guide as to the means by which it was possible to
effect ends which we have now all come to recognise as
desirable.

A much more permanent effect was produced when the
demand for the teaching of science was voiced by a man
of recognised intellectual prestige, Herbert Spencer, in a
series of articles issued between 1854 and 1859 and afterwards published in book form. But it was Spencer's reputation and not his arguments which produced the effect.
They display Spencer's weakness, not his strength. His
strength lay in the extent of his knowledge, especially on
matters which at that time were little studied, and in his
power of inventing new theories. His weakness lay in a lack
of judgment as to what constitutes proof and a sacrifice of
logic to pre-formed opinions. A mind which would have
excelled in the scholastic controversies of the Middle Ages
was filled with the scientific knowledge of the nineteenth
century and was set the task of supporting a philosophic
system by means of facts supplied by the natural sciences.
A bitter assailant of authority, he won his educational
reputation on the strength of the authority which the mass
of Englishmen allow to a man of science on any matter which
he discusses. Just as his political writing does little more than
give a philosophical flavour to the current individualistic
tenets of the Manchester school, and his ethical writing than

[1] *Op. cit.* pp. 181–184.   [2] *Op. cit.* p. 40.

suggesting an evolutionary basis for current Utilitarianism, so his educational writing did little more than voice the contemporary views of English Pestalozzians on method, of Utilitarians on curriculum, and of the followers of Rousseau on discipline. Yet his essays were long regarded as possessing weight when the contemporary writers from whom he had culled his educational views were forgotten. Milton's *Tractate* is perhaps the only other pamphlet or article which has been regarded as an educational classic by virtue of the author's reputation in other fields.

There is little or nothing in the articles which had not been said already by Combe or Wyse or other contemporary writers, and there is very little except the fourth article, on physical education, which will bear criticism. The first three deal with curriculum, method, and discipline. Spencer is satisfied that he has solved the problem of curriculum when he has answered the question, "What knowledge is of most worth?" He does not tell us whose knowledge it is or to whom it is of worth. He commits a well-known logical fallacy when he proves that it is of value to the community that there should be some persons who know each science and imagines that he has thereby proved that it is of value to each individual man that he should know them all. He does not even stop to enquire if, how far, and at what age a school child is capable of profiting by the physiology which preserves life directly, by the whole cycle of physical sciences which, as forming the basis of industrial processes, preserve it indirectly, by the psychology which enables parents to bring up their children properly, by the comparative sociology which is to make enlightened citizens, and by the anatomy and astronomy which are to make us spend our leisure nobly in the criticism of art from the standpoint of its scientific accuracy. When he proclaims the necessity of learning all the sciences, he has not a word to suggest whether he has in mind the captains of industry, the foremen, the skilled artisans, or the unskilled workmen, nor does he hint at the difficulty of carrying out his programme in the elementary school, which pupils of that day commonly left at twelve. As he could not altogether ignore the prevalent belief that the directly useful subjects are not the best for training—in other words that it is necessary to feed beginners on the intellectual milk which they can digest rather than on the strong meat of later stages—the champion of induction brushes the difficulty aside with the *a priori* assumption that "it is contrary to the beautiful economy of Nature" that one subject should be useful as knowledge and another as discipline. A still more remarkable betrayal of inductive philosophy occurs when he places history on the index and, like Combe, wishes to substitute for it an abstract course in comparative sociology, of which the laws, if true, can only be based on the recorded facts of history. But facts have an awkward way of upsetting *a priori* theories, and the political doctrinaire does not care for an uncensored study of them.

When he comes to deal with methods, Spencer finds his hands tied by the curriculum which he has already laid down. It is useless to assert that the "order in which the faculties" develop must be followed as regards methods of teaching when you have ignored that order in your choice of subjects. True, he never tells us what the order of development is, but we can hardly believe that he thought it to be of such a kind as would enable children under twelve to employ their critical powers on the abstractions of comparative sociology. The only justification for Spencer's chapter on curriculum would be that it was intended for university students: but in that case why did he follow it up by a chapter on method which could only apply to infants? For the second chapter gives us no concrete examples of teaching beyond the infant stage— presumably because the English Pestalozzians from whom he takes them were mainly concerned with that stage.

The article on discipline is a restatement of Rousseau's theory of the discipline of natural consequences, presumably handed down through intermediate sources, since Spencer declared that, when he wrote it, he had not read the *Émile*. A fundamental ambiguity deprives his version of the theory of all real meaning. At the outset he uses the phrase "natural discipline" as meaning the discipline which comes from the laws of inanimate nature, as equivalent to Rousseau's *discipline des choses*, which is opposed to the discipline of persons. But, having committed himself to the assertion that these consequences are "proportionate to the offence" and therefore just, he finds himself in difficulties. The discipline "of things" often punishes a small act of carelessness with death. He therefore tries to escape from the meshes by changing the meaning of the word "natural." It now comes to mean "such as we should reasonably expect," even where reasonable expectations would point to the displeasure of parents or teachers and not to a reaction of inanimate "things" at all. But he has now entangled himself worse than ever; for what is to exclude from our reasonable expectations the natural reactions of Dr Keate or of the policeman? So "reasonable" has to be explained as "sensible," and the whole theory of natural consequences has come to mean that parents and teachers ought to act in such a way as to produce the right effect on the child! He does indeed give some unexceptionable instances of sensible behaviour towards children; but they have nothing to do with the laws of inanimate nature, but seem to be instances of a sound principle of punishment which was afterwards enunciated by Gilbert and Sullivan.

Underlying the whole argument is a confusion of thought which enabled Spencer to convince himself that some moral quality attaches to that operation of physical laws whereby effect follows on cause. Actions, he holds, are wrong if they cause pain; natural laws secure that the pain follows, and there is the punishment! But what if it is *A* who sins and *B* who suffers the pain? Buddhists and Greek tragedians might hold that the punishment always ultimately recoils on the transgressor, because they allowed for agencies more moral than physical laws; but could Spencer hold that physical laws will bring all transgressions home to roost? No; acts are wrong which cause pain to others, but a child will be deterred from them on that account only if he has first become unselfish, and Spencer never probes to the heart, where unselfishness is to be found. He knows only of motives which appeal to enlightened selfishness. This implicit denial of altruistic motives is the worst point in Spencer's theory. Not that his training really provides even for the self-regarding virtues; for, if we were to wait for Nature's punishments for gluttony and sensuality, the harm would be done years before any indication of the punishment were foreseen. Spencer seems to think it is a merit in Nature that she never gives warning of her punishments. Rather, Nature is non-moral and Man has to step in with a more merciful justice.

In considering Spencer's article on discipline we have strayed rather far from the progress of science to a place in education; but it has been already pointed out that the scientific movement was closely bound up with other tendencies in nineteenth century education, and we cannot understand why science commended itself to some persons and roused the antagonism of others unless we see the company which it kept. If old-fashioned teachers suspected science of producing that kind of non-moral outlook which we have since seen fully developed in the Prussian intellectual caste, Spencer's third article was not calculated to allay their suspicions.

Spencer's claim for science was primarily utilitarian. But almost at the same time a plea for the teaching of science was put forward in a quarter from which it could hardly have been expected and by a writer who appealed to a totally different body of admirers. Ruskin, in a short appendix to the *Stones of Venice*[1], discusses briefly the subject-matter of a curriculum; and, though brief, his six pages present a coherent theory. His aim may be summed up in the one word "Outlook": the knowledge which is worth having is that which determines our mode of regarding life, our attitude to the universe and to our fellow-beings, the aims which we set before us, and to a large extent the sources from which we draw our happiness. The primary defect in the current disciplinarian conception of education was that it aimed only at producing a capable

[1] Vol. III, Appendix 7.

mind, but did not provide that mind with material on which to exercise its capacity. Ruskin's exposure of this defect was primarily directed against universities; but it is probable that, however true it may have been in his own undergraduate days, the progress of the newer humanism was fast making it untrue of contemporary Oxford. The schools, however, in spite of Arnold, were still devoted to the worship of form, and few of their pupils, save those who afterwards took honours at the universities, would be led to think seriously on political or social questions, on the new vision of the material universe which geology and biology were opening up, or on the religious questions which were perplexing the minds of thoughtful men. From the point of view of outlook Ruskin declares that an educated person "ought to know three things; first, where he is; second, where he is going; thirdly, what he ought to do under the circumstances. First, where he is: that is to say, what sort of a world he has got into: how large it is; what kind of creatures live in it and how; what it is made of, and what may be made of it. Secondly, where he is going"; that is to say, religion. And "thirdly, what he had best do under those circumstances; that is to say, what faculties he possesses; what are the present state and wants of mankind; what is his place in society; and what are the readiest means in his power of attaining happiness and diffusing it."

Ruskin's exposition of the failure of the existing educational system to produce "educated men" capable of understanding contemporary events on the Continent or social movements at home is excellent, but it does not concern our present purpose. On the neglect of science, with which we are here concerned, he says: "Our present European system of so-called education despises natural history." Even on the Continent the "result is that, unless a man's natural instincts urge him to the pursuit of the physical sciences too strongly to be resisted, he enters life utterly ignorant of them." "The main mischief of it is that it leaves the greater number of men without the natural food which God intended for their intellects. For one man who is fitted for the study of words, fifty are fitted for the study of things, and were intended to have a perpetual, simple and religious delight in watching the processes or admiring the creatures of the natural universe. Deprived of this source of pleasure, nothing is left to them but ambition or dissipation; and the vices of the upper classes of Europe are, I believe, chiefly to be attributed to this single cause." Here is a line of thought which would probably sound strange to most scientific men; it has little connection with the motives which have actually led to the admission of science to a place in higher education; but it has had much to do with the introduction of nature-study, as distinct from natural science, into our elementary schools. Ruskin's concern is with the aesthetic and emotional rather than with the intellectual side of our nature, and he discovered what many scientific men failed to discover, that there is a mode of studying nature which appeals to the former just as there is a mode which appeals to the latter. With this mode of studying nature Art has close connections; and an artist of genius could not fail to see them. Nature is the mother of Art, and nature-study is Art's act of filial devotion. At the elementary stage we believe that drawing and nature-study are so closely allied as to be practically one subject and that a child will never truly love one without the other. If he loves natural objects he will wish to depict them; and he will see no beauty in his productions unless they are reproductions of the beauty of nature.

However, nature-study is not natural science; nature-study belongs to that recreative side of life which Herbert Spencer rated so low; while natural science is a rigorous discipline of the intellect. We do not expect to see as the motto inscribed on the entrance to a laboratory the well-known lines:

> "He prayeth best who loveth best
> Both man and bird and beast,"

though, to their honour, there are many biologists of whom it is true.

The real protagonist of the scientific cause, however, was T. H. Huxley. To many devotees of the old literary subjects, his addresses must have revealed for the first time that hard scientific work may be a pleasure, that there is a satisfaction almost aesthetic in following a train of scientific reasoning, and that the solution of a problem yields a delight akin to that felt by the winner of a race. The utilitarian plea had indeed been overdone; many an opponent accepted the premise that the sciences had a greater marketable value than the humanities, and drew from it a conclusion precisely the opposite from that which was intended, namely that they were therefore ignoble and inferior. Huxley was not content with proving science to be useful; he proclaimed the grandeur of its subject-matter, the nobility of its quest, and the worth of the intellectual qualities which it developed. His addresses on this theme are no cold appeal to the intellect; indeed it would be difficult to preserve their flavour in a summary. The reader feels that he has been permitted to look into a noble mind, and his conviction that there is a value in what he has seen there is an act of intuition rather than of argument.

Indeed the humanities themselves owe a great debt to Huxley. For not only did he show up the half truth of Pope's old adage that "the proper study of mankind is man," but he made out a strong case for a still more serious charge against the school classics of fifty years ago, that they were not a study of man after all. They were a study of language and style, but not of literature. The true humanities are literature, history, philosophy, and sociology; the classics at their best are only an introduction to these true humanities and at their worst are pure gerund-grinding. Nor are Greek and Latin the only avenues to the study of man. Huxley outlined a curriculum which should consist, in addition to natural science, of the theory of morals and of political and social life, the history of our own country with incidental geography, English literature together with translations of the greatest writings in foreign tongues, English composition, drawing, and either music or painting[1]. Even now we doubt if any course of which natural science is the centre has attained Huxley's ideals on the humanist side; but there is no doubt that, whereas the classical curriculum of Huxley's time laid itself open to his criticisms, that of twenty years later achieved his aims more fully than any rival which has yet been discovered. An attack on a system often results in its improvement where the object was its destruction.

We said that it is impossible to make a satisfactory abstract of Huxley's writings. What follows is not an abstract of any particular essay, it does not reproduce his forms of expression, and it may not give the exact stress which he laid on each particular point. It is an attempt to run through the various functions of science which in different connections he brought to the fore.

First, children should in the days of childhood make friends with Nature. They should love and admire. The instincts which draw them to her must be given play before they are atrophied by disuse. Familiarity will breed knowledge, knowledge curiosity, and curiosity observation. It was many years before much was done to realise this ideal. Modern nature-study is only about twenty years old, and much teaching which passes under the name is still a miserable fiasco. In the future it may be hoped that a love of nature will really be fostered by schools, though perhaps not in the class room, and it may exercise a vast moralising influence. In boarding-schools natural history societies have come to revive this natural taste, which it was feared that games had finally driven out, and there is reason to hope that in the future it will humanise many a life which would otherwise become a prey to sensuality or discontent, will restore the sense of beauty to a nation which is tending to estimate values in terms of cash, will implant the seeds of the scientific attitude, and will re-introduce the spirit of reverence into subjects which may otherwise sell wisdom captive for thirty pieces of silver into the land of industrial bondage.

Secondly, an acquaintance with the results of science

[1] *Collected Essays*, vol. III, No. 7, Science and Art and Education.

changes our whole outlook on the universe. Instead of regarding the Earth as the centre of a tiny world created six thousand years ago, we know it to be a speck in an abysmal star-strewn space, but a speck with a wondrous story stretching over myriads of years; and we know that each of its infinite species of plant and animal inhabitants has an ancestry which goes far back into the past, an ancestry of strange forms which lived in vanished marshes or on the shores of forgotten seas as strange as themselves. And all these things must be taken into account when we ask, What is our life, and whence? why is it, and what is its goal?

Thirdly, the history of science is the history of the growth of the idea of causation and it may be that the study of science is essential in order to fix that idea in the minds of most human beings. Certainly no man who has not acquired this sense can be called educated. Legislators will only feel a sense of responsibility if they realise intensely, that, as is the sowing, so also is the harvest: the masses will recognise that hygiene is not a fad of sanitary inspectors only if they are accustomed to think in terms of immutable natural laws which will not yield to the customs or desires of man; in whatever sphere progress is to be substituted for conservatism, it is possible only when the change is seen to be no arbitrary preference of a school but is necessitated because Nature will only give us what we desire on condition that we seek it by the means that she lays down.

Fourthly—and this is a position which needs very careful discussion, and to which we shall have to return later—Huxley claims that there is one universal method underlying the methods of all the separate sciences. "The life, the fortune, and the happiness of every one of us, and, more or less, of those who are connected with us, depend upon our knowing something of the rules of a game infinitely more difficult and complicated than chess....The chess-board is the world, the pieces are the phenomena of the universe, the rules of the game are what we call the laws of nature. The player on the other side is hidden from us. We know that his play is always just and fair and patient. But also we know, to our cost, that he never overlooks a mistake or makes the smallest allowance for ignorance. To the man who plays well the highest stakes are paid with that sort of overflowing generosity with which the strong shows delight in strength. And one who plays ill is check-mated—without haste but without remorse....*Well, what I mean by Education is learning the rules of that mighty game*[1]."

Lastly, the crown of a scientific education is the capacity to conduct independent research. A few only may attain it; but progress depends on those few, and, through the neglect of science in its education, Great Britain was doing an amount of research absurdly small compared with that accomplished by Germany. With the chemists, such as Sir William Ramsay, the research argument seems to have outweighed all the others.

Huxley's campaign was therefore directed to attain all objectives which his predecessors had attacked singly, and others besides. Such strategy involved a considerable widening of the battle front, though it had the advantage that success at any one point would probably facilitate subsequent stages of the operation against others. The first aim necessitated an assault on the Kindergarten, the infant school, preparatory school, and elementary school. If these positions were taken, this first objective would probably be reached, whether the secondary school and university remained in the hands of the humanists or passed into those of the scientists. The strategy on this part of the line was, however, hopelessly mismanaged. It was essential to success that nature-study, not elementary science, should conduct this part of the attack; and Huxley's writings, as well as those of Ruskin and perhaps of Matthew Arnold, would suggest that this was what was proposed. Actually, physiography was the only unit of nature-study which was brought into action; the rest of nature-study was moved out of the line, not to reappear till the twentieth century; physiography actually obtained

[1] *Op. cit.* Essay 4, "A Liberal Education and where to find it."

a lodgment in the elementary school, where it found itself
so isolated that it had to be withdrawn and reorganised
as a section of geography. The motive for this mistake in
strategy undoubtedly was that the scientists did not take
the first aim as seriously as the remainder and believed
that physics and chemistry would be better able to secure
the next point in the line—the post-elementary annexes
of the elementary school and the secondary school—if they
could capture the upper standards of the elementary school.
The unsuitability of these two sciences for effective work
in the elementary zone was not recognised till after the
failure of Armstrong's attempt to secure success by arming
them with the new weapon of heurism.

The second, third, and fourth aims are all concerned with
the age from twelve to nineteen. They have as their
respective objects the widening of outlook, the creation of
an idea of causality, and the development of sound habits
of reasoning. But, though the teacher has in each case
pupils of the same age, he will have to adopt different means
to secure each of these three aims, and it was this problem
which the advocates of science did not clearly present to
themselves and which even now cannot be said to have
been solved.

The second aim, that of creating outlook, requires that
the results of many sciences should be taught, but it does
not necessitate a training in the methods of any one of
them. In a word, it asks for "popular science." Popular
astronomy extends our outlook in space, popular geology
and popular biology in time: our whole mode of thinking
is utterly different from that of pre-Copernican and pre-
Darwinian man. The intensive study of one or two sciences,
least of all of the two sciences which are now fashionable
in schools, physics and chemistry, will not give this knowledge. A real understanding of the means by which such
knowledge was attained would involve a study far more
protracted than is possible for the ordinary schoolboy.
He may be told in very rough outline the kind of considerations which influenced the scientific discoverers—how the
distances of the planets and consequently their velocities

were determined, how rocks containing certain fossils are
always found below those containing others, how variations
which increase adaptability to environment are found in an
increasing series. A clever pupil will appreciate the character of the proof; but the average pupil probably does not
reach even this stage; and not even the clever pupil can
be said to be in possession of the evidence as a juryman is
in possession of the evidence in a criminal trial, far less to
be in the position either of the barrister who has worked
it into shape or the judge who is an expert critic. In the
main it is a case of acceptance on authority; and the
majority of pupils at the end of such popular courses will
have scarcely any more idea of the reign of law than they
had at the beginning. Hence the opponents of scientific
teaching were somewhat contemptuous of any instruction
which might be given in furtherance of this aim and the
advocates of a scientific curriculum had an uneasy feeling
that to lay stress on it might expose their subject to a
suspicion of intellectual inferiority; and so it was allowed
tacitly to drop out of the programme[1], though, owing to
the prevalence of confused thinking, it is probable that it
is often regarded as one of the advantages to be gained
from the study of "science" even when "science" means
elementary physics and chemistry.

The third aim—the creation of an idea of causality—
opens up a wide field of controversy. One feels about it, as
about the second aim, that any conception of education
which does not recognise its importance is lacking in an
essential element. But many persons seem to acquire an
idea of causality without any formal training in natural
sciences. Their minds appear to be so attuned to that note
that they vibrate to it whencesoever it reaches them.
History, politics, economics, strategy, business, the every-

[1] This statement may at first sight appear to be an exaggeration,
but we beg the reader to ask himself what specific provision was made
in any school for teaching anything but a verbal smattering about,
say, nebulae, the evidence of ice action (till geography took it over),
the identification of local fossils, or the life of palaeolithic man, for
thirty years after the introduction of physics and chemistry into
schools.

day affairs of life, all seem schools in which they may learn it. It is its very universality which impresses them. Others seem never to acquire it even from natural science. The laboratory is to them a place where all experiments go wrong and Chance is king as much as elsewhere. The truth seems to be somewhat as follows. Common experience would suggest that events were divided into two classes, those where even babes and savages perceive uniformity, such as the sequence of day and night, and those which appear to be the sport of chance, such as the British weather. The effect on a flabby mind of a course, say, in chemistry is to convince it that the inside of a chemical laboratory may possibly have to be regarded as part of the domain of uniformity; but such a mind is not prone to generalisation, conscious or unconscious, and continues to assign to the realm of Chance all else which it so assigned before the assumed course in chemistry. The early advocates of science did not realise that the majority of mankind may be born with minds of such a description: consequently we do not know even at the present day what proportion of pupils are really capable of thinking scientifically all round, after the study of a single branch of science, or of several, and what proportion is incapable of ever properly forming the scientific habit of mind at all: hence we are still in the dark whether more science or whether none is what is needed for the majority.

The fourth aim needs the most careful consideration of all. It must be carefully distinguished from the third. We do not suppose that even the stoutest opponents of the transference of mental attitudes from one subject-matter to another would deny that really educated persons recognise the universality of law; but the most scientific mind may go wrong as to what the particular laws are which are operative in a field with which he is not well acquainted. How far can training in some branches of science secure a less chance of coming to false conclusions in others? Earlier in the chapter we argued that the history of scientific discovery seems to show that there is not, in any sense which helps the pioneer in a new branch of science, a

uniform scientific method. A training in some other subject
in which exact reasoning is needed will be of some assistance, but much modification in methods will be required
as the enquirer proceeds further in the new subject. Five
minutes spent with an archaeologist will convince you that
there is an archaeological sense as much as there is a
geological or a biological sense and that it can not be
comprised in a set of formulae. A master mind like
Huxley's can to some extent, if one may use the expression,
generalise such a sense. But can a fifth form boy? Apparently here again, as in the case of the formation of the
idea of uniformity at all, the effect on one mind is limited
in sphere to a particular subject-matter while its effect on
another is wider in scope. To one man particular processes
of scientific thinking may give a fuller appreciation of the
lines of procedure which are involved in all searches after
truth, to another they remain merely the tricks of one
particular science. But, if this is granted, a further question
arises. Is every branch of science equally fitted to produce
this wider appreciation of the methods by which truth is
attained? Huxley, without apparently realising to what
corollaries his contention might commit him, answered in
the affirmative. His answer was prompted by the charge
of "inexactitude" brought against his own speciality, the
biological sciences, which implied that they were less fitted
to produce the result than the mathematical sciences.
Huxley does not really meet the point of this charge. He
has no difficulty in showing that the particular facts of
biology are beyond a doubt, and that some of these facts
are established by experiment, that is by artificial isolation,
as well as by observation. But the point which his opponents intended to make was that the wide theories of
biology cannot carry the same absolute conviction as the
wide theories of astronomy, physics, or even chemistry.
It is implied that, when the pupil cannot see the certainty
of the conclusions so clearly that he cannot possibly think
otherwise, he has to some extent to depend on the judgment of another: he is in part dependent on authority and
to that extent lacks the "feel" how the thing becomes

certain. Hence he is at a loss when he is required to have
this feeling of certainty in another case. Huxley has not
disproved the position taken up, for instance, by Whewell
at an earlier date, that students should be introduced to
the less exact sciences through the portal of the more
exact. A number of further questions suggest themselves.
If Whewell was right, how far should the preliminary
training be carried, if it is on the one hand to save the
pupil from a careless attitude towards truth in the less
exact sciences and yet on the other hand is to avoid the
formation of a specialised physical or chemical demand for
certainty which might be actually prejudicial in botany
or zoology? Is it even certain that natural science in any
of its branches is the best instrument with which to start
the training of school pupils in the methods of scientific
thinking?

Thus, after considering the three aims which would seem
to dominate scientific teaching between the ages of twelve
and twenty-one—the period of secondary schooling and
the lower stages of a university course—we cannot feel
that Huxley or any of his contemporaries had either
estimated sufficiently the difficulties at any of the points
of attack or considered the relations between one point of
attack and another; and, though they succeeded in establishing physics and chemistry within the enemy's lines,
it is doubtful how much nearer they came to their ultimate
objectives.

The fifth aim, the encouragement of research, immediately
concerns only the highest stage of university work, but
it has a very great bearing on procedure at the lower
stages. Learning natural science means learning the elements of research. It is unfortunate that the difference
between the humanities and the sciences in this respect
is too often forgotten. Fifty years ago the predominance
of the humanities, and therefore of humanistic aims and
methods, was so strong that it was hard to convince people
that a scientific training means not the communication of
the results of research, not a critical estimate of the researches of others, but learning *how* to research. To-day

the predominance of natural science is tending to make a training for research appear to be commensurate with education not only in science but in the humanities; in Germany it has apparently already done so. In reality there is an important difference in the rôle of research between the sciences and the humanities. In the humanities, research may profit others but it is not their main educative value to the learner. Whereas in the sciences creativeness is but research carried to a high point, in the humanities the two things may be quite different. No man ever became a dramatist by discovering new facts about Shakespeare's life or a poet by a comparative study of the metres of two languages. Even in history the good to the learner and to the world ultimately comes from tracing the connections between events, from evaluating them, and from the development of a social sense; the discovery of new facts is only a step in the process. If the humanities are taught solely with a view of training critics and professors, they will abandon the higher task of making men wise for the lower task of making them learned. This is the truth which needs emphasis to-day; but the place of research in science was what needed to be impressed on the men of fifty years ago.

1859 is a memorable date in the history of science as it saw the publication of Darwin's *Origin of Species*. It also witnessed the first grants from the State towards scientific education and the establishment of science degrees in London University. The leading actors are now all on the stage and the controversy has begun. Unfortunately it was too often carried on, not with a desire to see the strong points in opponents' contentions, but simply to secure dialectical success. As if the *odium paedagogicum* was not enough, the *odium theologicum* must needs enter. Though the alliance between Aristotelianism and orthodoxy had set Catholicism and science in opposition in the days of the Renaissance, there had been no hostility in Protestant England during the seventeenth and eighteenth centuries. Milton took care that the universe of *Paradise Lost* should be strictly reconcilable with Copernican astronomy;

Newton was devoutly religious; and educationalists at the close of the eighteenth century were constantly and sincerely urging that a study of the creation would inculcate a reverence for the Creator. Geology provoked the first cry of alarm; but as yet there was no panic. Indeed with a man like Charles Kingsley geology became an intrinsic part of his religion. But the joint monopoly of classics and Anglicanism at the two ancient universities tended to promote a separation. The future theologians drifted as a matter of course to Oxford and Cambridge and never made the acquaintance of science or its votaries. The sciences were left in outer darkness where they consorted with all varieties of unorthodoxy. Of course the division was not hard-and-fast; Mark Pattison was not a man of science and A. R. Wallace was not an opponent of religion. But in the mind of the ordinary bishop Science was represented by the names of Darwin, Huxley and Spencer; and in the minds of this trio Charles Kingsley did not stand for a typical representative of orthodoxy. Enough passion had already been roused before 1859; the lightning-flash of the *Origin of Species* really cleared the air. The rapid acceptance of the evolutionary theory by scientific opinion made it obvious that, if orthodox science were to be pronounced heretical theology, educated men would be placed on the horns of an impossible dilemma. Temple, one of the small band of open-minded clergy who from the first accepted Darwinism, instead of suffering excommunication, lived to become Archbishop of Canterbury; and the *odium theologicum* was not handed on to the second generation.

While controversialists were "taking the side of the angels" or of the monkeys instead of deciding the relative importance of the various aims which were being urged for the teaching of science or the kind of curriculum which would combine those aims, utilitarian considerations were very naturally deciding what kind of scientific curriculum would ultimately emerge. In 1839 a committee appointed to enquire into the best method of encouraging the fine arts had recommended the establishment of a Normal School of Design. Science had come in as an ally of the arts and crafts; and the Science and Art Department, South Kensington, resulted. The great Industrial Exhibition drew attention to the defect of British handicrafts at the moment when science was "in the air," and in 1859 Parliament consented to the system of what became known as South Kensington grants. In 1851 there had been only thirty-eight science classes with 1300 pupils in the country; encouraged by these grants there were in 1861 seventy science schools with 2543 pupils. But the all-important problem of a supply of teachers was not effectively grappled with. The proposal to set up a strong central School of Science which would have produced a crop of efficient teachers was abandoned, and in its place was adopted the miserable substitute of an examination for science teachers. Before this examination was abandoned the pathway of scientific teaching was already clogged by a body of teachers who mistook cram for education and had no idea how to extract from their subject its inherent educational value, who had acquired a knowledge of facts without being really trained, narrow specialists from whom no broad outlook could be expected. The Public Schools Commission of 1868 reported in favour of introducing two kinds of sciences into the seven schools, the first represented by physics and chemistry and the second by "comparative physiology" and natural history; and the chairman of the Endowed Schools Commission afterwards stated[1] that it was the intention of that Commission to insist on one branch of science being taught in all schools and two in schools with a "modern" curriculum. The second demand sounds moderate beside the first, and it is evident that the Public School Commissioners had a very inadequate conception of the demands on time which branches of science make. Eventually the Royal Commission on Scientific Instruction, generally known as the Devonshire Commission, sat from 1871 to 1875, and presented a series of reports on the place of science in every grade of education.

This Commission was intended to act as a general headquarters for the scientific army to decide the plan of

[1] *Sixth Report of Devonshire Commission*, p. 3

operations, and as such it was urgently needed. The allied armies of mathematicians who were proud to discover a truth "which could not possibly be of any use to anybody," of chemists intent on preserving British industry against foreign competition, of biologists and geologists setting out with a missionary zeal to spread a new outlook on the universe, of naturalists intent on using Nature as a purifying agent on the pettinesses of economic man, and of physiologists eager to improve sanitary conditions and the national physique, had each found that they had rushed certain positions and each believed that the next position on its own front was the key of the situation. Amongst them they had established honours examinations in Natural Science at the older universities, set up Colleges of a predominantly scientific character in London and other large towns, instituted classes for the diffusion of scientific knowledge among artisans, secured South Kensington grants for "Science and Art" classes, devised examinations for science teachers and made the public schools invite down a few perambulating scientific lecturers! Yet they had only taken the outworks. In 1870 the vast bulk of candidates for honours at the old universities were still studying the humanities or mathematics, the provincial colleges even where they existed had not yet attained university rank, the secondary schools scarcely taught science at all, there were few teachers of science and most of these had received a very narrow training, the smatterings of facts taught in a few elementary schools could not be called scientific teaching, and technical instruction was sadly deficient.

The Commission investigated the teaching of science at every grade of education—elementary schools and training colleges, South Kensington classes, the universities, museums, colleges and secondary schools, and published reports on each grade as soon as their work on it was complete. Their work showed the barrenness of the land beyond a doubt and inaugurated a rapid spread of scientific teaching in every branch of education. As regards the merit of its policy, it may be roughly said to have been best at the higher and worst at the lower stages.

The elementary stage does not fall within our scope. Action at the next stage was taken rapidly, the reorganisation of the South Kensington "Schools of Science" being largely carried out by Huxley in 1872. The result was a very doubtful success. Huxley, as we have seen, showed in his essays that he had a clear idea in what a good general education should consist, but his reorganised schools did not give it. Eighteen out of twenty-four hours were devoted to science and mathematics. In the remaining six hours what room was there for his moral and social training, his civic training through history and geography, his literature, music, and one or two languages? The problem was not approached from a broad point of view: instead of starting with the idea of a complete education in which science should have its due place, it was treated purely as a question of pushing the claims of science. Schools of Science were neither technical schools following a sound general education nor schools giving such an education. Without any such intention, but as a direct consequence of this partial view, the reformers practically brought it about that science was consoled for a subordination in the higher grades of secondary education by being given undisputed sway over a lower grade of quasi-secondary schools[1] with an earlier leaving age and an inferior status. Twenty years later the Bryce Commission unreservedly condemned the system on the ground that South Kensington schools suffered from a permanent examination fever. Nowhere was the insidious system of payment by results worked out so elaborately, and nowhere was education so completely replaced by "cramming." One of the first acts of the Board of Education after its constitution in 1899 was to assimilate these schools to the broader type of secondary schools which they encouraged.

In the ordinary type of secondary school the Devonshire Commissioners found that science had very little place. In 65 out of 128 endowed schools from which returns were

---

[1] A "school" of science was not really a school at all, but usually a portion of a school, secondary or elementary, organised to receive South Kensington grants.

received, no science at all was taught. Of these only thirteen possessed laboratories[1]. It may be safely assumed that almost every school in which it was taught would send returns. The Report recommends that science should be allotted six hours weekly on the time-table of all public and endowed schools and should be allowed one-sixth of the marks in all internal or leaving examinations. It may be noted that the Report assumes that the advice of the Public Schools Commissioners against a division of schools into sides would be taken, an assumption which a few years' experience showed to be incorrect. More significant than anything which the Report contains is a vital point which it omits—the character of the scientific teaching to be given. No wonder. All the scientific specialists could agree in urging that "science" should be taught; but unanimity would have ceased the moment they tried to determine *what* science. On this point the most they tell us is that many authorities believe physics to be a better school subject than chemistry[2].

The absence of all thought concerning curriculum and method from the minds of academic adherents of science makes it desirable to notice one of the few expositions of the scientific standpoint which came from the pens of practical schoolmasters—the essay by Wilson, science master at Rugby, in Farrar's *Essays on a Liberal Education* (1867). Wilson is one of those who believed physics to be a better school subject than chemistry and he sees the need of thinking out a policy on the vital points which the Commissioners ignored.

His main idea is that the study of two unlike branches of natural science is a necessary part of any complete education which is to give an all-round power of intelligent thought. In other words, the education of which science is a part, not science by itself, is to fulfil our third and fourth aims. His general view of the advantages of science does not substantially differ from that of Huxley. By appealing to native interests, science puts the pupil into the right active attitude of mind; it increases his grip, as

[1] *Sixth Report*, p. 1.   [2] p. 5.

is seen by his progress in other subjects, especially as regards activity of thought and sustained attention; it arouses and utilises curiosity; it is exact, it is "an applied logic." He lays stress on accurate observation, exact reasoning, and power of judging evidence, "than which there is no characteristic so marked of the educated man." Mathematics does not serve the same purpose. Science serves also as a preliminary to the research aim; for it is the business of the school to discover special aptitudes. He does not forget outlook; but he quotes from a report of the British Association to the effect that giving a literary acquaintance with scientific facts is not teaching science. Such an acquaintance can be easily given in addition; but it will be taken from sciences other than those which are formally studied—from astronomy, geology, and physical geography[1]. Here we have the usual aims, but in addition a clear conception as to the means which elsewhere we have lacked. He claims no monopoly for science; we have to deal with Man as well as with Nature; and he regrets that so many advocates of science have ignored the claims of the aesthetic side of our being.

He next discusses the choice of the two subjects for formal study. Since science proceeds from facts to laws, not from laws to facts, a certain broad array of facts must be known to the pupil before he can apply scientific methods; it is useless to supply foreign facts and forthwith expect him to deal with them scientifically. With what branches of science can he most easily deal scientifically? Geology and chemistry lend themselves too readily to cram. Botany and physics he does not think suffer from this defect, at least intrinsically, though "what they may become with bad text-books and bad teachers it is hard to say, but it is an important consideration." The next twenty years indeed were to see the teaching of science ruined by neglect of this consideration! Wilson's methods, unlike those of Armstrong later, made no attempt to delude the schoolboy into the belief that he was discovering everything for himself. But they distinctly aimed at

[1] *Op. cit.* p. 262.

making him think. "The teacher ought to make the pupils teach themselves, by thinking out the subject with them, by taking up their suggestions and illustrations, by criticising and hunting them down, by starting them on a fresh scent when they are at fault, by reminding them of some familiar fact which they had overlooked, and so eliciting out of the chaos of vague notions that are afloat something of order and concatenation and interest before the key to the mystery is given, even if after all it has to be *given*." He starts in the middle of the school and proposes to extend science teaching a class lower each year till experience determines the lowest point at which effective teaching can be given, and, when once that point has been determined, to carry on the science teaching therefrom up to the stage where the boys begin to specialise.

Had some such policy as regards curriculum and method been officially adopted, the history of science teaching during the next twenty years might have been very different. During the seventies and eighties it gradually found its way into secondary schools. But, amid the welter of confused opinions as to aims, utilitarianism naturally triumphed. The subject which was commonly introduced was not physics, which would have formed the best introduction to scientific method, nor any of the open-air sciences which would have aroused a sense of the wonders to be found in Nature, but chemistry, the subject which appeared most likely to provide an immediate source of livelihood, and chemistry taught by rule of thumb. "What science may become with bad text-books and bad teachers" and bad examinations was now to be seen. The London Matriculation Examination had most influence on the schools which were most likely to take science; and in that examination it was possible to pass in chemistry without entering a laboratory—indeed it was the easiest way. The headmasters of the first-grade schools, whose prejudices needed to be overcome, were confirmed in their belief that science was an uneducative "cram" subject; and, faced with a utilitarian demand from certain parents for a subject in whose merits they did not believe, they solved the difficulty by dividing their schools into two sides, a classical and a modern, and relegating science to the modern side. The more promising pupils were kept in the classical side to be prepared for university scholarships; and the modern side was welcomed as a means of disposing of stupid boys who would otherwise retard their progress. Then the failure of these stupid boys to get on in life was used as an argument for the inferiority of science as an intellectual discipline.

We must hurry over the later stages and postpone the technical and university sides of science teaching to a later chapter[1]. In the nineties Armstrong, enthusiastic in his belief that chemistry was the finest of educational organa, but recognising that it was a tool blunted by bad modes of using it, started a crusade in favour of the "heuristic method," by which the pupil was supposed to discover everything for himself. Of course the pupil did nothing of the kind, as was discovered as soon as the London School Board allowed its pupils to be used as *corpora vilia* for this impossible experiment. But other causes were at work to improve the position of science. The technical schools which were established in the eighties brought out the fact that technical education can only be based on a sound general training in science, not on scientific cram. The provincial colleges developed into universities and began to produce an adequate supply of teachers in addition to furnishing recruits to industry. Science steadily increased the number of its followers in the older universities. Examinations were improved. A tradition of sound methods of teaching was established. In all the larger schools physics was introduced and was begun before chemistry. Botany, always popular in girls' schools, began to be taught so as to produce scientific habits of mind. There are, however, still schools in which chemistry is the only branch of science taught, and these can hardly be said to give a scientific training. The Board of Education has reformed the curriculum of the old Schools of Science. Finally the war has created a rush to receive a scientific

[1] Chapter X.

training. Though in part this will probably prove to be a transient phenomenon, it will correct the balance which has hitherto inclined too strongly in favour of the humanities.

There has been an attempt to represent the nearness with which the Germans came to victory as due to a supposed predominance of science in German education. In point of fact classics play a greater part in the school education of Germany than of England. The real error in English education is that it has been too specialised, leaving the man who has been trained in the humanities, and who naturally gravitates into the government of men, without even that bowing acquaintance with science which leads him to see where it is needed and when to call in the expert. German education is proponderatingly scientific only in the sense that in German universities the humanities have been studied in what we may call a scientific instead of a humanistic spirit; and this loss of the humanistic spirit is far from calling for imitation. The humanistic spirit is the soul of civilisation. The Greek world shows us that nations may be civilised with a very poor knowledge of natural science, though it is equally true that scientific enquiry will be one of the results which flow from civilisation. But the inventions of modern science do not make a nation civilised—for two reasons; because science appeals only to the brain and not to the heart, and because it primarily demands the training of a small intellectual class. Russia is proving this fact. Russia had her small band of scientific experts; she had all the externals supplied by a century of scientific discovery; but below this was a proletariat unacquainted with literature, economics, and history, who were incapable of intelligent thought on morals, religion, politics, or social relations; and they have acted as men unacquainted with the rudiments of the humanities must act. Germany's case has been different and the consequences have been different. Germany suffered from an intellectual caste who thought purely in terms of physical cause and effect and disdained that outcome of the humanistic way of studying the humanities which Thomas Arnold called moral thoughtfulness. They studied literature, history, and philosophy, but with the head alone and not with the heart. Nemesis delayed, but when she struck her blow, she struck deep.

REFERENCES

William Whewell, *Thoughts on the Study of Mathematics*, 1835.
—— *On the Principles of English University Education*, 1837.
—— *Of a Liberal Education in general, and with particular reference to the leading studies of the University of Cambridge*, 1845.
—— 2nd edition with addition of a second vol. Part II, *Discussions and Changes*, 1840–1850, 1850. (References are to this edition.)
William Jolly, *Education as developed by George Combe*, 1879.
Herbert Spencer, *Education*, 1859.
John Ruskin, *The Stones of Venice*, 1853, vol. III, Appendix 7.
T. H. Huxley, *Science and Education* (vol. III of Collected Essays), 1893.
Royal Commission on Scientific Instruction and the Advancement of Science (Devonshire Commission), eight reports, 1871–1875.
F. W. Farrar, *Essays on a Liberal Education*, 1867 (essay by J. M. Wilson).
H. E. Armstrong, *The Teaching of Scientific Method*, 1903.
British Association, *Report for* 1889 (report on teaching of chemistry).

CHAPTER VI

FIRST STATE INTERVENTION:
THE ROYAL COMMISSIONS

NOTHING perhaps accounts for the suggestion of dullness which the mention of Education conveys to the ordinary reader of the newspaper so much as the vision which it calls up of reports, blue books, and debates in Hansard. He instinctively feels that, if Education be a living thing, its true history must be found elsewhere: and he is right. The living force of education has always sprung from movements of the human mind and aspirations of the human heart; legislation and administration are mere tools which these movements and aspirations use. We may therefore view the Royal Commissions as marking the time when the educational zeal which had been developing for half a century became conscious of its power and able to carry public opinion with it.

The educational function of the State is now accepted by everyone except Mr Harold Cox. New State-controlled types of schools and colleges outnumber the old institutions. The old institutions themselves have been radically changed by the State. It is hard to put ourselves into the mental attitude either of Whigs or of Conservatives in 1850. The Whig attitude to education of those days was more conservative than the attitude of Conservatives to-day. Yet the way of regarding the educational duty of the State which is well-nigh universal to-day would have been impossible but for the triumph of the Whig views in the middle of last century.

At that time Whigs, Conservatives, and even advanced Radicals restricted State activity within narrow limits. To the Whigs State action seemed to have had its day under the absolutist system of the Tudors, of Cromwell, and of the Stuarts: and in two directions especially had they been occupied in limiting its activity—control of trade and

control of conscience. Nor were extreme Radicals more
friendly. Their ideals had grown up in France, the country
where Louis XIV had truly said *L'état c'est moi*, and democratic prejudice against State action had not died out with
the old *régime*. State control was associated, not with
democracy, but with the "benevolent despots" of the
eighteenth century, with the absolutist monarchies of
Austria and Prussia. "Liberty" was the battle-cry both
of Whigs and Radicals: State socialism had not arisen.
As for the Conservatives, though they supported the
retention of State control in departments of life where it
already existed, yet they were equally opposed to its
extension to new fields.

No party, however, was prepared to apply its principles
with unfailing consistency: facts were often too strong for
theories. Thus, though the absolutist governments sought
to control education because they suspected it, yet Prussia
in the sphere of higher education used its control to develop
it. The failure at Jena was too powerful a fact to be overlooked: Humboldt and Stein felt that the autocracy must
make an ally of the middle classes and were wise enough to
trust their new ally. Hence the efficient scheme of higher
education which they produced! Democratic opinion too
was driven in one direction by theories and in another by
facts. Theoretically, to let the State control the schools
seemed to the French Revolutionaries like handing soul
as well as body to the rule of a master. Practically, however, the wiser among them saw that an uneducated
democracy would be unable to last and that without State
control, State supply, and State compulsion the democracy
would not become educated. A similar divergence of
theoretical and practical views prevailed among English
admirers of the Revolution and reappeared when by the
establishment of the Committee of Council on Education
in 1839 the State took the first serious step in the direction
of educational control. Alongside of the two parties which
on practical grounds supported the establishment of undenominational State schools or the State support of
denominational schools stood a third party—the "Volun-

taryists"—who on theoretical grounds rejected educational action by the State as outside its sphere. But, whereas the last party was small in numbers and, in the sphere of elementary education, facts were proving too stubborn for it to survive, yet in the sphere of secondary and university education everyone was a voluntaryist. The reason is obvious. Whereas the State was driven by an imperious necessity to intervene in regard to elementary education because without such intervention great masses of people would remain uneducated, some sort of a system existed already in regard to higher education and theory was not confronted with an irresistible obstacle of fact.

In setting up the Royal Commissions there was therefore no intention of introducing permanent State control over higher education. On this matter the "common-sense" man did not differ substantially from the doctrinaires of the Manchester school. A "nation of shopkeepers" applied to education the principles of the market-place. No one valued what cost him nothing; competition was the best security and the parent the best judge of efficiency. If governors were to carry out their functions well, they must be interested either as buyers or as sellers of education, that is to say either as parents (or friends of parents) or through a feeling that they were competing with other institutions. The headmaster was the manager; as long as the business succeeded he must have a free hand with complete power over his subordinates. The application of these principles during the second half of the century produced a high degree of efficiency along certain lines, and those presumably such as parents desired. It involved, however, two great defects. First, it worked as it was intended only in regard to non-local institutions where competition was really free; it left unsolved the problem of local day-schools, since competition between several schools in a small town could only be wasteful. Secondly, it failed to see that the form of education which each parent would desire for his own child would normally be that which enabled him most successfully to compete with the children of other people and that this would not

necessarily be the form of education which the interests
of the community rendered desirable for children as a
whole. These problems will face us later: for the present
it is enough to notice that the period of competition created
two standards possibly higher than could otherwise have
been obtained, the standard of attainment which could
be expected of the picked pupil and the standard of discipline on which an experienced teacher could insist.   It
did not create equally high standards in other directions
as, for instance, the level of attainment which could be
expected from the duller pupils or the level of teaching
which could be expected to reach them.

The ideal of the authors of the Royal Commissions was
therefore individualistic and the best way to regard these
Commissions is as temporary socialistic means for securing
a permanent individualistic policy. The Whig individualists
found in existence a number of institutions which had come
down from days when schools and colleges were regarded
neither as competing businesses nor as State agencies, but
as quasi-ecclesiastical foundations. They were governed
by archaic regulations of which the purpose had passed
away; and their considerable endowments were in consequence being largely wasted. The Whigs took the common-
sense view that, since by no possibility could these institutions now carry out the exact intention of their
founders, it was best to accept their modern aim, but to
compel them to fulfil it more adequately by adopting the
competitive principle, and to scrap all founders' conditions
which ran contrary to that principle. Harrow School, for
instance, was intended by its founder to teach elementary
classics to any boy in the parish whose parents wished for
such an education; but its present income was many times
more than would suffice if every Harrow parent had desired
his son to learn classics. In point of fact it had for a
hundred and fifty years been an aristocratic school and
most of its present income represented capitalised profits
from the fees of its aristocratic pupils. Hence the Whig
policy, after providing an education—classical or otherwise
as they desired—for the inhabitants of Harrow, was to

spend the rest of the income on the aristocratic school, to conduct that school on competitive business lines, and to sweep away all existing regulations which prevented this being done. Nowadays this policy would have to face a powerful rival; it would be proposed to apply the endowments neither to the founders' nor to existing purposes, but to those which seemed best to the State as represented by the majority in Parliament. But this view commanded little effective support in the middle of last century; and the only opposition to the Whig view came from that body of Conservative opinion which was alarmed by every supposed assault on vested interests or on tradition.

The policy of the Royal Commissions may not have been the best possible; but, when the coach is stuck fast in the mud, it is something to have got it out and set it moving. Subsequently to change its course is a much easier process than originally to make it move at all. It is hard nowadays to realise how deeply embedded universities, colleges, and schools were in the mass of founders' regulations, mediaeval and Reformation statutes, and other unalterable decrees. Pious founders had no conception of future changes; even at the time of the Renaissance, when they were deliberately improving on "the barbarous grossness of the Middle Ages," they never envisaged the possibility of a time when their own arrangements would appear equally out of date. The more pious the founder, the more carefully did he prescribe for his foundation the details of its administration. He fixed salaries regardless of future changes in the value of money; and by the nineteenth century they were generally inadequate to secure the services of any man fitted to be a headmaster. He generally prohibited the taking of fees, or fixed them so low that there was no means of legitimately increasing these inadequate salaries. He imposed curricula which were subsequently enforced by the law-courts in so literal a manner that, in the Leeds case, a classical school was prohibited from giving a "modern" education even when there was no demand for classics. He often imposed oaths to do things which were no longer possible, to the scandal

of onlookers who regarded oaths seriously and to the confusion of recipients who found it hard to distinguish those
which had become mere forms from others with which
compliance might still be expected. Naturally there was
much straining at gnats and much swallowing of camels.
The same general principles of sweeping away obsolete
statutes, providing new constitutions, and then leaving
administration—and legislation, subject to the consent of
the Queen in Council—to the institutions themselves, were
applied to the universities, to the public schools, and to the
smaller endowed schools, by the Acts which followed the
various commissions[1]. Each class of institution will now
be considered separately.

(1) **The Universities.** The Oxford Commission was a
result of the wave of academic liberalism which swept over
the University after 1845. As Mark Pattison[2] claimed,
"All her recent reforms have been the work of a minority,
it is true, but still a minority of her own family. The
movement commenced from within. Is it too bold to say
that more enlightened views as to her proper destiny and
worth are entertained by those whom she has trained than
are to be found elsewhere in that public opinion by which
she is most seriously arraigned." At Cambridge too the
movement for a commission originated with a progressive
minority. The majority of the old academic governing
bodies was, however, opposed to change, and the reformers
appealed to the Prime Minister, Lord John Russell. Feeling
ran high, as any reader may see who cares to peruse a skit
called *The University Commission or Lord John Russell's
Postbag of April 27*, 1850, by William Sewell, fellow of
Exeter and founder of Radley. Its general style is often
to be found to-day in undergraduate journals, but these
would usually refrain from describing the Cabinet as thieves
and from attacking the Royal Family as Sewell attacks

---

[1] The Brougham Commission (1818–1837) and the Chichester
Commission (1849–1853), the latter of which led to the passing of
the Charitable Trusts Act, 1853, are important chiefly to those interested in educational law.

[2] *Suggestions on Academical Organisation*, p. 5.

the Prince Consort. Commissions were appointed for both universities (1850), and, on their report, Acts of Parliament were passed to carry out parts of their recommendations (Oxford, 1854, Cambridge 1856). Another period of controversy followed, both sides producing a shower of pamphlets, amongst which those by Mark Pattison and Goldwin Smith state the reformers' position most clearly, till a fresh commission was appointed to enquire into the property and income of the universities and their colleges, and, on its report of 1873, a fresh Universities Act was passed in 1877. It will be convenient to treat the reforms of the whole forty years under a few main headings.

(a) *Constitution.* The need of change is shown by the fact that Cambridge was still governed by the enactments of Queen Elizabeth and Oxford by those of Archbishop Laud. These archaic constitutions they could not change in any important feature even if they wished. Real power was vested in the heads of colleges, who alone could initiate legislation; a final veto, but without the power of amendment, was given to the whole body of masters who had "kept their names on the books," *i.e.* continued to pay a yearly fee. Heads of colleges were usually elderly men who, in an age of rapid change, had probably fallen behind the times; and the bulk of masters of arts who kept their names on the books were country clergy, for the most part ultra-conservative. The college tutors as such had no voice in the government of the university. The Acts of 1854 and 1855 swept away the old enactments, substituted a changeable for a rigid constitution, reduced the heads of colleges to one-third of the initiating committee, added a new body composed of resident masters of arts (who would be mainly college tutors) who could amend as well as reject the proposals of this committee, but left the final right of veto to the whole body of masters resident and non-resident. On the whole the new constitution has worked well. The tutors have proved to be alive to the need of progress and have in the last fifty years transformed the universities almost out of recognition; and the non-residents have in most cases been deterred by the trouble of a journey to

Oxford or Cambridge from opposing their reforms. But on certain issues, notably the admission of women to degrees, the abolition of compulsory Greek, and the admission of Nonconformists to theological degrees and examinerships, the wishes of residents were time after time over-ridden by the veto of the non-residents. Since the war Oxford has, however, adopted all three changes, though Cambridge still refuses degrees to women. The Act of 1877, through the schemes made by a body of commissioners appointed under it, has similarly swept away the old college statutes and given the colleges new constitutions.

(b) *Fellowships and Scholarships*. The revenues of the universities and their colleges taken together were very substantial; but by far the greater part belonged to the colleges. On the fellows of colleges fell the bulk of the teaching in the university; and college scholarships constituted almost the sole provision for helping needy students. But both fellowships and scholarships were so tied up by founders' restrictions that they could not be used to the best advantage. Life fellowships without duties, the well-nigh universal requirement of celibacy, the general insistence on holy orders, restriction of fellowships to persons born in particular counties or educated at particular schools, automatic progress from scholarships to fellowships, were all subjects of attack. The earlier commission gave the death-blow to geographical restrictions, and the later completed the work of reform on all points. Life fellowships are now confined to those who have long held tutorial or administrative posts in their colleges, the requirement of orders has been removed, and the present generation is perfectly familiar with the married fellow who resides outside the walls of his college. The Oriel plan of electing fellows by competitive examination has not, however, been generally followed. When once the tradition of favouritism had been broken down, the main reason for such a method of selection ceased; and, in choosing a man who will become a college tutor, colleges prefer selecting the person whose record shows him most fitted for the post, just as electors to any other office would. Scholarships were almost universally thrown open to free competition.

It is still not unusual to hear regret expressed for the loss of certain features in the old system; but there can be little doubt that a big balance of advantage has accrued from the changes.

The alteration in the tenure of *fellowships* has abolished the drone, who was rewarded for early scholastic successes by being freed from the necessity of using his abilities for the benefit of the community; nor has the institution of married fellows resulted, as was feared, in their losing interest in college life or influence over the undergraduates. Great as was the importance attached to this influence by supporters of the old order, it cannot be inferred from independent sources that it was ever so strong as at the present day, and in many colleges it was almost negligible. Indeed modern times have created a number of tutors whose relations to the undergraduates, like those of the modern assistant master to his boys, would have been inconceivable to the stiff old days. Leslie Stephen, as fellow of Trinity Hall, Cambridge (1854–1864), was probably the first tutor who coached his college boat, appeared in "shorts," and shared every intellectual and social activity of his men.

As regards *scholarships*, it is sometimes suggested that the old system did more to provide for the needs of poor students. It is true that in the middle of the last century, a period of almost unreasoning belief in competitive examinations, many people expected them to secure an equality of opportunity which it is not in their nature to produce. Success in a competitive examination was bound to depend in a large measure on previous educational advantages, which in those days were not open to all classes. But the obvious remedy was to open up the avenue of secondary education, not to choose scholars on grounds other than their proved abilities. Now and again no doubt a poor boy who happened to be born, say, in the Channel Islands may have won a close scholarship which, had it been open, might have gone to a wealthier competitor; but there is nothing in the nature of the case which would tend to produce such a result. One advantage at least has accrued from the change, that no eleemosynary suspicion attaches to scholarships; they are regarded as rewards of merit, and, with a nation like the English which loves a contest, the respect felt for victory in a competition has come to attach a value to industry. It was a sound instinct which prompted the reformers to consider it their first task to stimulate a working spirit in the universities; only after that had been accomplished would admission to them become a real advantage to the poorer student.

(c) *Religious tests*. Up to the time of the first commissions admission had been refused to Nonconformists at Oxford, and at Cambridge they could study but not graduate. The earlier Acts secured them admission and initial degrees; and a special act passed by Gladstone's government in 1871 swept away tests altogether save for degrees in divinity. Even this restriction has been recently removed.

(d) *Diminution of expense*. A much debated question in contemporary pamphlets was the increase in accommodation and particularly provision for a poorer class of student. The importance attached to this question is a sign that the universities were beginning to prove attractive on real educational grounds. The mere provision of additional room was easily secured at Oxford by allowing members of a college to live for part of their time outside the college walls, as they already did at Cambridge, and at both universities by extensive additions to college buildings. The steps taken to provide a less expensive mode of life, however, did not fulfil the expectations of their authors. The permission of "private halls" by the earlier Acts was a vain attempt to restore an institution which had passed away in Tudor times; and the institution of non-collegiate students in 1868 has been a doubtful success. Sumptuary legislation is always difficult. Neither rules nor college tutors were responsible for the cost of living in Oxford and Cambridge; hence neither changes in rules nor the efforts of tutors could do much to diminish it.

Even so stout a reformer as Goldwin Smith gave up the problem as insoluble. The right atmosphere in a university is only possible where there is no feeling of social inequality, and in this respect there was a great change for the better in the second half of the century. Social equality, however, tends to produce at each end of the scale an approximation to equality of expenditure. While extravagance has decreased among the wealthier, the poorer, finding that a smaller increase in expenditure is needed to keep them in the full swing of college life, spend more than they would if they were able to set the prevailing scale for themselves. However, the opening up of the universities has been facilitated in a number of ways. The boy of real ability, whatever his means, is better able to get a good secondary education; and scholarships are won from an extended range of schools. Sport has helped to end the supremacy of the wealthy "set." The river, as a dominating factor in college life, is said to date from 1843; "before that year the college races were a mere pleasing incident in a summer term[1]"; and cricket, played in black coats and beaver hats, soon followed. Football, the least expensive and most democratic of all games, came in over thirty years later. Partnership in such sports tends to bind all members of a college together; whereas the old expensive recreations of hunting, shooting, and riding inevitably kept the wealthier men apart: and, in an athletic society, the best athlete, not the man who can afford to entertain most, will take the lead. It is true to say that nowadays brains, athletic prowess, the gift of public speaking, or any other clear capacity, counts for more than wealth.

(e) *New professorships.* Perhaps the most hotly debated point in the war of pamphlets was the real or supposed antagonism between the "professorial" and "tutorial" systems. In all countries save England, not even excluding Scotland, university instruction has been given by professors, that is to say, experts specifically responsible for lecturing on some one subject or branch of a subject. In

[1] W. Tuckwell, *Reminiscences of Oxford*, p. 113.

Oxford and Cambridge alone the university had been subordinated to its colleges, which had been originally designed
purely as places of residence, and university lectures had
become only a small excrescence on a system of college
tuition. Long ago a different system had prevailed. Unable to provide paid instructors, the mediaeval university
had compelled every master of arts to undertake lecturing
for a certain period as a condition of receiving his degree.
Henry VIII, to encourage humanism, had endowed a few
professorial chairs at each university, and other professorships, mostly miserably paid, had come into existence.
Most of these represented subjects which lay outside the
somewhat narrow scope of the existing degree courses;
hence the bulk of the teaching was in the hands of the
college tutors. The theory that the decadence of the university had been due almost entirely to this cause was
first propounded by Sir William Hamilton in 1831. Both
his Scottish birth and his German training helped to make
him favourable to professorial instruction; and he was able
to prove by researches in existing statutes that it was still
legally obligatory in Oxford, and that all degrees given
for the last century and a half were probably void! The
existing system certainly involved a needless reduplication
of lectures, and, by requiring college tutors to teach every
branch of a subject, prevented them from becoming expert
in anything. In fact Hamilton summed it up by saying
that it replaced one great university by twenty small ones.
The two purposes for which specialist lecturers were most
needed were to give the highest instruction to candidates
for honours in the older subjects and to provide altogether
for the teaching of the new subjects. Candidates for these
new subjects were still too few for each college to provide
a tutor in them; and the introduction of further honours
schools would increase the difficulty. The reformers also
recognised the width of the older subjects and foresaw
that many of the best candidates would be attracted
towards different aspects of them. They did not wish to
mould everyone in one pattern. Though the linguistic,
literary, historical, and philosophical sides of classical

antiquity covered a wonderfully wide range of interests, there might be among the more original minds some to whom classical art, archaeology, comparative philology, or some yet unexplored aspect of classics, might appeal more. Moreover, the tutorial system had been devised for the ordinary pass-man; and, at the very time when the majority of tutors were uniting to urge that only by its means could real teaching be secured, practically every candidate for high honours was paying for private "coaching" because he could not get what he wanted from his college tutors.

But the defence of the tutorial system, which even Mark Pattison wished to see surviving along with the other, was by no means entirely the outcome of stolid conservatism. Its defenders understood the meaning of education better than some of its opponents. They knew that the majority of undergraduates needed not mere lecturing but real teaching, not very different from what they had received in the higher forms at school. Question and answer were required to make them think, exercises were required to develop skill and mastery of their subject, regular preparation for classes was required to secure steady work. For the brilliant student lectures by specialist enthusiasts would do all that was needed; they would inspire, would suggest new lines of thought, and would point out where he could find information for himself. But on the man who was not susceptible to inspiration and did not wish to seek information for himself, they were wasted. Modern experience confirms the belief that instruction which confines itself to lecturing leads to mere receptivity, uncritical acceptance of others' ideas, and "cram." But, on the other hand, a university in which the teachers do nothing but drill pass students is little more than an adult school. It will hardly furnish the atmosphere in which new scientific discoveries, new interpretations of history, new ideas on social and political questions, or a fuller appreciation of art and literature are likely to develop.

Both parties had their extreme wings. To the one extreme it appeared that knowledge and wisdom had quitted

Olympus to dwell only with the Greeks, and that, after their rescue from a long captivity by the knight-errants of the Renaissance, they had consented to dwell with the moderns only on condition that they would speak no other language than Greek or Latin. At the other pole were men who appeared to think nothing to be true but what is new, nothing admirable but what is paradoxical, nothing native so good as what is foreign. Solid insular narrowness was set against unsteady eclectic brilliance. To the one side subjects existed to train men, to the other men existed to develop subjects. Training of character was set in opposition to the enlargement of knowledge. The older school claimed to give men of action to the nation, the newer to give inspiring ideas to the world.

The result, as finally reached by 1881, was a compromise. The professoriate has a considerable voice in determining policy through the faculties, it organises and conducts research, and takes a large part in teaching subjects for which there is not a sufficient demand for the colleges to provide. In natural science, where the laboratory is the centre of work, its influence is more felt than in the humanities. New chairs have been established and old chairs adequately endowed. College fellowships have been attached to university professorships. But now that college lectures have been practically opened to the whole university—a change which has grown up gradually since 1870—college tutors in fact fulfil the duties of additional university professors; and the conduct of a college lecture on the lines of sixth form work in a school is now a rarity.

(f) *Higher degrees.* The new examinations had only affected the qualification for the initial degree of B.A. Mere seniority and payment of fees qualified the bachelor to become a master and the master a doctor of law or divinity. A half-hearted attempt was made to impose conditions for the mastership of arts but was soon dropped. In more recent times research degrees of B.Litt. and B.Sc. have been set up to take the place which the M.A. and M.Sc. occupy in modern universities, and degrees of D.Litt. and D.Sc. to recognise original work of a high order. The doctorate of divinity has likewise in recent times been made a reality.

(g) *Research*. The desire to encourage research had much to do both with the demand for a professorial system and with the desire to make the higher degrees a genuine mark of distinction. Research is a modern idea. In the Middle Ages a university had two functions, to establish truth by argument and to hand it down by lectures. The establishment of truth was believed to depend on syllogistic reasoning from indisputable premises; observation and experiment in the sciences, the investigation of records in the humanities, were unknown. The Renaissance almost wholly extinguished the work of the universities in finding out truth. The idea that all knowledge worth having had been possessed by the ancients confined discovery within the narrow limits of finding and studying classical manuscripts. The authors were then treated as authoritative, and for several centuries the functions of a university were almost limited to handing down what was already known. Scientific discoveries might be made more copiously than ever before; but the universities had little share in the work. Even the scholarship of Bentley and Porson, and the discoveries of the great mathematicians, were regarded as something exceptional, not as illustrations of what might generally be expected of university teachers. The abandonment of all attempt to add to the sum of knowledge has a deadening effect on the teaching of existing knowledge. Research revived in Germany, in the middle of the eighteenth century. By the middle of the nineteenth century the idea had made such progress in that country that an addition to knowledge was expected not only from every professor but from every candidate for a degree. Power of research became almost the sole test of academic merit and the sole passport to academic promotion. The transmission of existing culture and the training of men of action were altogether subordinated to the research aim. These two views of the function of a university were now to cross swords in this country.

Mark Pattison may be taken as representative of the adherents of research. He wished to set up a professoriate of the German type and to give up some of the colleges wholly to researchers. As teaching institutions, he held, the German universities were no better than our own; but as centres of research they were unique. The falsity of some of the German hypotheses had been urged in condemnation of the system; but Pattison contends that "a fertility of ingenious hypotheses is a well-known condition of any period of scientific activity," and he urges the stimulating effect of Wolf's influence on philology, Niebuhr's on history, and Baur's on theology, irrespective of the truth or falsity of their particular conclusions. "The highest education cannot be given through a literature or a science which has no higher than an educational value." "The university is largely distinguished from the school, that the pupil here takes leave of disciplinal studies and enters on real knowledge. The student comes to the university to grapple with those thoughts which are occupying the men of the time." The teacher who is also a student can inspire us as the mere teacher cannot. But, though "the university is an association of men of science, it is not for the sake of science that they are associated. A professoriate has for its duty to maintain, cultivate, and diffuse extant knowledge."

A generation was to elapse before these arguments were to bear fruit. The professoriate of the Scottish universities and of University College, London, were far ahead of the older universities in research in the domain of natural science. The last thirty years have seen a great change in Oxford and Cambridge as regards both scientific and historical investigation. The university now sets out to train researchers and to guide research in both spheres. So assured is the position of the older universities that another thirty years will probably see them pre-eminent in this as in other spheres. The newer universities certainly secured a start upon them; but it is very probable that they attempted to imitate Germany too closely by assuming that research is within the reach of every young graduate who has taken an honours degree. Arts and science here differ widely; and the distinction has been too often forgotten. Industrial processes give an inexhaustible field for scientific discoveries, great or small; but the third-rate historian, the mediocre critic, and the semi-scientific economic researcher are rather a danger than an aid to the cause of truth. There is no inherent virtue in contact with original authorities which trains a man to estimate a policy, to judge of character, to acquire a sense of values, or even to know when a thing is proved and when it is not. The older universities may have hit the happy mean in confining research in the humanities to their first-rate men.

The lapse of another fifty years since 1870 has seen another commission appointed to investigate the work of the older universities, the result of which belongs to the future.

(2) **The Public Schools.** The Commission reported in 1864, and such of its recommendations as required legislation were embodied in the Public Schools Act of 1868. These, however, concerned only the administrative side, and followed the lines which have been indicated at the beginning of the chapter. Adopting the principles of the University Commission, the Commissioners formulate them in the words of the *Edinburgh Review*: "The statutes of founders are to be upheld and enforced whenever they conduce to the general objects of the foundation, but they are to be modified whenever they require a closer adaptation to the wants of modern society." Reformed governing bodies were set up, and on them was imposed the duty of so revising the statutes as to remove local restrictions on masterships and scholarships and to reorganise the expenditure on prizes and scholarships. The revised statutes were to be approved by the Queen in Council. It may be noted that, while the Commission dealt with the two large day schools, St Paul's and Merchant Taylors', these two schools were omitted from the Act and left to be included in the subsequent Endowed Schools Act.

More interesting is the part of the report which dealt

with the internal affairs of the schools. For purposes of comparison, information was secured from the newer foundations of Cheltenham, Marlborough, and Wellington; but the Commission was in no sense an enquiry into these schools. However guarded was the language in which the commissioners couched their conclusions, it is clear that their general verdict, while not too condemnatory (because they recognised that there had been a considerable improvement in recent years), emphasised the need of far more amendment before the schools could be regarded as doing their duty. Rugby and Shrewsbury seem to escape the general condemnation. Idleness is the chief count in the indictment. There is little suggestion of sins of commission on the part of the public schoolboy; but his sins of omission are so great that we are left at the end with a picture of a good-natured, easy-going youth, without intellectual interests or any conception of a purpose in life, who is almost certain to succumb, the moment he leaves school, to the temptations of self-indulgence, frivolity and carelessness. As they pass from the consideration of curriculum to this section of their report, they observe: "We have found no difficulty in ascertaining what is *taught* at these schools; to discover what and how much is *learned* in them is difficult and is only roughly practicable." Then they trace how one-third of the candidates fail in the Christ Church matriculation, how it would be useless to try the bulk of the candidates with an unseen, and how only one piece of Latin Prose in four is free from bad blunders; and thus they work up to their conclusion that, though the best scholars usually come from the public schools, they "send also (and in this Eton has a certain pre-eminence) the idlest and most ignorant men." Holding, as they do, that the classical languages are the best of all educational instruments, their condemnation of the narrowness of the course is all the more remarkable. "A young man is not well educated—and indeed is not educated at all—who cannot reason or observe or express himself easily and correctly....He is not well educated if all his information is shut up within one narrow circle."

There can be little doubt that, as regards curriculum, they took the German *Gymnasien* as their model. They pronounce against the attempt to divide the school into a classical and a "modern" side, possibly foreseeing what happened within a few years, when, in spite of their advice, the system spread from Cheltenham, Marlborough, and Wellington to the older schools. Nor do they appear to contemplate the possibility of a first-grade "modern" school; the *Ober-realschule*, with a leaving age of nineteen and admitting to certain faculties in the university, was still to come. Specialisation at the top of the school is to be limited to such minor variations as substituting additional non-classical work for Latin and Greek verse. Here again the progress of events in England has been in a diametrically opposite direction, though German schools still keep the pupil engaged in all his subjects of study to the sixth form inclusive. For the commissioners, classics is still, as in the *Gymnasien*, to be the chief study, but not, as heretofore, the only subject taken seriously. "The writing of brilliant Latin verses is not, however, the ultimate end of school education." "The one main object for which boys learn the dead languages is to teach them to use their own." They are even a little distrustful of the Arnoldian tendency to emphasise subject-matter: "the mind of a boy must indeed of necessity be principally directed to the style and language of his books, since it is chiefly with a view to language that he is employed upon them." They sound the death-knell of the old original theme: in this respect current practice follows them to greater lengths than they were perhaps prepared to go, for it has been entirely replaced by translation of English into Greek or Latin. Indeed it has been left to the direct method to revive free composition even in the case of modern languages. Mathematics—again as in the *Gymnasien*—holds second place, and such absurdities as the treatment of mathematical masters as a subordinate caste receive their *coup de grâce*. The remarks on modern languages seem to belong to a different era from our own—so great is the improvement which the direct method, not then dreamed of, has effected. It is strange reading that the teaching of modern languages was, in spite of current opinion, as bad abroad as in England! Arnold's plan of making form masters teach French is declared to be passing away, but the report laments the deficiency of Englishmen competent to become specialist teachers of the subject. The section on history does not suggest the "barbarous grossness" of the Middle Ages quite so much as that on French; but it is only the first streak of dawn which is visible. Indeed one headmaster, questioned on the subject, frankly told the Commission:—"I wish we could teach more history, but as to teaching it in set lessons, I should not know how to do it." Their conclusion may be described as feeling after the truth "if haply they might find it." It runs thus: "To gain an elementary knowledge of history, little more is required than some sustained but not very laborious efforts of memory; it may therefore be acquired easily and without any mental exercise of much value—which, however, is not a sufficient reason for not acquiring it....But a good teacher who is likewise a good historian will always, we believe, be able to make the acquisition of even the elements of historical knowledge something more than a mere exertion of memory—to make it, with the more advanced boys, a real introduction to the method of historical study, and a vehicle for imparting some true insight into history and interest in it." Apparently the device most in favour with progressive teachers was to experiment with Guizot and other French or German writers, with the object of seeing if they could produce a modern equivalent for Arnold's lessons on Thucydides and Tacitus. It is interesting to note that Rugby, Marlborough and Wellington were the scenes of this experiment —another trace of Arnold's direct influence. Geography is not recognised like history as something which may grow out of being a mere memory subject. It is, as in Germany, a kind of handmaid to history. But in nothing is the influence of the *Gymnasien* so noticeable as in the section on natural science. The influence of those who were in a few years to make it a bedrock subject shows no trace in the report. Class-teaching for one or two hours a week is contemplated, just as in the case of German *Naturkunde*. So little did the Commissioners appreciate the subject with which they were dealing that they evidently believed that in this time two kinds of science—the physico-chemical and the biological—could be profitably handled! Such is the danger of substituting attempts to imitate for first hand acquaintance with the matter with which you are dealing. How much of the handling of education by "educationalists"—as distinguished from educators—has in England during the last fifty years been of this kind! Finally the "many-sided" aim which the *Gymnasien* had not very successfully attempted to transform from Herbartian theory into class-room practice is completed by the demand that either music or drawing should be introduced to meet aesthetic requirements.

(3) **Schools Inquiry Commission.** The Report of this Commission in 1868, which was followed by the passing of the Endowed Schools Act in 1869, marks the middle of our period in point of time, and may in addition be regarded as a turning point in the direction of our interests which will henceforth be directed to the great mass of secondary schools which had hitherto been quite unable to assert themselves. The newer type of university had not come into being, and the majority of the schools had little connection with Oxford and Cambridge. The Commission found that 550 so-called grammar schools sent no boys to the universities and of the eighty or ninety schools which did, only forty sent three every year. The "seven" accounted for 529 undergraduates, St Paul's and Merchant Taylors' for 48 and seven of the newly founded schools for 235, and two of the old grammar schools which had forced their way recently into public school rank—Repton and Uppingham—were responsible for 71. This would account for almost half the total number of undergraduates in residence and a far higher proportion of scholarship-holders. Moreover the Commission discovered that few endowed schools prepared boys for the examinations of London University or even sent them in for the newly-

instituted Local Examinations. Nor did these schools make up for their weakness on the more strictly academic side by superiority in the new fields of intellectual activity. The newer foundations like Cheltenham were the pioneers in this direction.

It is not implied that the progress of the last fifty years is entirely, or even mainly, due to the Endowed Schools Commission. Walker was already showing at Manchester what could be done with a large city day school. Day schools of new foundation were already proving themselves efficient: King's College School had been founded in 1829, University College School in 1832, Liverpool College in 1840. Proprietary schools, founded by the inhabitants of various towns for the benefit of the town rather than for profit, were already fairly numerous. Cheltenham (1841), Marlborough (1842), Rossall (1844), Epsom (1855), Wellington (1859), Clifton (1860), Malvern (1862), Radley (1863), and Haileybury (1864) were trying to imitate the good features of the old boarding schools and to avoid their defects. Woodard had founded his three Church schools—Lancing, Hurstpierpoint, and Ardingly—to meet three different levels of income. Thring was at work at Uppingham; and Sherborne, Repton, and Tonbridge had emerged into prominence from being local grammar schools.

On the whole these schools catered for the more prosperous part of the middle class, with whom there was a genuine interest in the education of their sons. Not exclusively; Manchester, Birmingham, and Bradford at any rate were already means of enabling the children of the lower middle class as well to reach the university; Woodard aimed at seeing how far the boarding school system could be made suitable to the needs of a poorer class than that which would supply his first grade school at Lancing; and the Commission notices the recent attempt to found "County Schools," *i.e.* boarding schools of a fairly cheap character to meet the needs of rural districts, of which the Surrey County School at Cranleigh (founded by subscription in 1865, with 153 boys) and the Suffolk school at Framlingham (310 boys) were examples. "As far as they have been tried," the Commissioners remark, "there have not, perhaps, been anywhere more successful or more promising undertakings than those great modern schools." But the success of a few large day schools and of private efforts in the case of a few middle class boarding schools only brought into bolder relief the needs of the bulk of towns and counties alike, where it made clear that provision, were it only made, would be eagerly accepted.

The Commissioners interpreted their reference in no narrow spirit. They regarded enquiry into the existing supply of schools as merely a preliminary task. Their first duty was to suggest how existing endowments could be utilised to extend that supply. They found that very much could be done simply by the best use of such funds as were already available; and this part of their recommendations was carried into effect by the Endowed Schools Act which followed their report. But they did not regard this as the end of their work: the creation of a complete system of secondary education could not, in their opinion, be effected out of existing endowments; to establish a system at all comparable to that of Prussia, State aid was necessary, and their report boldly aims at securing some measure of State control and some measure of public supply such as was secured in the domain of elementary education in the following year (1870). In this hope they proved to be in advance of public opinion; their wishes were only partially included in the Bill, and even those proposals had to be dropped to facilitate its passage through Parliament, on the understanding that they would be brought forward again in a subsequent session—an intention which was not carried out till after a second commission had reported in 1895. The country had thus to wait over thirty years for the Act of 1902.

In one respect the Commissioners almost exceeded their instructions, or at any rate acted upon them in a way which was hardly in the minds of those who drew up the reference. They took the bold step of construing that reference as covering the secondary education of girls as well as boys, thereby opening a new era in girls' education.

This part of their work will be treated in the chapter on the education of girls and women.

We will take first the proposals which were finally passed into law by the Endowed Schools Act. The procedure was similar to that adopted by the Universities and the Public Schools Acts. A special Commission—called the Endowed Schools Commission—was set up to approve new schemes for all the foundations not covered by the Public Schools Act and with powers so wide that it was said that it could convert a boys' school in Northumberland into a girls' school in Cornwall, though of course it never did anything so revolutionary. Its powers were renewed several times and, after its immediate work was accomplished, they were transferred to an augmented Charity Commission, and later still in 1899 to the Board of Education, when that body was established. There was nothing absolutely novel to English law in the exercise of such a power: foundation deeds could already be altered, if they were clearly obsolete, by the Court of Chancery; but readers of Dickens know what the Court of Chancery was in those days, and fortunate would the institution be, having once applied to that Court to modify the conditions on which its funds were to be expended, if, when it emerged from the Court, there were still any funds to apply. Not only was the new procedure quick and cheap; but the new Commission felt at liberty to make changes more freely. The Act, for instance, ordered them, wherever possible, to make provision for girls' as well as boys' schools; and, where the funds of any foundation permitted, they did so. It is hardly likely that such an intention was ever in the minds of founders, though the contrary has been sometimes maintained. The Inquiry Commission had dealt with 782 grammar schools and 2175 endowed elementary schools, but the latter were excluded from the Act and the subsequent scheme-making commission. 235 schemes were made by the Commissioners before the transfer of their powers to the Charity Commissioners, though, as we shall see when we come to the life of Thring, a considerable opposition to their activities developed.

This was a substantial work; for it meant that the scandals described in Chapter IV were henceforth impossible and that a large body of schools began to do solid work, to send pupils to the universities, and to inherit the spirit which the scholastic generation that followed Arnold's death had called into being. Between thirty and forty of these schools are now first-grade schools represented on the Headmasters' Conference.

The Commission was the first official body to recognise the policy of the "ladder." It may come as a surprise to many readers to learn that this ideal had entered into practical politics so early: for it is often regarded as a vision in the mind of Huxley which has only materialised since 1902. It is true that the provisions of the Act did little directly to help in its realisation; secondary school exhibitions were hardly made obtainable in practice by elementary school pupils, except where this was already the case; and in some instances, as at Bedford, where the number of free places was found to cause a neglect of elementary education, it was reduced. But, by improving the education in schools which were already available to elementary school pupils, it indirectly helped forward the policy of the ladder; for the Commission of 1895 was able to point to the actual successes of ex-elementary pupils at the universities and so to overcome the reluctance of English people to believe in the possibility of anything of which they have no practical experience.

The results, as the Commission of 1895 discovered, were, however, a patchwork. In the first place, as regards the kind of school, the Commission reported that three grades were needed, first-grade with a leaving age of eighteen or nineteen and closely connected with the universities, second-grade with a leaving age of sixteen or seventeen, and third-grade with a leaving age of fourteen or fifteen. It must be remembered that Robert Lowe's reactionary code of 1860 had practically fixed the leaving age for elementary schools at twelve, and that the last of these three grades, which later was partially supplied from the grants assigned to elementary education, was treated by the Commissioners as unmistakably secondary. It was in regard to this third grade of school, which would be frequented by the children of small farmers, small shop-keepers and well-to-do artisans that the report discovered the greatest deficiency of supply and the most unsatis-factory character of the supply which was available. The classical curriculum of the local grammar school, consisting of elementary Latin and possibly "less Greek" (as in Shakespeare's day), led to nothing and was in no demand; the gap was filled, so far as it was filled at all, by private schools, mostly inefficient. The numbers of pupils who might be expected to attend this grade of school were the largest of the three; and it was here that the Commission rightly judged that government aid was most imperative. It was here, however, that least was effected as the result of their report. The meagreness of the result cannot be put down altogether to public apathy or to ministerial lack of imagination. Two changes were necessary before this type of education could be stimulated and directed to a clear-cut aim. The first was the creation of provincial universities with a technical bent. Such universities offer a goal to which the pupils can aspire; they provide a supply of capable teachers; and finally they extend the influence of science over industry. The public was only beginning to realise in a very vague way the use of physical and chemical science to artisans; and the possibility that persons engaged in agriculture could profit by a scientific education was to the generality of agriculturists incon-ceivable. The second change therefore needed was the development of science teaching on sound lines.

But the patchwork character of the result did not merely concern the unequal stimulus given to different types of schools: it was also marked as regards their geographical distribution. Educational endowments were in a large measure distributed in accordance with the distribution of wealth and population in the reign of Queen Elizabeth, and were deficient in areas which had then been either thinly inhabited, like the modern industrial areas of the North, or poor, like Wales. This inequality was only partly remedied by the work of the Commission. The deputy commissione appointed by the Commission of 1895 to report on the schools of Lancashire handed in a map in which a dot was assigned to the abode of every boy attending Manchester Grammar School and showed that the number of dots appearing in any district was in inverse ratio to the adequacy of local provision. At St Helens, for instance, money which had been diverted to elementary education was found, when applied by the Commissioners to secondary purposes, sufficient to establish a really good school; and Bury Grammar School was praised for the fact that there boys of all social ranks mixed to a degree elsewhere unknown: but at Rochdale there was still in 1895 only a school of nineteen boys and at Oldham the school had developed at a period much later than the Commission out of South Kensington grants.

We now pass to the side of the report which was not carried into effect. Briefly it would have set up a system of State and local control. As originally drafted, the bill included the proposals for State but not for local control. An examining council was to be set up consisting of twelve persons, half nominated by the Crown and half by the Universities of Oxford, Cambridge and London. This council would examine schools and also intending school-masters. In short it was to establish the Teachers' Register which subsequently proved so thorny a question, and to introduce the thin edge of the wedge in the direction of securing the training of secondary teachers. These ideas were so novel to the ordinary member of parliament that they stood little chance of success. Beresford Hope voiced the general opinion of schoolmasters and the public when, in the discussion on the bill, he declared that surely a degree should be enough for a teacher! Even the 1895 Commission found a prevalence of this opinion. More reasonable was the view that an examination of schools would introduce and stereotype a system of "cramming." To persons living in the heyday of Robert Lowe's "payment by results" no other opinion was possible, and the nearest approximations to a central examination system in the case of secondary schools—the Central Welsh Board and its Irish counterpart—show that even thirty years later the importance of examining as opposed to inspecting might be over-emphasised. It is by no means certain therefore that the postponement of State control till inspection had received its proper recognition was not the lesser of two evils. As this section was omitted from the bill, a mild substitute was provided in most of the schemes approved by the subsequent Commissioners requiring that the schools should submit themselves to examination by some external authority, such for instance as the Universities by means of their Local Examinations or later by the Oxford and Cambridge Joint Board.

The local authority was a feature on which the Commissioners laid great stress, but it was not even mentioned in the bill. They had enquired into continental and colonial systems of secondary education and had before them Matthew Arnold's valuable report. "Before all things the wishes of the parents and of the people at large must be met. The management should in some reasonable manner be in their hands. The people perhaps cannot give guidance, but they can give life, which is even more valuable than guidance." In the last sentence the true basis of democratic control is laid down. In one sense democratic control is impossible. Not one man in a hundred has thought out an educational policy. Elected bodies, Parliament itself as much as any other, are not composed of educational experts, and the means which they propose to secure desirable results are often fantastic. They are too prone to think that enthusiasm and personal influence can be secured by ordering them to come into existence. If they delegate their powers to officials, we too often get a class of persons who regard themselves as experts by reason of a contact with education no closer than the other end of a telephone. But popular control, exercised on the spot and not entirely delegated to officials, has advantages entirely independent of the regulations which it ordains. It gives an opportunity for the few who have ideas to ventilate them; it provides a medium for the interchange of opinions between the teachers and the outside world; it educates administrators and parents; it creates an educational atmosphere. Where it exists, parents who would otherwise be indifferent become keen. The Commissioners suggested quite a number of alternative plans on which such a local authority might be constituted, in all cases independent of any authority which might be created for elementary education; but the dread of possible harm felt by existing efficient schools was too strong for those who thereby hoped to create efficient schools where they did not already exist. It was at this moment too that we have the nearest approach to an incursion into the domain of secondary education of the "religious difficulty," which did so much to hamper all attempts to improve elementary education. Beresford Hope in the debate expressed alarm for the maintenance of the Church character of existing foundations, though a "conscience clause" and an exemption from any obligation upon holders of scholastic posts to take Holy Orders were all which the bill offered in regard to the religious question.

It is certain that the Commissioners proposed a State system of secondary education and that the State refused to undertake the burden. At first sight it would appear that a great chance was missed. Undoubtedly a modern House of Commons would adopt a very different policy. To some extent a supply will create a demand, but to do so the supply must be good. It is not certain that a State system imposed in 1869 by a progressive minority but administered by indifferent representatives of the average citizen would have been good. It is hardly a case for blame. You do not blame a savage or a man of the Middle Ages for being a savage or a man of the Middle Ages; you merely record what he was and what he thought and felt. Why do otherwise with a Mid-Victorian? He was a snob, but in many ways a very kindly person. He was an ultra-individualist, but he had a shrewd political sense. He had no idea of the application of school learning to industry, but he built up the industries to which it was subsequently applied. He had little aesthetic taste, but he produced a race of writers for whom we have no substitutes. He did not realise the close connection of intellectual and moral development, but he had his own philistine morality. He did not appreciate the virtues of organisation, but he was not the slave of red tape. He did not try to evolve schemes for educating his neighbours' children, but he discovered empirically what a good school is and left it as a legacy to the next generation to create more of them.

REFERENCES

Oxford University Commission, *Report*, 1854.
Cambridge University Commission, *Report*, 1856.
Commission into the Property and Income of the Universities of Oxford and Cambridge, *Report*, 1873.
Goldwin Smith, *Reorganisation of the University of Oxford*, 1868.
Mark Pattison, *Suggestions on Academical Organisation*, 1868.
H. H. Vaughan, *Oxford Reform and Oxford Professors*, 1854 (defence of professorial system).
W. M. Campion, *Commissioners and Colleges*, 1858 (attack on professorial system).
Sir William Hamilton, *Discussions on Philosophy and Literature, Education and University Reform*, 1852.
F. W. Maitland, *Life and Letters of Leslie Stephen*, 1896.
C. A. Row ("A Member of the Oxford Convocation"), Letter to Lord John Russell on the Constitutional Defects of the University and Colleges of Oxford, 1850.
Public Schools Commission, *Report*, 1864.
Schools Inquiry Commission, *Report*, 1869.
Secondary Education Commission, *Report*, 1895.
Acts of Parliament: Oxford University Act (17 and 18 Vict. c. 81); Cambridge University Act, 1854; Universities Test Act (34 Vict. c. 26); Universities of Oxford and Cambridge Act (40 and 41 Vict. c. 48); Public Schools Act (31 and 32 Vict. c. 118); Endowed Schools Act (32 and 33 Vict. c. 56).
Schemes made under the various Acts, catalogued in State Papers and Accounts.

CHAPTER VII

THE AGE OF THE PROPHETS

W E have seen in the last chapter how the State, confronted with the task of organising secondary education, refused to take the leap. For forty years secondary schools, many of them, it is true, revived by the State, were conducted independently. During most of this period the headmasters regarded State interference as an overhanging peril which they must spend every effort to avert. Englishmen judge institutions as they work; and, judged by the working of a State department in the sphere of elementary education, the headmasters had reason on their side. From 1861 till the nineties, elementary education groaned under a tyranny of mechanical routine. The official view was that elementary education was synonymous with the "three R's." It was something in which the formation of character, broadening of outlook, rousing of intellectual activity, training of mental habits —everything which the universities and public schools set forth as their aim—had no part. It could be judged by "results," which, as Matthew Arnold said, "were an illusion." The State had succeeded in subordinating teaching to an examination which did not test, in driving out every subject which could give nutriment to the mind, in deadening the pupils' intelligence, in making drudges of the teachers, and in inventing a training for them based on the idea that, till you had turned a man into a machine, he would decline to do the machine-like grind which the Department expected of him. This was State education as it presented itself to Thring when he resisted it as the "dead hand."

It has been said that a nation generally gets the government which it deserves, and we suppose this is true of its education. How then came England to "deserve" such an education as this? Matthew Arnold, Ruskin, Maurice, Kingsley and the other prophets supply the answer. There was much that was noble in Victorian England; but it co-existed with a self-complaisance which it will be impossible for future generations which have not grown up in it to understand. It was truly an age of prophets; for everyone to whom the gift of vision had been granted could find abundance of material against which to take up his parable.

The nineteenth century accepted class distinctions as axiomatic. In this point at least all classes were agreed. Beyond it, the current of thought in Victorian times can only be understood by taking as a starting-point the inherited tradition of the three great classes into which Matthew Arnold divided the nation. The working class was still prone to take its ideas from the other two classes, whom Matthew Arnold named the "barbarians" and the "philistines." Now-a-days we would fain believe that we have shaken off the belief in class distinctions. We are lavish in our use of the word "snobbishness." It would be nearer the truth to say that we wish that we had shaken ourselves free of the belief, but feel that we have not. The modern phenomenon of an inverted snobbishness, the "class consciousness" of Marxism, is one proof among many that we have not. It is not easy therefore to treat the Mid-Victorian ideals in a dispassionate historical spirit; but the true background of educational difficulties in the middle of the nineteenth century cannot be understood except by realising the good and bad features in the ideals of the "barbarians" and the "philistines" and their attitude to one another and to the working class.

The "barbarian" set of ideals had a long pedigree. Feudalism, chivalry, the "courtly ideal" of Queen Elizabeth's age, the feelings of the cavaliers, the toryism and high churchmanship of Queen Anne's time, had all left their mark upon it. This mode of thought had extended far beyond the landed aristocracy. It pervaded the Church, the professional classes, and the universities. The "philistine" ideals were of later growth. They owed something to earlier Puritanism; but in their Victorian form they became recognisable only after the industrial revolution had created a powerful manufacturing class. Speaking generally, they were the ideas alike of the wealthy manufacturer, the shop-keeper, and the clerk. All nonconformists were "philistine" and not "barbarian," though all "philistines" were not nonconformists. Most "philistines" were liberal in politics, and their liberalism was more usually of the "Manchester" brand than radical; most "barbarians" were conservatives, but, if they were liberals, it was almost always of the Whig brand.

It cannot be said that the intellect made any great appeal to Victorian Englishmen as a body, whatever their class. When we speak of the educational ideals of a class, we are therefore thinking of a small minority of that class. In this sense the public school of 1868 represented the educational ideals of the "barbarians." Though the House of Commons tended to be dominated by the ideals of the "philistines," the Royal Commissions, through the powerful part played by the Church and the universities in educational matters, tended rather to represent the "barbarian" point of view. We might therefore have expected that the "barbarian" would wish to educate other people's children on the same lines as those on which he educated his own: and this is very much what in the long run has come to pass, for the "barbarian" code is at bottom based on the native instincts of the Englishman, developed in freedom from the restraints of circumstances and untrammelled by opposing ideas.

Why then did this not occur? Because of the exclusiveness of the unintellectual majority in the class. The exclusiveness of the "barbarians" may not have been half so potent for evil as the race for wealth among the "philistines": the country squire did not alienate the workers to anything like the same degree as the self-made capitalist. All the same it cannot be denied that, tempered though it might be by Christianity, by patriotism, and by fellowship in sport, there was in the "barbarian" something of the old Greek feeling that the highest life was one which could be lived free from "banausic" labour and that the hand-workers existed to make such a life possible for his own class. Their claim to a share in the good things of body and soul as a fair reward for accomplishing their *raison d'être* was recognised—though they were too prone, as a class, to close their eyes to the evils of an industrialism with which few of them came into direct contact—but what the land-owning and professional classes never recognised was the claim of boys and girls born in the hand-working classes to the good things of the intellect. Possibly it was because the majority of "barbarians" did not appreciate them very much themselves. But in this respect the Victorian era contrasts unfavourably with the Middle Ages, when the Church gave an opportunity for a poor boy to rise to the highest rank which a subject could hold, an archbishopric, and to be the companion of kings.

Besides this lower motive there was another aspect of "barbarian" exclusiveness which we must not overlook. Classes are always afraid of losing their ideals and are far more prone to keep their children segregated from those of other classes than to remain in isolation themselves. The "barbarian" really had much which we can admire, which he wished to hand on to his sons. The Hanoverian type, with which the present age can have little sympathy, was dying out. His Victorian successor was far superior. We know Tom Brown's father: admiration for his type leavened Charles Kingsley with an element of toryism, despite his zeal for social reform; Disraeli's policy was to appeal from the mercenary instincts of the manufacturers to the sense of fair-play which he believed he could find in the squires. Honour and duty sum up the better side of their tradition. On this foundation the religious leaders of the century following the Wesleyan and Evangelical revivals sought to build a more self-conscious morality. Thomas Arnold had set himself to make the public schools instruments in accomplishing this task. In those days, when such men as he talked of "a gentleman and a Christian," they meant one in whom a sense of honour and a sense of duty had taken root from his earliest years and

in whom the other virtues had been more consciously
developed by Christian influences from this starting-point.
If we had similarly to pick out the special virtues of other
classes, we should probably select honesty and industry
as the virtues of the "philistine," and helpfulness to
distress as that of the worker. In a vague kind of way we
believe that the "barbarian" felt that a mixture of classes
might result in the complex possessing the virtues of none
and the faults of all. Headmasters had learned how to
build on the virtues of the young "barbarian" and wanted
him segregated so that they could accomplish their
task.

The average "barbarian" was not much given to abstract thought, and it rarely occurred to him to consider
how the young "philistine" and young worker ought to
be educated. The public school headmaster had carried
him away by force of character. Even the careless boy
usually respected the "head"; and, when he grew up, even
if he was a man of no great moral zeal, he wished his son
to be educated by a man whom he respected. Members
of parliament had thus a clear idea what the school to
which they would send their own sons must be like. But
they were not convinced that the same kind of schooling
would suit any other class. As regards the young worker,
they found an easy way out of their difficulty; they handed
the matter over to the clerical members of their class, who
had inherited the notion that what was needed was the
Bible and the Catechism. It never seemed to occur to the
clergy that the direct teaching of religion played only a
small part in the Arnoldian "Christian education": they
went on valiantly struggling on the platform for religious
teaching in the elementary school, regardless of the fact
that it provided no counterpart for the other elements in
Arnold's training. Arnold emphasised the close connection
of intellectual and moral education; but the moralising
effect of broadening the intellectual horizon, outside the
shape which it took in the public schools, was still to seek.
The public school class on the whole saw through the
pathetic fallacy, in which many "philistines" believed,

that the knowledge of reading was by itself a moralising agency, but they had nothing more to offer.

As regards the education of the young "philistine" the "barbarian" was completely at a loss. He could not hand this over to the clerical members of his class; for the young "philistine's" parents were as often as not nonconformists, sometimes were free-thinkers, and nearly always took a point of view which the "barbarians" could not understand.

What then of the standpoint of the adult "philistine"? On the whole he had more definitely formulated ideas than the "barbarian." Unfortunately they were often narrow. Instinct is often a surer guide to conduct than ideas, especially second-hand ideas. The intolerance of a far-back age and the conservatism of recent days had denied the nonconformist, who constituted the backbone of the "philistine" class as far as strength of character and conviction was concerned, a share in such liberal education as was provided in the recognised places of learning. The "philistines" of early Victorian days consequently lacked among their numbers the counterpart of the public school headmasters. Their ideas were largely borrowed and crude. The traditions of Puritanism rendered Art and most Literature suspect. Political ideas were borrowed freely from continental liberals; but other intellectual ideas from this source were tainted with infidelity. John Stuart Mill probably influenced the Oxford of the seventies and the small number of working men who were able to educate themselves by their own efforts far more than he influenced the genuine "philistine." The result was to leave the "philistine" class divided and educationally powerless. Many were won over by Arnold's religious zeal to a belief in the public school system. Some were adherents of new and transient forms of education like George Combe's. The majority were frankly utilitarian and kept their children at school no longer than was necessary to teach them commercial arithmetic and a little of informational subjects. As regards the education of the young workers the "philistine" was a firm believer in the three R's, and as regards that of the young "barbarians," he washed his hands of it. Of the great movements in thought which reacted on education, the scientific movement was consequently the only one with which the "philistines" had any noteworthy connection.

Finally, can the workers be said to have evolved any educational ideas? Of course we must expect to find a much smaller proportion of this class possessed of ideas than of the other two; for it required the sternest grit for a worker to find opportunity for getting them. This small hard-headed minority displayed great interest in education: Mechanics' Institutes, Working-men's Colleges, the co-operative movement, and the educational side of the Chartist movement are evidence enough. But the time had not yet come when their policy could look beyond the elementary and lower technical sphere. They would support an educational leader, when they found one, through thick and thin. They were more ready to set prejudices aside than either of the other classes. But for the present the leaders in working-class educational movements came from outside.

This analysis of the educational ideals of the three classes into which for this purpose Victorian society may be divided is sufficient to explain why the State was unable as yet to establish a system of secondary education. The public school system was the only system worthy of the name; the public schoolmen gloried in having produced it without State interference; and the system of State education which the "barbarians" and "philistines" had between them imposed on elementary schools was its direct antithesis and filled secondary schoolmasters with alarm. Obviously a very different attitude of mind all round must be produced before State secondary education could be a success. Hence the next stage requires explanation by forces which lay outside the school walls. We must ask ourselves what new elements have been added to the mental outfit of all classes which were lacking when Queen Victoria came to the throne, and it is convenient to label the process by which each of these elements was added as a "movement."

The first was the scientific movement already discussed in Chapter v. It offered a new form of intellectual education; it presented education to the workers and to lower middle class parents in a form in which it seemed to be of practical "use"; it held out prospects to the manufacturers, whose influence was perhaps stronger than that of any other class in the House of Commons, of obtaining more competent managers and more efficient "hands"; it came as a relief to politicians who were expected to do something to maintain England's commercial superiority. If Science was associated with a somewhat narrowly utilitarian view of education, it was partly because it turned into adherents of education persons who otherwise would not have been educationalists at all. Thus we see how it came to pass that for a time Science was regarded as solving the problem of educating the young "philistine" while it hardly affected the education of the young "barbarian" for several decades.

The second movement was the aesthetic. Matthew Arnold and Ruskin may be taken as its representatives. It was a reaction against "philistinism." Puritanism had tended to regard all pleasures as evil. In the long run the "higher" pleasures were the losers. The ordinary man would not believe, for instance, that it was his duty to abstain from the pleasures of the table, which a heathen philosopher would certainly have classified as "lower"— besides, was not fasting a Romish superstition? But he was quite willing to abandon music, painting, sculpture, and architecture—besides, were not these the vehicles of Romish worship? Even literature should only be enjoyed within the narrow limits where it made for edification; and the love of natural scenery, though not formally condemned, shared in the general loss of the aesthetic sense. Evangelicalism in its origin was not like Puritanism, based on a mixture of legalism and asceticism; planted in a different soil, it would naturally have encouraged Luther's love of music and St Francis's feeling for nature: but most Evangelicals inherited a strain of Puritanism in their spiritual pedigree. Moreover, the base purposes to which art and literature had been put wherever neo-Paganism had prevailed since the Renaissance blinded them to their nobler uses; while a suspicion of Romanism prevented the use of art by religion, without which it first became secularised and then demoralised.

Matthew Arnold (1822–1888) is peculiarly interesting to us because he was both educationalist and prophet and because he succeeded in influencing the education of the succeeding generation by his work as a prophet, whereas he failed to influence that of his own generation by his professional work as an educationalist. His educational views were the direct outcome of his attitude as a prophet, and they can be read in the present age with approval. But they were in advance of his time and, though what he wrote was highly valued by Royal Commissions and by educational reformers, as far as immediate effect on educational legislation and administration was concerned he was a voice crying in the wilderness. What better proof can we have that educational advance is due to the efforts of individuals than this instance of the State appointing a man of genius as one of its educational officials and then finding that he re-shaped educational ideas during his leisure hours devoted to literary criticism, while his official work largely consisted in ineffectively denouncing the policy of his official superiors!

Arnold was, as we might imagine, a thorough product of the classical movement, and came under many of its varied influences. His schooling at Rugby was responsible for the serious attitude to life which underlay a somewhat light and bantering mode of expression; to it may be attributed that view of literature as a criticism of life which at first sight appears more consonant with the outlook of a moralist like Plato than of an apostle of beauty like Arnold. As scholar of Balliol and fellow of Oriel he came under the more critical elements in the many-sided humanistic movement: above all he was filled by enthusiasm for the Greek spirit and set its love of "sweetness and light" in opposition to the unlovely compound of Puritanism and money-making for which he employed the undying name of "philistinism." Chance made him an educationalist by profession; for, after a short career as an assistant master at Rugby, he was offered the post of private secretary to the Marquis of Lansdowne who, as Lord President of the Council, was responsible for education; and in 1851 he was appointed an inspector of schools. His vigorous attacks in his *Reports on Elementary Schools* upon the system of payment by results at a time when examination was an obsession in the minds of educational administrators almost brought about his resignation; but this part of his work belongs to the volume on the history of elementary education. In secondary education he was one of those who, in their reaction against British insularity. strove to awake the country to the superior merits of continental systems. He was employed by the Royal Commissions to investigate continental education on the spot; the task was highly congenial to him, and he became the recognised authority in England on the subject. His publications were *Popular Education of France* (1861), *A French Eton* (1864), and *Schools and Universities on the Continent* (1868). We have seen how his conclusions as to the grave deficiency of middle-class schools and the need of State intervention as the only means of supplying it were adopted by the Schools Inquiry Commission but fell on deaf ears in Parliament and failed to produce any immediate result. Though very necessary at the time, this tendency to look abroad for educational guidance was not an unmixed blessing at a later date; for it tended to substitute imitation for thought and to place industrious compilers in the seats of authority over public opinion where creative genius was needed. It also irritated the teachers of the older universities and public schools to be constantly told that all good things in education were made in France and Germany; and conservatism was fostered by the failure of some of its opponents to see that a national education must be based on a foundation of national aspirations and traditions.

But it was as the author of *Culture and Anarchy* (1869) and in his various critical writings that he did his most real educational work. His influence was quite as strong in intellectualising the "barbarians" as in leavening the "philistines" with sweetness and light. He thus tilled the soil in which the educational seeds which he sowed could ultimately take root. He lived in the heyday of the scientific movement—if we mean by the movement the crusade for spreading the teaching of science rather than the results of that crusade. His criticism of the movement was far more effective than the opposition of theologians or the academic opinions of faculty psychologists, because there was nothing obscurantist in his ground of attack. He approached the problem from the point of view of the pupil who had to be educated, a point of view which was liable to be disregarded so long as attention was fixed on the character of the subject-matter. His experience brought him into contact with elementary school pupils and students in training as teachers, so that the humanities had for him a wider meaning than the classics of the public schools. He was the first man insistently to voice the need of a literary element in the training of working men and the middle classes. "The only use the Government makes of the mighty engine of literature in the education of the working classes amounts to little more, even when most successful, than giving the power to read the newspapers[1]." "The animation of mind, the multiplying of ideas, the promptness to connect in the thoughts one thing with another and to illustrate one thing by another, are what are wanted; just what letters, as they are called, are supposed to communicate[2]." In 1876 he ended his report by replying to a speech made on behalf of the teaching of science at the meeting of the British Association. "Whatever else," the speeches had said, "a man may know, viewed in the light of modern necessities, a man who is not versed in exact science is only a half-educated man, and, if he has substituted literature and history for natural science, he has chosen the less useful alternative." Matthew Arnold replies by quoting paraphrases of a passage in

[1] *Reports on Elementary Schools*, p. 157.
[2] *Op. cit.* p. 175.

Macbeth written by students in a training college as a proof of what a failure to teach English may produce. He adds that to make people obey the laws of health a knowledge of science is not enough. "To have the power of using (which is the thing wished) these data of science, a man must in general have first been in some measure moralised, and for moralising him it will not be found easy, I think, to dispense with those old agents, letters, poetry, religion[1]."

It is doubtful, however, if Matthew Arnold had been in the position of an educational dictator and had been able to impose on the schools the means which he thought necessary to effect his aims, whether he would have been successful. He still clung to the old faculty psychology enough to believe that English grammar was needed in elementary schools to fill the place of Latin in secondary schools; and surely science has rarely been so little of a civilising agent as the technicalities of so-called English grammar usually are. He firmly believed in making children and students in training colleges learn poetry by heart, regardless of the fact that such a course may inspire a life-long hatred of poetry in the victims. And, when his campaign had won examining bodies to his side and English literature became a regular subject in secondary schools, what a travesty of his intentions did it become! It is probably true that far more valuable study of literature took place in public schools in the old days when classics were the only regular subject of the curriculum, when examinations were unknown and when boys were guided in their leisure reading, than is usually found in any type of boys' school—in many girls' schools it is happily different—where English is taught as an examination subject. The truth is that, given a teacher who really loves literature, whether he has ever passed an examination in it or not, his pupils will read and read in the right way; but that, given a teacher, however high honours he may have taken in English, who approaches it as school "business," it would be much better that he should not "teach

[1] *Op. cit.* p. 200.

literature" at all. Arnold's real glory is in having spread a love of literature amongst many who would never otherwise have felt it and so increased the probability of the right kind of teachers being found.

Ruskin (1819–1900), albeit that his direct educational views are fanciful, was in some ways the greatest indirect force on education during the century. It is almost true to say that before his time art was to the "philistines" a stumbling-block and to the "barbarians" and the workers foolishness. Of course he neither created the Gothic revival nor the pre-Raphaelite school of painters. But he did something far wider. From the Renaissance art had been aristocratic and in England confined to a small minority of the aristocracy. Since it had been taken from the religious soil in which it had flourished in the Middle Ages it had been a hothouse exotic. Deep in the English heart is a love of nature: classicism had for over a century divorced art from nature: and what the romantic movement did for literature, that Ruskin did for art. Here then are the three things which Ruskin did; he re-united art to craft, he re-united it to religion, he re-united it to the love of nature. The "fine arts" were no longer to be regarded as a hobby of ostentatious princelets and idle aristocrats, but as the invention of artist artisans. They were to be associated not with the *Quartier Latin* and its bohemianism but with the builders of cathedrals in the ages of faith. Art was not artificiality; it was to be won by studying the trees of the forest and the flowers of the field. Ruskin treated art as Matthew Arnold treated literature—as one of the moralising agencies. As soon as this change of attitude became at all general, art was bound to become an instrument of education. The earlier teaching of drawing and of arts and crafts had been purely utilitarian, and confined to those to whom skill and a sense of beauty were to become commercial assets. Henceforward it was to be a part of the education of all, necessary to a full development of human nature, to the enjoyment of life, and to the banishing of sordid, morbid and petty attitudes, and, like language, a medium of expression and a carrier of thought and feeling.

But Ruskin did something even greater than setting up art as the companion of literature in the sphere of education. He did more than any individual—though it is little that a single individual can do in this direction—to break down class exclusiveness. The basis of class distinctions is the belief that there is something "banausic" in manual work or that a life of leisure is necessary for developing the higher qualities in human nature. Ruskin did not succeed in showing how, under present conditions, it is possible for every man to develop his whole being. In the old Greek days when practically the only source of mechanical power, save for a little use of other beasts of burden, was man himself, slavery, open or disguised, was probably the one basis on which a cultured free society could be built up. Machinery would appear, from the point of view of purely mechanical science, to have solved the difficulty, by reducing the amount of muscular work which was necessary in the old days to manageable proportions. But, directly the laws of nature had been converted into allies, the laws of political economy seemed to spring up with hydra-like multiplicity; and the problem appeared more desperate than before mechanical sources of power had been discovered. In his titanic struggle with the economic hydra Ruskin wore out body and brain, and the end is not yet. He dared to contemplate and to feel in its fulness a problem which, fully realised, must make the head reel and, fully felt, must make the heart melt as wax, namely, that we do not yet know how to enable the bulk of mankind to be what we feel that their possibilities mean them to be and that, so far as we ourselves are able to approach the ideal, it is by the sweat of the brow, the deadening of the sensibilities, and the loss of the capacity of living, of other men. The agony of Ruskin's yearning cannot be realised by the "philistine" who does not know of these lost possibilities, by the revolutionary who believes that the favoured classes could give them if they would, or by the socialist who thinks he has a panacea which will shortly be applied. What Ruskin succeeded in doing was, first, to make his contemporaries see that we must never rest till the solution is found and that, in proportion as we recognise our duty, we shall cause society to approximate more closely to the ideal; secondly, to proclaim a ground of hope, to be drawn from the fact that, though most work is a bar to the higher life under present conditions, yet all idleness is a bar by its very nature. When God made man in His own image, He made him a creator; his instinct as a child is to create; and he can never properly see that the larger creation of God or the smaller creations of men are very good till he has in some measure exercised his creative powers. The notion that human superiority is to be based, not on capacity for intellectual work, which may make it quite desirable that a judge, for instance, should not spend too much of his time on manual work, but on the mere fact of never having done any serious manual work, was shown up as destructive of art, an ignoring of human nature, and blasphemy against God. The paganism of the Renaissance was now detected in its last hiding-place. While Jupiter feasted in his palace on Olympus, man was godlike in so far as he did the same. The Christian concept is, "My Father worketh...and I work." In some way or another the goal to which progress must tend is one where all work is done in the spirit of the artist, aims at the perfection of the artist, and arouses the joy of the artist. Then will the worker be the full perfection of manhood.

Obviously the first step towards the ideal, so far as educational machinery is concerned, lay with the elementary school; for little could be done with the adult workmen if the foundations were not truly and wisely laid. Hence he frequently returns to the demand for a free and compulsory education, physical, moral, and manual[1]. His idea of the school is, however, so bound up with his views of the relation of the State to industry that it would take too much space to consider it here. Secondary education has been influenced more by the corollaries from his teaching on the part which art, handicraft, and a love of nature should play in life than by deductions arising from his economic writings.

[1] *Crown of Wild Olive*, Part IV; *A Joy for Ever*, §§ 127–136; *Unto this Last*, Introduction; *Time and Tide*, letter 16.

Amongst the corollaries which he himself definitely drew were the necessity of beautiful class-rooms and the use of paintings in teaching pupils to understand the past[1]; the teaching of a trade to boys of all ranks[2], a conclusion at which he would probably have arrived even if it had never been expounded before; the place of science in education, which we have discussed in a previous chapter; the value of nature-study[3], at that time an unknown subject for which not even a name had been found; and the necessity of putting girls' education on a foundation on which it could build for real development and not for display[4]. He must have startled schoolmasters of that day by proclaiming "all emulation to be a false motive and all giving of prizes a false means," another echo of Rousseau, and a view which almost necessarily goes with Ruskin's elimination of competition in the economic sphere. Emulation never receives fair treatment from men who have not played games; they have never felt it in its healthiest form. But these direct educational passages are of minor importance; Ruskin's real influence on education would have followed from his general outlook on life equally if he had not written a word directly on the subject.

Though we began considering Ruskin's work as a contribution to the aesthetic movement, it has led us on to a third movement, for which it is somewhat hard to find a name, which is represented by Frederick Denison Maurice and Charles Kingsley. It was a religious reaction against the individualism of Puritanism and even of Evangelicalism.

Industrialism had naturally fostered men's money-getting instincts; and, since money-getting is facilitated by banishing ease and living laborious days, persons of puritanical descent and tendency were generally well to the fore in the race for wealth and were inclined to "compound for sins they were inclin'd to by damning those they have no mind to." The continental conception of English-

<hr />

[1] *A Joy for Ever*, §§ 104–109.
[2] *Op. cit.* § 128.
[3] *E.g. Time and Tide*, letter 16.
[4] *Sesame and Lilies*, Part II, "On Queens' Gardens."

men as a race of hypocrites is of course a gross exaggeration: but it remains true that among the Victorians thrift, attention to business, and perseverance were as often degraded into vices as was an excessive love of ease. No time in fact was left for the higher pleasures: and the unvaried relation of competition was hardly likely to foster the generous instincts towards their fellow men. The results, in the case of the orthodox, were uncharitableness and gloominess in the less buoyant natures, and a restriction of outlook in all; while among those who were brought up in this atmosphere and found the yoke of orthodoxy too hard there was naturally a reaction towards the lower pleasures. Among the working classes too it created a tendency to regard respectability as a class code evolved for the furtherance of amassing capital in the hands of that class. Is it not a curious fact that in Mohammedan, Buddhist, and Jewish communities, and in Mediaeval Europe, a strict fulfilment of the accepted moral code has always earned a certain measure of respect from the laxer members of society, but in modern Western Europe alone has it been a cause of ridicule and contempt among many individuals of every class and a majority of individuals in particular classes? Surely the basis of the difference must be this: the laxer Mohammedan or Buddhist somehow feels that his more devout co-religionist is seeking his neighbour's good while the laxer Westerner suspects that he is seeking his own good.

The movement, then, which we are considering protested against the conception of religion as a process of "saving one's soul"—that is saving it, not from selfishness and sin, but from their physical punishments in the hell of popular theology—and represented it as a process of developing love of God and love of one's neighbour through and by means of one another. It held up religion as something social. From a social state of mind social conduct must result. Social reform of all kinds was constantly in the minds of this school. Sanitation, housing, conditions of work, opportunities for recreation, thrift, all received their attention. To these men education had a new meaning which it did not possess to its ordinary clerical advocate. The latter divided education strictly into secular and religious; the former was only an indirect while the latter was a direct means of saving souls. Secular education had three uses: first, if administered in very small doses, it made a man a better economic producer; secondly, it gave him certain intellectual tools for understanding religious truths; thirdly, if education were given by the right persons, it exposed the pupil to the influences which would make for the acceptance of sound religious principles. But in itself it was no better to be educated than to be uneducated. To the school of Maurice and Kingsley secular and religious education were alike holy. They conceived Heaven as a state where every faculty which is born in man will be developed to a point beyond our present conceptions, in perfect harmony with every other faculty, and with the purpose of God and the blessedness of all His creatures; and, as Man is a "social animal," the social and altruistic faculties would constitute an important element in his redeemed manhood, in which intellect and the sense of beauty would somehow conduce *ad maiorem gloriam Dei*. Earth was a training school for Heaven; and men would only be able to enter the preparatory class in Heaven if they were sent there in a state of lop-sided development. "Whatsoever ye shall bind on Earth shall be bound in Heaven." The words had an awful significance to those who interpreted their priestly commission in this sense. Not merely do ignorance and the cramping of parts of our nature *lead* to sin; they are themselves ἁμαρτία, a missing of the mark which man is meant to hit. So far as the Christian Church allows conditions to exist which cramp man's development and fail to educate him, it is "binding him on Earth."

This movement touched others at many points. It does indeed embrace a "social" movement in education, but it is so much wider that we have hesitated to call it by such a name. It touches the scientific movement, especially in the case of Kingsley—one of those natures to whom "the Earth is the Lord's," who was more likely to picture himself in Heaven with a geologist's hammer than with a harp, ever learning more and more, in Milton's phrase, "to know God through His works." It touches the aesthetic movement so closely as to turn the feeling of beauty into one of adoration. It touches the hygienic movement, for our bodies are "the temples of the Holy Spirit"; and Kingsley "wishes to think" with the mystics that somehow our minds create our bodies and not our bodies our minds.

F. D. Maurice was the son of a unitarian minister. He was educated at Cambridge in the days when it was possible for a nonconformist to study at that university but not to take its degree, which involved subscription to the Thirty-nine Articles. He spent the next few years in London as a journalist, but gradually came to a belief in the tenets of the Church of England; and it is characteristic of the man that he joined the Church at a time when he had no material benefit to derive from the act, though a few years earlier he could have retained his scholarship at Trinity Hall by subscription. He now went up to Oxford and in 1833, after taking his degree, was ordained to a country curacy at Bubbenhall in Warwickshire. It is strange to think that he was actually put forward as a candidate for the chair of political economy at Oxford by the Tractarians. As he was clearly not an evangelical, they concluded that he must necessarily incline to their own school of thought. On his real views becoming known, his name was hurriedly withdrawn. In 1840 he was appointed professor of English literature and modern history at King's College, London; and in 1845 theology was also assigned to him.

Hitherto his interests had been mainly religious and educational, but the Chartist movement of 1848 made a deep impression on him. Though doctrinally he was a convinced churchman, having definitely broken with the unitarianism in which he had been brought up and holding Calvinism in horror, he had not inherited the tory traditions which in these days were dominant among the clergy. He faced the situation in an attitude of fearless enquiry and came to the conclusion that the dissatisfaction of the working classes with the existing order was justified. He saw as clearly as his panic-stricken colleagues that Chartism was the lineal descendant of the French revolutionary movement and that the religious beliefs of most of its leaders were those of Tom Paine. But he believed, what his colleagues did not believe, that, though the Chartists did not support Christianity, Christianity supported them, and that the brotherhood preached by Christ was no more a form of words than the fraternity proclaimed by the followers of Rousseau. He set himself the double aim of making Christians of Chartists and making social reformers of Christians. On December 7th began the meetings of that band of enthusiasts who acquired the name of Christian Socialists. From May he had been publishing a series of penny pamphlets entitled *Politics for the People*, to which Charles Kingsley contributed under the title of Parson Lot. He started an adult school in Little Ormond Yard, "a place so disorderly that no policeman liked to venture there alone at night," and Tom Hughes helped in the teaching. He threw himself vigorously into the co-operative movement. The following year came the cholera, and sanitation became an important plank in his social programme. In 1850 the tailors formed a Working Men's Association, and a Society of Working Men's Associations was rapidly developed, the principles of which Maurice explained and defended in his *Tracts on Christian Socialism*. Soon after, his social activities were disturbed by an attack on his religious views arising out of his criticism of the prevailing belief in regard to eternal punishment. Maurice was victorious in so far as he obtained from the law-courts a decision that acceptance of the generally accepted belief was not required of clergy either by the Prayer-book or by any other lawful authority; but it cost him his pro-fessorships.

This, however, left him the more free to carry on his social programme, and in 1854 he formed his Working Men's College. The Mechanics' Institutes, which have been described in a previous chapter, had passed their zenith. They had struck on the rock which prevented Maurice's own institutions from becoming a permanent part of the educational machinery of the country, the lack of previous training. Both movements left behind them a certain number of institutions which in modern times, when this difficulty had been removed, have been absorbed in the technical system of later days. But, even had they been still flourishing, they would not have fulfilled Maurice's purpose. Their aims were too utilitarian and informational; Maurice sought rather those studies which would humanise and moralise. The "College" was taught by volunteers such as Ruskin, Alexander Monro, Woolner, Lowes Dickinson, Rossetti, Frederic Harrison, W. J. Brodribb, C. H. Pearson and Grant Duff, a list sufficient to show that it was animated by no spirit of religious exclusiveness. He was helped by a stream of young men from the universities such as at a later time carried on the work of Toynbee Hall or the Oxford House in Bethnal Green. Maurice's boldness in refusing to compromise with convention, where compliance was opposed to what he believed to be the truth or the general welfàre, is shown in his stand on the matter of Sunday pursuits and recreations, which was a very vital question in the case of manual workers who were hard at work all the week. His attitude is so much commoner to-day that it is hard to realise that no "respectable" person, unless he were inspired by deep religious conviction, would then venture to attack Sabbatarianism. A hard-drinking, hard-swearing, loose-moraled, gambling- mid-Victorian would have regarded anyone who suggested playing cricket on Sunday as outside the pale. Maurice never sought conflicts but, when the success of any cause which he prized was at stake, he never flinched from them: and in this case he felt that he was following not merely the general tenour of his Master's principles, but His direct precedent on at least three occasions. "I have felt," he wrote, "that a Working College, if it is to do anything, must be in direct hostility to the Secularists—that is to say, must assert that as its foundation principle which they are denying. But to do this effectively it must also be in direct hostility to the Religionists—that is to say, it must assert the principle that God is to be sought and honoured in every pursuit, not merely in something technically called religion."

Maurice's work was twofold. With the exception of St Francis there is hardly any man since the first three centuries of Christianity of whom it is as true to say "*To the poor* the gospel is preached." Hanoverian official religion was exploded. The difference between an evangelical like Westcott and a high-churchman like Gore in succeeding days is a trifle compared with the gulf which yawns between them and a Georgian pluralist. His second task, however, was to put education in the forefront of the social movement. When society is all wrong and seditious discontent is rife, education is almost the last thing·which the dissatisfied demand. More food, better clothes, more pay, less work, more amusement, all come first. Yet in a sense education is both the means to these things and their end. By increasing a man's value as a worker it helps to improve his material position. When he has acquired means of sustenance and leisure, it enables him to enjoy his leisure. It enables him to live fully; and without this knowledge increased wages are of little value. Changes in wages only alter the distribution of the good things of life: education actually multiplies them. We are at the present time sufficiently familiar with kinds of unrest which, while searching to produce universal happiness, run the risk of producing universal misery; but, if the unrest of the "fifties" had not been turned into a healthier direction, we might now be in the condition of Russia. Christian Socialism did not create much in the way of educational machinery, but it produced an attitude of mind. Governments came to realise that, though education was not what the workers were consciously seeking, it would, when once they had obtained it, do more than many more popular demands to satisfy their unconscious cravings; and working men themselves came to aspire after it. The foundation was laid of the belief that is now becoming widespread that no human being's education should end with the elementary school.

The fourth movement for us to consider is the hygienic. It was immediately occasioned by the bad sanitary conditions which resulted from the uncontrolled growth of towns after the Industrial Revolution and especially by the visitations of cholera. But it has a wider significance; it represents the passing of an age-long attitude of mind and the spread of an attitude which, except to small intellectual minorities, had been previously unknown, but once accepted, alters the whole mode of looking at the physical world. This is the scientific aspect of the movement. Of course in all ages, man has been compelled, in order to adjust himself to his natural environment, to acknowledge some sort of uniformity in nature; empirical agriculture and empirical medicine both imply such a belief. But, the further we go back, the more we find mankind believing in a multitude of variable factors entering into the result along with a few invariable uniformities. The weather and disease are so elusive that popular opinion continued to regard them as such variables long after it had acknowledged many of their companions as subject to law. We would hesitate to define the scientific spirit in terms which suggested that it totally denied such variable factors—the existence of conscious beings by itself introduces one such factor: nor, in regard to disease, does the scientific spirit, in the best sense, deny the effect of mental condition on bodily health. The scientific attitude of mind, however, believes that, apart from such mental influences, disease will obey physical laws as fully as a material body, apart from the operation of the human mind on human muscles, will obey the law of gravitation. It is an attitude totally opposed to two beliefs, one or other of which has satisfied popular thought in all past ages, that the weather and disease are either the sport of "chance" or else in a special sense "acts of God." But pure intellect has no driving-power ($\nu o \hat{v}_s \ o \dot{v} \delta \dot{\epsilon} \nu \ \kappa \iota \nu \epsilon \hat{\iota}$); as a cold philosophic belief the uniformity of nature would have made few converts among the masses. Yet cholera showed the need that it should be believed; it soon became apparent that the most serious obstacle to the adoption of hygienic habits was the incapacity of the bulk of the population to think in a scientific manner. Unless people are habituated to think in terms of cause and effect all round, they will not do so in regard to some one specific matter where at any particular moment it is needed. Thus it came to pass that a movement which originated in science became associated with the social and philanthropic activities and the religious opinions of Maurice and Kingsley. With the theory of chance science could deal easily, for, while it had many adherents, it had no devotees. But with the theory of "act of God" it was different; strange as it seems now, there were in those days many who regarded sanitary measures as a direct attempt to resist the decrees of Providence. Against such Kingsley was the best fighter who could be found. The cause enlisted two of the strongest elements in his nature—his social sympathies, and his enthusiasm for *mens sana in corpore sano* as the ideal of the entire man. Born a naturalist, a sportsman, and a lover of the country, he detested equally the view that science is irreligious, the identification of bodily feebleness with spiritual strength, and the existence of slums. His attitude on the second point was so specially his own that it was accepted as his main contribution to contemporary thought; he was spoken of as the inventor of "muscular Christianity." It is easy to see that the popular imagination would easily be seized at the sight of a parson playing cricket on Sunday afternoon with the lads to whom he had preached in the morning, or setting out in the middle of service at the head of his congregation to put out a fire in the pine woods.

Medical science and "muscular Christianity" have between them had a considerable effect on education. Though it is a far cry to the Medical Inspection Act of 1907, men of science and followers of Kingsley both began to demand hygienic instruction in schools. Not that even now do we consider the problem has been solved. Matthew Arnold showed up the futility of the physiological teaching in elementary schools which was put in to satisfy the demand. Most of the modern teaching of hygiene is equally academic. The general diffusion of a scientific spirit through the whole of education appears to be doing more than the specific teaching of hygiene. Making games an integral part of education was an easier task. In the public schools they had grown up of their own accord; and the example of the public schools has infected the whole nation. The "barbarians" of course always loved sport. Before they rowed or played cricket, long before they played football, they had hunted and shot. At school they fought with their fists; and that ardent muscular Christian Thomas Hughes was by no means ashamed that, as Tom Brown, he had fought with a future cleric, "Slogger Williams." But no headmaster of 1800 regarded school games as anything but a concession to human frailty which unfortunately would not allow boys of twelve to study at all hours when they were not sleeping or eating. The dangers of over-athleticism which we recognise in 1920 had not become pronounced during Kingsley's lifetime, and the headmaster of 1860 had come to regard games not merely as excellent means of promoting health, or as a harmless way of occupying leisure hours, or as a safety-valve, but as a direct and important element in moral training. Dons were not quite so unanimous; but the unbelievers were dismissed as old-fashioned or as oddities or as admirers of things foreign, especially of German universities. By the eighties every player of Rugby football had come to believe at the bottom of his heart that the boy or man who had never dropped on the ball at the feet of an opposing rush, or found himself, two minutes before time and with a try to win, pushing in a scrum on his opponents' line, had never truly lived. Even though the war has made such things seem child's play, he probably still believes, that whatever the playing-fields of Eton (on which Rugby football was certainly not played) did for Waterloo, his game doubtless won *this* war. To the spectator from Mars all this would no doubt appear sufficiently absurd; but man is very human, and surely these deep, bedrock, primeval instincts, before which self-interest seems utterly forgotten and the thing to be done seems of transcendent importance, are

not of the ape and tiger but of the man, not to be crushed
but to be used, not something devilish but an inexhaustible
hidden spring whence altruism, determination, nay heroism
may be drawn.

It would doubtless be possible to mention other influences
which helped to mould the attitude of different classes of
Englishmen to education, but none, we venture to think,
are as important as these four.

The High Church movement, for instance, might be
expected to have had a wide influence through the many
headmasters who have been devout high churchmen.
These men have undoubtedly done much to spread both
the sense of social duty which we have considered in connection with Maurice and the methods of school government associated with the name of Arnold; but it does not
seem easy to fix on any specific educational ideal which we
can associate with the followers of Newman and Pusey.

Nor does it seem possible to regard the democratic
movement, apart from the social movement, as having
produced as much effect as might have been expected.
Properly speaking, democracy is a theory of government
"by the people and for the people." A logical connection
there certainly is between political democracy and social
reform. A practical connection does not necessarily follow.
Now that political democracy has been established for
some little time, the Labour party is beginning to put
forward an educational policy. But hitherto the influence
of educational questions has been negligible at elections,
except where the "religious difficulty" has been brought
in; and, till the introduction of Mr Fisher's Bill of 1918,
education debates were usually conducted in an empty
house. Not until the working man had been given a taste
of education was he likely to ask for more; and it was
Robert Lowe, the very man who on the granting of the
vote to the working man remarked "Now we must educate
our masters," who showed as minister of education that
his whole conception of schooling consisted in the "three
R's." The truth is that you may be a democrat for one of
two reasons. You may believe in the equal claims of all

men to be able to develop their possibilities to the utmost, and you may regard the vote as a means to this end; but, if you believe this, you are an educationalist before you are a democrat; your democracy is a corollary. Or you may be a democrat because it is the line of least resistance, as for instance if you believe that you will ultimately have to choose between extending the franchise and a revolution. Then you are an opportunist democrat; and education needed zealots, not opportunists. Possibly we ought to add a third class, those who accepted democratic formulae as they accepted other facts and theories about which they had never thought. And it would be hard to find a Victorian statesman of the first rank whom an impartial judge would unhesitatingly put into the first division. Maurice, Kingsley, Ruskin he certainly would.

Indeed these four movements by themselves well-nigh cover the possible ground. The scientific movement has taught us that education is necessary to national efficiency in the economic sphere, the hygienic movement that it is necessary to individual well-being in the bodily sphere, and the other two movements that it is thus necessary in the spiritual sphere.

REFERENCES

Matthew Arnold, *Reports on Elementary Schools*, 1889.

—— *A French Eton*, 1864.

—— *Schools and Universities on the Continent*, 1868.

—— *Culture and Anarchy*, 1869.

John Ruskin, *A Joy for Ever*, 1857, §§ 104–109, 127–136.

—— *A Crown of Wild Olive*, Part IV, 1866.

—— *Time and Tide*, letter 16.

—— *Unto this Last*, 1862 (preface).

—— *Sesame and Lilies*, 1865 (education of women).

Frederick Maurice, *Life of Frederick Denison Maurice*, 1884.

J. Llewelyn Davies, *The Working Men's College*, 1854–1904, 1904.

F. E. Kingsley, *Charles Kingsley*, 1878.

CHAPTER VIII

THE WORK OF INDIVIDUAL ENDEAVOUR

THE prophets prophesied mainly during the "fifties" and "sixties," but it took some time before the gradual leavening of national thought resulted in producing a state of mind capable of devising and supporting a State system of post-elementary education. In the technical sphere up to the passing of the Technical Instruction Act of 1889, in the secondary sphere up to the Bryce Commission (1894–1895), and in the university sphere up to the giving of government grants in 1889, we may call this the age of individual endeavour.

As regards secondary education, this endeavour was naturally most successful at the upper end of the social scale, where there was least need of financial assistance from the State. Many of the schools which had been set on a sound financial basis as the result of the Commission began to do excellent work; they copied all the best points in the Arnoldian tradition, and sent their most promising pupils to the universities, where they held their own well with the products of the older schools. These schools were less expensive and appealed to the professional class; and they avoided more than the older schools the tradition of idleness and the new tendency to over-athleticism. But there were still lamentable gaps. Most of the reforms by which the educational value of the newer subjects have been brought out belong to a more recent date: witness the new geometry, the direct method of teaching languages, and reformed geography. The majority of the schools founded modern sides but relegated to them all their unpromising pupils. Classics continued therefore to be the great educative agent. The non-classical "middle" schools were deficient in numbers, lacked a clear-cut educational programme, and, till the rise of newer universities and places of professional and technical instruction, led nowhere.

In describing the work of individual endeavour, it is easiest to take some one outstanding example; and, in this case, it would be generally agreed that the premier place belongs to Edward Thring of Uppingham, who gathers together the effects of all the movements described in the last chapter. He was the first notable example of a headmaster who realised the effect of an artistic element in the school environment, who introduced manual training into the secondary school, and who used school missions to awake in the minds of his own class an understanding of the workers and sympathy for them. The introduction of the first school gymnasium likewise connects him with the hygienic movement. In the novelty of his ideas, the force of his personality, his influence over his contemporaries and his reputation after his death, he is almost the equal of Arnold; but he does not possess the supreme importance of breaking up entirely fallow ground.

Thring was educated at Eton and King's College, Cambridge. Even in boyhood his experiences at Eton turned his attention to the evils of the public schools of those days before the Commission. The material conditions of "Long Chamber" were so bad and the tone so low that, though Eton foundationers had the privilege of automatically proceeding as scholars to King's, with a good chance of a fellowship to follow, Thring's father like many others sent him at first as a paying pupil and entered him for a scholarship at the latest moment compatible with his holding it for the necessary three years. As a "colleger" he and many other boys could only work by getting up in the middle of the night when the other pupils were asleep. At King's, as at New College, Oxford, there existed the curious privilege by which undergraduates obtained their degree without undergoing the University examinations. Thring was thus cut off from the hope of winning a first class; but he proved his scholarship by gaining the Porson Prize and subsequently, as a fellow, he took part in abolishing the obnoxious regulation. Possibly to a mind so bubbling over with intellectual interests as Thring's, the opportunity of working in his own way free from examinations was an advantage and may have had something to do with his subsequent policy of laying stress on the literary and artistic sides of school work which do not help to win scholarships. After his ordination he was for a time curate at St James's, Gloucester; and of all the branches of his clerical work that which interested him most was his teaching in the National school connected with the church. He regarded it as experimental work; he felt that education in all its grades was based on bad foundations, and the task which he set himself was to look for better. All his life he looked back to this time as his formative period: thus his views took shape before he ever began to teach in a secondary school and, though expanding in detail, were never substantially changed. He became profoundly convinced that, the younger the pupil, the more was teaching ability needed, that few teachers ever really got into the minds of their pupils, that they thought too exclusively of the subject-matter, and that they were committing a grave injustice in confining their interest to their clever pupils. He regarded a stupid boy as a most interesting problem, as a challenge to his skill as a teacher. When ill-health compelled him to abandon parochial work, he undertook private coaching as a form of light duty, and thus, like Arnold, passed directly to a headship without ever being an assistant. As in Arnold's case, this private tuition opened his eyes to the need of dealing with individuals as individuals and not losing them in the mass, which is a cardinal feature of his educational theory. In 1853 he was appointed headmaster of Uppingham, at that time a small country grammar school with two masters and twenty-five boys, and, in spite of much opposition from the governors, he raised it to a school of thirty masters and 320 boys, beyond which limit he refused to allow it to increase.

It will be best to consider the leading features in his character before we pass on to his work. The first was his thoroughness. "An archbishop was asked 'What kind of a man is Edward Thring?' The archbishop was about to poke the fire. 'Why, he was this kind of a man; if he were poking a fire, he would make you believe that the one thing worth living for was to know how to poke a fire properly[1]." Another man said, "I do not believe he would have omitted one portion of the day's routine, if that omission had injured a single boy, for the position of the highest eminence his country could bestow[2]." The effectiveness of this quality is obvious; but it had one disadvantage —it made his writings seem somewhat exaggerated: his condemnations of politicians, officials, his governors, and others who did not agree with him, at first sight suggest a man who could see no good in anything which was not in accordance with his own ideas. Yet no man was less conceited.

The second striking characteristic of Thring was his sympathy. This quality was combined with an absolute masterfulness. Arnold was sympathetic with very small boys and, at the other end of the scale, he won the friend ship of his Sixth Form, but his sternness was somewhat awe-inspiring to boys in the middle of the school. But it must be remembered that Arnold had to reform a school where bad traditions had taken root, whereas Thring could build up what was practically a new school on his own lines and, beginning with a few boys, was able to get into such touch with them at the beginning that he never lost it. Nevertheless, in spite of Arnold's remark that he should resign as soon as he could no longer run up the library stairs, one has a feeling that Thring had something of the boy in him which Arnold never had; and his impulsiveness, his tendency to rush from gloom to the full enjoyment of a holiday, and his unwillingness to brook opposition are all characteristics of a bubbling, boyish nature which made him understand boys. Unlike Arnold, he had too a strong sense of humour. He was ready to do anyone a good turn either by help, time, or money. He

[1] G. R. Parkin, *Life of Edward Thring*, vol. II, p. 300.
[2] *Op. cit.* p. 301.

kept in constant touch with his old boys. In his diary little school incidents seem to occupy his attention as much as big questions of administration: he was always thinking of individuals. Gratitude or confidence shown by pupils touched him deeply and misconduct made him miserable.

Thirdly, we have already spoken of his masterfulness. Up to a point all great headmasters are masterful, at least in their dealings with their pupils; but it was not mainly with his pupils that Thring showed this quality. Though he made it clear that he took a serious view of misbehaviour in class, this was a natural outcome of his securing smaller classes, better masters, and more congenial surroundings. He considered that he had done away with the causes which naturally led to idleness and inattention and that he could justly claim a higher standard of order. He secured his higher standard, but he was no martinet. "A master came to him and said, '*A* must be caned; he has been very insolent.' Thring agreed and *A* was caned. A week later the master came and said, '*A* must be crushed; he has repeated his insolent conduct.' Thring turned and said, '*A* shan't be crushed; he is a very good boy, but just at present he is standing at bay like a rat in a corner. Punish him slightly for this, for the next month shut your eyes resolutely to everything you are not obliged to see.' The plan answered[1]." Though we find from Thring's diary that he was strict with his staff on such points as being late for school and going off to read the newspaper, and though at first there was some little inclination among them to regard him as faddy on matters which seemed to them to be trifles, yet he had their solid support in all his great struggles with the governing body. He insisted firmly on his absolute right to dismiss his assistants, but he was too kind to use it on the rare occasions when he had a master who was not up to his usual standard. In fact his masterfulness was not displayed against those who were under him but against those who claimed to be over him. He held an autocratic theory as to the independence of a headmaster and showed an almost rebellious spirit

[1] *Op. cit.* p. 143.

to any power, whether the State or the governors of the school, who claimed to limit that independence. His fighting instincts were aroused by opposition. When he engaged new masters, he made it clear that, even though they were sinking money in the school by the conditions on which they took boarding houses, his right to dismiss them was real, that he was no constitutional ruler, much less the instrument of a committee, that even when he asked for advice he was not bound to act on it, and that the masters' meetings were merely advisory. The least sign of opposition on the part of the governors is met by an outburst of wrath in his diary; and against the Commissioners appointed under the Endowed Schools Act he declared open war. He has nothing too bad to say of government interference in education or about any attempt to impose inspection on secondary schools.

Lastly we may notice his religious earnestness. His diary reveals an almost Cromwellian belief that every detail of life is specially determined by Providence for some end. It was the humility and constant searching of heart which this belief inspired which prevented his masterfulness from becoming of such a kind as to over-ride the legitimate claims of others. His religion was very practical: it led him to found the first school mission in a slum and to take an active part in working the local "Mutual Improvement Society," to which he gave a less formally religious turn than that which hitherto prevailed in such organisations. Nowadays, perhaps, religious bodies are inclined to run to death the idea of reaching the people by means of amusements; but the danger then was in the opposite direction. This society therefore, with its concerts, classes, lectures, and tennis and cricket clubs, was a move in the right direction, an attempt to educate informally. His scripture teaching left a deeper impression than any part of his work, though it would have surprised any examiner. He used the supposed matter of the syllabus merely as a peg on which to hang his own ideas, which were always marked by freshness and individuality; he would sometimes devote a whole month to a single chapter.

We pass now to his leading ideas, which, as has already been stated, were formed before he went to Uppingham.

He lays it down as the main point of difference between his own practice and that of the old public schools that a school, to be honest, must educate every single pupil and not concentrate its main endeavours entirely on the ablest. Even at Rugby, which had since Arnold's death come to be popularly regarded as a model—a view which Thring somewhat resents—he declares that there were three forms which averaged over sixty boys and that in the headmaster's house there were between sixty and seventy. (In justice to Arnold it should be said that the restriction which he had set on the total number of the school had been removed since his death.) He attacks, as "the greatest heresy against educational truth ever expressed," the belief that "the first, second, and third duty of a schoolmaster is to get rid of unpromising subjects[1]." If he is attacking Arnold, the charge is hardly fair; for Arnold only removed boys whose moral influence he believed to be bad: but he has more show of reason if he is attacking the system of "superannuation" recommended by the Public Schools Commission and since pretty generally adopted in the public schools, by which any boy who fails to gain his promotion to a particular form by a given age is automatically removed. No stigma attaches to such removal; the plan is due as much to the tremendous competition for places in these schools as to the acceptance of Arnold's theory that intellectual dullards are more often than other boys a bad moral influence. Thring's championship of the claims of the average boy is eminently reasonable, though he seems to have pushed it too far in claiming the right of the stupid boy to remain at school after sixteen. Surely the true principle is that, so long as the boy is at school, he has a right to his fair share of attention, but that there must be an age at which it is not worth while wasting the energy of teachers in continuing the education of less able pupils. It is merely an application of the law of diminishing returns. Thring's sincerity on this point

[1] *Life*, vol. i, pp. 68–69.

was so well-known that he felt it a cause of grievance that certain parents sent their less able children to Uppingham and the clever member of the family elsewhere!

Though his personality was doubtless the largest factor in his success, he himself attributed it largely to organisation. He was always emphasising the need of adjusting every detail in the school to the fulfilment of its aims, with this object in view he began with the buildings. "The almighty wall is, after all, the supreme and final arbiter of schools[1]." We are used to this doctrine now; it was revolutionary in the days of ill-lighted, ill-ventilated class-rooms, their heavy oak desks carved with the names of countless generations, without a picture on the walls, ink everywhere, and everything of such a colour that the day's dirt made no difference. "Never rest till you have got all the fixed machinery for the work the best possible. The waste in a teacher's workshop is the lives of men." "There is a large percentage of temptation, criminality, and idleness in the great schools to be got rid of even by mere mechanical improvements. Bullying is fostered by harshness in the masters and by forcing boys to herd together in promiscuous masses. Lying is fostered by general class rules which take no cognisance of the ability of the individual to keep them. Idleness is fostered when there are so many boys to each master that it becomes a chance when it will be detected. Rebellion is fostered when many boys who are backward or want ability find no care bestowed on them. Sensuality is fostered when such boys are launched into an ungoverned society without any healthy instinct."

His general principles thus glide into the careful working out of minutiae. To begin with, he limited the number of boys to 320, and in his later years had one big fight with his governors on this point. "As long as a headmaster knows every boy," he used to say, "he is headmaster"; otherwise, if a boy whom he does not know is reported to him by one of his staff, he must take the master's opinion and the latter "is so far headmaster" and the head "sinks

[1] *Life*, vol. II, p. 116.

into the position of his policeman[1]." He likewise limited the size of houses to thirty and of forms to about twenty-five boys.

Though he loved architecture, he denounced the building of stately piles which were intended for architectural effect rather than to serve their purpose of training boys. As soon as he was able to collect the money, he built a hall to hold the whole school (1863) and a chapel (1865), in order to provide for their life as a community. As we have already said, he was the first headmaster of a large school to see the bad results of the old bare untidy class-room, of which the worst existing elementary school which survives in some isolated parish gives us but a faint idea. "Another grave cause of evil," he writes, "is the dishonour shown to the place in which work is done. Mean treatment produces mean ideas. Honour the work and it will honour you[2]." So he instituted well-lighted comfortable class-rooms with autotypes on the walls, installed new desks which he would not allow the boys to cut, and insisted on tidiness.

"Every boy can do *something* well": this was the principle on which he dealt with the problem of the "stupid boy." He confined the ordinary school subjects—classics, mathematics, English composition (on which he laid great stress), English grammar, scripture, history and geography —to the morning: in the afternoon came music and the various optional subjects, of which every boy had to take one or two, viz. French, German, chemistry, drawing, carpentery, and turning. The gymnasium, which was opened in 1859, was the first in any English school. So were the workshops, laboratories, school garden, and aviary. Though not particularly musical himself, he attached great importance to music, wrote the words of school songs, engaged good musicians as teachers, and instituted school concerts. Before his time a school choir for the chapel services and a little music on speech-day were all that any school ever attempted, and most public school-boys would have been as surprised to be offered instrumental music, which a large percentage of Uppingham boys

[1] *Life*, vol. I, p. 73.   [2] Vol. II, p. 119.

learned, as their successors would be if they were expected to learn sewing. Sport was of course already well established in schools and Thring often turned out to play football with his boys; but he may be considered as the originator of the other activities which no less than the class-room form part of the educational machinery of the modern school.

As regards curriculum, though he was thus a pioneer in the work of introducing the aesthetic and hobby subjects into schools, he was opposed to the superficiality which he believed would come from an overloaded curriculum. He was a firm believer in classics. His point of view was not exactly that of the old-fashioned "scholarship" nor yet Arnold's, in which the emphasis was laid on the thought of the authors. His old pupil Nettleship writes to him, "The way in which you taught what they call 'scholarship' tended distinctly to make one think of the *form* of ancient and modern artistic expression rather than of language as a subject of philological or even (primarily) grammatical interest[1]." Thring replies, "Philology I look on as a scientific toy totally unfitted for school training. I have always striven to make our literary training here a great artistic lesson in the sense you speak of art; to make it a living thing, to join together the ages, and show how thought in heathen times worshipped form and beautiful shape, and how thought in Christian times worships expression and beautiful life, and to weave together the principles of skilful power at work so as to show the proper proportions, the true sources, the right use, and enable a right judgment to judge correctly of each[2]." Similarly in English, he regarded all teaching of the history of the language, which was just beginning to find advocates, as pure cram, but, like Matthew Arnold, he retained the old disciplinary idea that English grammar, treated inductively, furnished the best basis for language teaching, and he wrote several grammars intended for younger pupils. English composition was to his mind as important as classics. He does not seem to have taught English literature, doubtless believing that to insist on reading it in the

[1] *Life*, vol. I, p. 279.   [2] p. 281.

class-room was the surest way to prevent it from being read anywhere else. Latin verses still found in him a defender[1]. Like the Public School Commissioners he was opposed to modern sides, believing in the German system of establishing separate *Realschulen*.

He was one of the first secondary school teachers in England to become conscious of method as such. He was interested in the training of elementary school teachers, but we are not aware of any evidence that he definitely contemplated the establishment of a system of training their secondary colleagues. He wanted everyone to think out his own methods. "In teaching, the structure of the work is everything, and the power of turning out the perfect result nothing. If for one year all rules and lesson books could be swept clean out of the world and the performers be brought face to face with mind, the little boy mind, and be compelled to trade on their own resources and forced to meet the real problem of mind dealing with mind, there would be much tearing of hair, but a new creation would have begun[2]." The first sentence of this quotation possibly shows his attitude towards the professional training of teachers. As conducted in elementary training colleges in Thring's time it was naturally affected by the unfortunate necessity imposed on teachers by the Lowe Code of aiming at "results." Secondary training, he may have thought, would have followed the same lines. Possibly too he may have feared lest it would cause the teacher to lose his originality and not to think for himself. The same fundamental views may lead two men at different periods to directly opposite policies on what *seems* to be the same issue. Training now aims less at inculcating cut-and-dried rules than at encouraging the student to think out things for himself.

It was a somewhat novel thing for a headmaster to write books on his educational views. Thring, however, felt that he had a message and he delivered it in his *Education and School* (1864) and *Theory and Practice of Teaching* (1883). In these publications he shows himself not so much as

---

[1] *Life*, vol. II, p. 192.   [2] Vol. II, pp. 211–212.

the author of a system but as a suggestive writer, with a penetrating intuition dealing with a variety of practical points and setting out his intuitions after the manner of an essayist. They owe their value to his thorough understanding of boy nature.

His interests were not confined to his own school. He was a keen supporter of the movement for the better education of girls and women, and invited a conference of headmistresses to Uppingham. He strove to promote adult education among the townsfolk and inaugurated various classes for discussion and the teaching of cookery and handwork. He was the first headmaster who conceived the idea of using a public school as a means of interesting the wealthier classes in the social conditions of their poorer brothers: his mission in North Woolwich and subsequently in Poplar was the forerunner of numerous university and public school settlements. Herein we see the effect of the social movement started by Maurice and Kingsley.

An account of Thring's work would be incomplete without a reference to one of the best-known incidents in his headmastership, the outbreak of diphtheria and removal of the school for a time to an hotel at Borth on the Cardiganshire coast. The incident illustrates Thring's invariable promptitude, energy and resource.

There died in 1919 an Uppingham master who followed in Thring's footsteps and proved that the twentieth century can still produce men in the old heroic mould. This was G. W. S. Howson, who was appointed in 1900 to be headmaster of Gresham's School, Holt, by the Fishmonger's Company, the endowments of the school having suddenly increased. Like Thring he started with such small numbers that he was able to follow his own lines. He carried the system of trusting boys' honour successfully beyond the point at which Arnold and Thring had left it. He had no written rules, and an absolute minimum of punishments. He did not lock the doors at "lock-up"; he proceeded on the assumption that boys were the same beings at a boarding-school as at home and would respond to the same treatment. On one matter only did he break away from Thring; he abolished Greek. But he gained many scholarships in non-classical subjects. His school was thoroughly conducted "on public school lines"; he limited its numbers, however, like Arnold, to 250, and on the same grounds; he trusted to surroundings as much as Thring; and he kept out the modern over-athleticism. He dealt a final blow to the "natural enmity" theory between teacher and taught.

We have reserved to the end the story of Thring's war against government control. It began with the Schools Inquiry Commission, before which he gave evidence. He was received in a thoroughly friendly spirit, but the report contained no reference to his views, and he soon showed his disapproval of its tenour. He described it as "a great indirect glorification of the old and new shams[1]." "I feel quite certain that the question 'What constitutes a good school?' must be raised." "The Commissioners have not raised the question at all but tacitly assumed" that the seven public schools "are models" and that "a happy combination of ability and fortune may possibly raise some others to this level." "What great school, even in theory, has faced the problem of teaching and training *each boy* in the best way?" "I desire to separate my lot entirely from the fashionable schools and to cast it in, come weal come woe, with the smaller schools."

When the Act was passed and the Commissioners who were appointed under it drew up their scheme for Uppingham he resolutely fought it on the following grounds. (1) The masters who had practically been the financial reconstructors of the school were only to be represented on the governing body by two members. (2) The functions of governors should in his opinion be strictly limited, whereas "there are sundry things in the scheme which practically give absolute control of the construction of the school to the governing body, and that deadest of all dead hands, the hand of living external force, can at any moment be applied to the heartstrings of the work and the workers

[1] Vol. 1, p. 169.

here[1]." (3) He feared the loss of the Church character of the school. He was a stout believer in denominational teaching, holding that under an undenominational system "religion must be treated as a by-subject of intellectual knowledge"; "but religion *is* education[2]." On all three points the Commissioners gave way. It is natural to sympathise with a man like Thring who was really origina- tive and felt that an educational experiment was at the mercy of committees who can never originate. It must not be forgotten, however, that the policy of a body like the Commissioners has to be based on the Kantian principle so to act that the principle of your action may be able to serve as a universal law. It would be impossible and, if possible, undesirable for all local grammar schools to be turned into big first-grade schools. It would be equally harmful for all the headmasters of grammar schools to waste their energies in a useless competition to be the few who succeeded, as all would have neglected their own proper work, whether they succeeded or not, in doing that for which they sought to exchange it. Thring's case was in its nature an exception to a general rule: the Com- missioners wisely treated him as an exception, as pioneers and men of genius necessarily are; but Thring had no right to claim that exceptions should determine general rules. History necessarily selects big men to illustrate their time; in so doing it often sees things through the eyes of big men and from their standpoint; and it sometimes forgets that there is any other standpoint. In this particular case of Thring's struggle to make Uppingham into a "new model," it is easy to forget, for instance, that there was an Oakham standpoint. Oakham was a sister grammar school on the same foundation, founded for the same purpose as a local grammar school for Rutland, and till Thring's time it was the more successful school of the two. Yet Thring proposed to convert it into a preparatory school for Uppingham!

In order to secure a permanent machinery for resisting encroachments, as he considered them, by the State, Thring took the lead in turning a special meeting of headmasters,

---

[1] Vol. I, p. 187.   [2] Vol. II, pp 222–3.

convened to consider the Bill of 1869, into an annual
Headmasters' Conference. At first the old public schools
held aloof, but they soon came in. After fifty years we can
only look on the Conference with mixed feelings. It was
almost the earliest of scholastic associations. The National
Union of Teachers was founded in 1870, the Headmistresses'
Association in 1874, the Private Schools Association in
1883, the Assistant Mistresses' Association in 1884, the
Teachers' Guild in 1885, the Headmasters' Association in
1890, the Assistant Masters' Association, the Headmasters
of Private Schools' Association, and the Headmasters of
Higher Grade and Organised Science Schools Association
in 1892. Sectional societies were necessary before any
solidarity could be gained in the scholastic profession:
sectional they had to be if their deliberations were to deal
with the practical problems which their members had to
handle every day; and in 1870 anything but sectional
bodies was impossible. At any rate the Conference has
done something to put an end to the separation of the old
public schools from a hundred smaller schools doing the
same work. But it has proved an ultra-conservative body.
Its first work was to anticipate the danger of a State
examination by inducing the old Universities to set up
an examining body of their own for first-grade schools—
the Oxford and Cambridge Joint Board. Probably this
was a good piece of work. Most examinations have led
to cram, but the Joint Board least of all. It is hard to
pronounce a verdict on an examination which never existed
outside the minds of a Royal Commission; but we do not
believe a State examination would have been so good.
State examination in the case of elementary schools was
as bad as it could possibly be. On the other hand a State
examination would have not only performed the work of
the Joint Board, but it would have absorbed a hundred
other examining bodies whose multiplicity was forty years
later revealed to be working havoc with school timetables.
But, after it had done this, it is difficult to point to anything else which the Conference has ever done. Probably
Thring was right in insisting that its discussions should

be merely designed for the interchange of views and that it should make no claim to pass binding resolutions. But it is hard to imagine anything which would so bind the members of the Conference to adhere to set paths as Thring's action in preventing the very discussion of making Greek optional by threatening to resign his seat. From that time onwards the Conference has tended to become a trade guild for preserving traditional customs and to miss its chance of becoming an educational cabinet which should convert ideas into working realities. There is not much use in an educational House of Lords which accepts new ideas only after everyone else has accepted them, even if its members are wiser than some persons outside it in seeing the value of old ideas. People who are all agreed need not come together to tell one another that the world needs literature as well as science, and character as well as instruction: they would be better employed in preaching these truths to those who have forgotten them or never knew them.

Thring's opinion that government action in education was essentially evil may need modifying into a statement that government action about 1880 was accidentally but invariably evil, and we can then dissent from his premises while we recognise the value of the action which he based on them. The foremost belief which he regarded as rooted in the mind of government officials as such was an unlimited faith in examinations. "Where examinations reign, every novelty in training, every original advance, every new way of dealing with the mind, becomes at once impossible. It is outside the prescribed area and does not pay." "Do our universities, the government, and the parents want memory or mind? Do they want knowledge or strength?[1]" "The inspector destroys teaching because he is bound by law and necessity to examine according to a given pattern, and the perfection of teaching is that it does not work by a given pattern." He feared too that, by insisting on additional subjects, the government would produce superficiality. "The government during the last twenty years

[1] Vol. II, p. 131.

has practically been legislating against the schools, demanding everywhere either fresh subjects or a different kind of them or both, thus calling into existence an army of crammers and pulling down the schools in the direction of more branches of superficial knowledge[1]." In 1885 he writes: "The professional body are beginning to chafe under this terrible slavery. The present exponents of education in London won't do. As far as I know them, they are the strangest mixture of red tape, crude dissatisfaction, narrow sciolism, revolutionary fumes, unworkable old and unworkable new, kneaded up into an infallible pudding, that can be imagined[2]." The important thing to note is that this kind of talk, which assumed that the Education Department was incurable, has cured it. State education under Robert Lowe would have been a curse; under Mr Fisher it may be a blessing. Long after Lowe's time the central authorities treated teachers as the army before the Boer War treated recruits—"their's not to reason why."

The result was that a progressive educationalist like Thring was led, on the political side of education, to a high Toryism which would strike the present generation with amazement. He denounced free elementary education as theft, and the arguments which he uses against it would logically apply to all State subsidy of schools. (1) You place judgment on educational questions in the hands of the general community, *i.e.* the ignorant. (2) You place the teachers who are skilled workmen under officials who are amateurs. (3) You decide all questions on authority and so prevent experiment and improvement. (4) You prevent individuals from starting new types of school. (5) When parents pay or subscribers subscribe, they are interested in the education which they maintain; when they are taxed, they wash their hands of the whole matter. (6) State education must be undenominational, and he did not believe that undenominational education could be really religious. The weakness in Thring's conclusion does not arise from any fault in his arguments—there is much truth

[1] p. 199.   [2] p. 211.

in many of them—so much as from his failure to see the considerations on the other side. The essential fact was that there was a huge gap which private endeavour in the years between 1868, when the gap was made clearly evident by the Schools Inquiry Commission, and 1894, when the Bryce Commission was appointed, entirely failed to fill. It was the work of the prophets to arouse the country to a sense of the meaning and value of education; it was the work of progressive schoolmasters like Thring to set examples of it in concrete form; but either it was the work of the State to diffuse it on a large scale, or else such diffusion must be pronounced to be impossible.

We have had numerous occasions to refer to the increasing hold which examinations were gaining upon schools, and it is time to treat their history a little more fully. Perhaps the belief in their efficacy originally dates from the part which they were supposed to have played in the recuperation of the old universities. It was rife everywhere by 1850. England succeeded in imposing the incubus not only on itself but even over other countries with which it came into contact. Examinations have been the bane of Indian education. They were undoubtedly encouraged at home because of their use for competitive as well as testing purposes. Some substitute for appointment by influence was needed in government departments; and examination afforded an obvious method of ensuring fairness though it does not necessarily secure efficiency. They were first adopted for the Indian Civil Service in 1854; the higher positions in the Home Service followed almost immediately; within twenty years the system had spread to all branches of the civil service, to entrance into Woolwich and Sandhurst, and to commissions on passing out of those institutions. We have already seen how Oriel opened its fellowships to competitive examination, how the Universities Commissions extended competition to all scholarships, how the Public Schools Commission insisted on competition for scholarships in the large secondary schools, and how Robert Lowe in 1860 introduced the system into elementary schools. Its defects were ignored.

As a means of entrance into the State service, it was forgotten that examination at its best tests only certain kinds of ability, and that a good examinee may from the lack of other qualities prove a very poor civil servant. At its worst it only tests memory or even luck in choosing an expert "crammer" who can "spot the questions" likely to be set. Our scholarship system is excellent in intention, since it is an attempt to open our educational institutions to poorer candidates of ability; and its application in the universities was successful in encouraging industry and did something towards admitting poorer pupils. Its adoption in the public schools was a more doubtful blessing, since its direct effect was to encourage premature specialisation in expensive preparatory schools.

But it is of examinations for testing purposes that we here wish particularly to speak. Five main examinations have been invented for testing the work of pupils at schools.

(1) The College of Preceptors, founded in 1846, began its work of examining in 1853. Its examinations were of three grades, and it provided mainly for the lower branches of secondary education. It did a useful work in its early days in the way of widening curricula and giving something for private schools to aim at; but later on its examinations were used as an easy mode of advertisement, and young pupils were greatly harmed by being kept constantly in an examination atmosphere. This danger has in recent times been mitigated by the refusal of the Board of Education to allow pupils in grant-earning schools to be sent in for external examinations below the age of fifteen; but it lasted throughout the period of which we are now speaking.

(2) The Local Examinations (1858) of Oxford and Cambridge were of a higher standard and intended for second-grade schools. The authorities proceeded to add a junior and a preliminary examination which fostered the same evils as the examinations of the College of Preceptors; but their senior examination has on the whole stimulated and guided.

(3) The Oxford and Cambridge Joint Board Examination, of which we described the origin in the account of Thring, is intended for first-grade schools. Girls were admitted in 1878, and a junior examination was added in 1882. On the principle that less harm is done by examinations to older than to younger pupils, the " Joint Board " has been the most innocuous examination of all.

(4) The London Matriculation Examination was not intended as a school testing examination but came to be used for this purpose. To avoid the evils incident to applying to one use an examination intended for another, London and other modern universities have in recent times instituted school-leaving examinations.

(5) The South Kensington examinations in science and art (1861) were intended to test evening and other classes rather than full-time schools. Some of them (1859–1867) were also intended as qualifications for teachers of science and art—a poor substitute for a proper course of training. This particular incursion of government into examination was due to the fact that, at the time these examinations were instituted, science and art were supposed to lie quite outside the scope of secondary education. They had the further peculiarity that they were a part of the grant-earning machinery, like the later examinations of Robert Lowe's Code. When science classes developed into schools of science (1872), these examinations became a part of the regular examination machinery of schools which would now be considered as secondary, and completely dominated them, with very uneducational results, till the reconstitution of these schools as Schedule A Schools at the beginning of the new century (1902). South Kensington was a branch of the Board of Trade from its full constitution in 1853 to 1856; but it had already become attached to the Education Department when it started its examining work; however, it retained substantial independence till the passing of the Board of Education Act, 1899. It is difficulty to say whether more good was done by securing that science was taught at all or harm by encouraging bad methods of teaching it.

But these five by no means exhaust the list of examina-

tions taken by school pupils. The number was ever increasing. At the end of the period there were examinations
in technical subjects such as those of the City and Guilds
Institute and the London Chamber of Commerce, and
examinations conducted by various professional bodies for
admission to their respective professions, such as those of
the Law Society, the General Medical Council, the Chartered
Accountants, Actuaries, Architects, Civil Engineers, and
Pharmaceutical Society. Though in time these bodies came
to recognise other examinations, they still retained their
own. Indeed the Consultative Committee of the Board of
Education discovered in the early years of the present
century that there were more than a hundred examinations
for which school pupils were being entered; and the Board
has set itself to reduce their number, to co-ordinate those
which remain and determine their equivalence, to abolish
examinations at the junior stages and to approximate to
the Prussian system of two examinations, one intended for
pupils aged about sixteen and the other for pupils aged
about nineteen. An examination at the end of a pupil's
career is inevitable; but it does not involve either a subordination of the whole school teaching to what will "pay"
in examinations or the incessant taking of the machinery
to pieces to see how it is working. By the end of the century
it had actually come to pass that a pupil was frequently
sent in for the same examination several times from pure
motives of advertisement; and schoolboys and schoolgirls
came to be so used to working for an examination every
year that they lost the power of working without such a
stimulus. University scholarship examinations, which test
promise rather than performance, have, however, rather
mitigated than augmented the evil.

The years from 1868 to the end of the century witnessed
a growing encouragement of school activities outside the
class-room. The old public schools gave us games, the
school magazine, and debating societies, at an earlier date;
and these have of course become well-nigh universal.
During this period games came to be so emphasised at the
old type of school as to arouse considerable misgiving.

A games master became a regular institution, and athletic ability came to count too much in the appointment of his colleagues. The love of playing—but, alas! too often only of watching—games spread to the whole nation. It was during these years that football, both Rugby and Association, came to be played at the universities, where rowing and cricket were already well-established, that both forms of the game became an adult as well as a boys' amusement throughout the country, that League football almost surpassed the turf as a national institution, and that Australian cricket teams began to visit the mother country. Cricket had already produced its greatest exponent in W. G. Grace before football gained its popularity. The exaggerated stress which is laid on sport in boarding schools must not blind us to the good effects of its spread in day schools, where it would appear that its physical and moral advantages can be secured without its monopolising attention. At many day schools games are now compulsory, and, from a wide point of view as to the nature of education, the arguments for this course would appear irresistible. Since Thring's time all large schools have built gymnasia; but gymnastics have not become so popular as games have. Herbert Spencer, the apostle of physical education, regarded them as an artificial substitute; and his testimony is that of a cold-blooded scientist, not that of an athletic enthusiast. Popular opinion regarded them as a foreign importation. Educational theorists called to mind the saying of Plato, the founder of educational theory, that those are wrong who hold that "gymnastic," *i.e.* physical training, is for the body and "music," *i.e.* intellectual training, for the soul, but rather both are for the soul. They argued that the modern gymnasium, however much it might develop the muscles, fell far short of games in its influence on character. Finally, modern hygiene showed that muscular development and health are by no means identical, and that enjoyment is a great factor in giving bodily exercise its health-giving value. Nowadays systems of physical drill which take account of the internal organs as well as of the muscles are tending to supersede the parallel and horizontal bars and the other appliances of the gymnasium.

Plays, concerts, and natural history societies are of later growth. Latin plays were a regular school institution in the days which followed the Renaissance, but the Westminster play was the only survival. The Bradfield Greek play, acted in a disused chalkpit and reproducing the original methods of staging, is the most famous of modern developments in this field. The decline of the Puritan hostility to stage plays has been followed by their recognition as a legitimate form of art, to which equally with other forms a school education should introduce its pupils. The recognition of play-writing and play-acting as a training in self-expression, especially for the younger pupils, is a more recent development. Musical teaching in boys' schools developed out of the chapel services which in large boarding schools, partly through Arnold's influence, quite superseded attendance at the parsih church; but music is now established in its own right. Natural history societies are of course an offshoot of the scientific movements and are probably a more effective way of reviving the interest of boys in the animal and plant world, which the predominance of games had tended to displace, than any formal lessons in "nature study." In the old days boys' natural instincts had tended to satisfy themselves in poaching, birds'-nesting, and other undesirable exhibitions of the Englishman's motto: "It's a fine day; let's go out and kill something"; and headmasters had naturally discouraged such activities. During the last thirty years photography, boys' magazines, and the modern scientific trend have provided better outlets for the open air instincts.

Finally, there can be no doubt that the relations between boys and masters had improved before the bulk of the new schools revived and has been improving ever since. Partnership in games and in hobbies has been of great assistance, but the main cause has been the changed attitude of the teacher towards his work. Improved methods of teaching will probably complete the change; for, so long as boys hated their work, there was always a clash of motive.

They might respect the man, but they were bound to chafe against the taskmaster. This is one reason why discipline has proved easier in girls' schools.

These changed relations are well brought out in the biographies of Edward Bowen, who became an assistant master at Harrow in the sixties, and Almond, headmaster of Loretto (1862).

Bowen's criticism of Arnold shows the points in which the opinion of teachers was changing. He objects to the over-serious, over-dignified master, who will not venture a joke in the class-room; to the stiff attitude of boys in class which was regarded as essential to good discipline; to the excessive use of emulation; to a half unconscious belief that work which is to be beneficial cannot be enjoyable; and to a suspicion that a teacher with outside interests cannot be devoting himself whole-heartedly to his school work[1]. Bowen was one of the first masters in a classical school to value the importance of making the work interesting. Without interest he held it to be impossible to secure the true aim of scholarship, which was to get to know the mind of the ancients, that is from their mode of expression to reach their mode of thought, and from that "to get a kind of intellectual parallax in contemplating the problems of life." He took a vigorous part in the campaign for finally exterminating memorised syntax, he was prepared to legitimise the use of "cribs," and he was so ultra-modern as to oppose compulsory Greek. There was, he held, "a point beyond which the claims of scholarship are not paramount," and that point was passed when work was an unwelcome burden. In 1869 he became master of the newly-formed modern side, and fought hard for keeping its intellectual level as high as that of the classical side. But it is not in his fine teaching power and his gift of moral inspiration that he is so strikingly modern as in the way in which, as a house-master, he set the example of sharing the life of the boys, by writing school songs, by playing football up to the age of sixty-five, and by personal interest in each individual boy.

[1] W. E. Bowen, *Edward Bowen*, pp. 371 *sqq*.

This changed relation to the boys is the leading feature too in the work of Almond. Almond may be thought to have pressed the claims of athletics too far and to have rated the claims of scholarship too low. His career was one long reaction against contemporary Scottish philistinism. "All work and no play" as a means of getting on in business, with a consequent atrophy of the finer sides of human nature, seemed to him to be the ideal of the Scottish middle-classes. In this spirit he had been brought up till, at Oxford, the river revived the dormant impulses in his nature. He became a fanatical adherent of the *mens sana in corpore sano*. "The laws of physical well-being are the laws of God[1]." The luxury of the rich and the rushing of the poor into towns were undermining the physique of the nation. Only games could save it. But, what was even more, games were the best corrective of a conventional morality which had its true roots in selfishness; they would restore spontaneity, forgetfulness of self, and the pristine joy of living. They would counteract the craving for luxury by revealing that true happiness comes from the unfettered activity of our own nature and not from external possessions. He justified the subordination of scholarship by the order in which he placed the aims of education—"character, physique, intelligence, manners," and last of all "information." He determined, not merely to modify convention by progressive changes, but to break with it altogether. "The English public schools seem to me bound not so much by red tape as by barbed wire[2]." His position as headmaster of a private school, which, when he bought it, contained only fourteen boys, enabled him to do as he liked. He hated rules. The right use of rules "is one of the chief points of the magnificent training which cricket affords for the greater game of life. Don't be a slave to rules. Use them as short and easy *memoria technicas* of the principles on which they depend and the ends which they aim at. But always be ready to refer your actions directly to first principles. All the

[1] R. J. Mackenzie, *Almond of Loretto*, p. 76.
[2] *Op. cit.* p. 146.

miserable mismanagement of red-tapeism springs from a servile adherence to rules, good in ordinary circumstances, destructive when these circumstances change. Rules are simply a nuisance, and armies and nations, schools and clubs, would be better rid of them altogether, if they are preferred to common sense[1]." He lived among his boys; and, as their numbers grew from fourteen to a hundred, he still continued to be more a foster-parent than a master. Hints and persuasions, mainly of course to the prefects but not exclusively, were the means by which he introduced, one at a time, those breaches of ordinary convention which became to the outside world the special marks of Loretto and its "mad" head. In 1862 came open windows, tweed knickers, and flannel ties, in 1864 the morning tub, in 1866 the discarding of coats, in 1868 the disuse of waistcoats and the practice of runs in wet weather, in 1869 the sacrifice of "grub" between meals (could there be a greater evidence of a headmaster's persuasive powers?), in 1870 the abandonment of hats, in 1872 "anatomical boots" and changing into flannels for games, in 1874 the habitual use of flannels. Some at least of these hygienic reforms have spread to the whole nation. Almond must really close the chapter; for the antithesis to committees and the special contributions of individual endeavour could go no further.

REFERENCES

G. R. Parkin, *Life and Letters of Edward Thring*, 1898, 2 vols.
Edward Thring, *Education and School*, 1864.
—— *Theory and Practice of Teaching*, 1883.
"The Times," *Educational Supplement*, Aug. 14, 1919 (Howson).
Board of Education, *Report of Consultative Committee on Examinations*.
Rev. the Hon. W. E. Bowen, *Edward Bowen, a Memoir*, 1902.
Robert Jameson Mackenzie, *Almond of Loretto*, 1905.

[1] *Op. cit.* pp. 21–22.

CHAPTER IX

REFORM OF FEMALE EDUCATION

"THE education of women was probably at its lowest ebb about half a century ago," wrote Miss Cobbe in her *Autobiography*, published in 1904. "It was at that period more pretentious than it had ever been before and infinitely more costly; and it was likewise more shallow and senseless than can easily be believed. To inspire young women with due gratitude for their present privileges, won for them by contemporaries, I can think of nothing better than to acquaint them with some of the features of school life in England in the days of their mothers. I say advisedly in the days of their mothers, for in those of their grand-mothers things were by no means equally bad. There was much less pretence and more genuine instruction as far as it extended[1]." She goes on to describe one of the numerous fashionable schools which clustered in Brighton. The cost was £500 a year! Work lasted from morning till night. During the one hour's walk, when alone the girls were in the open air, French, German, or Italian verbs were recited. During the rest of the time, they were reading or reciting in one of these languages amid the din of four pianos in various rooms, or practising accomplishments. On Saturday they were all hauled before the assembled mistresses and told what "cards" they had lost for any crime from lying to stooping, both of which were treated alike! Then girls at the top of the school along with the rest were made to stand with their faces to the wall. Everything was done for "society." Music, dancing, and calisthenics counted highest in the scale of subjects, writing and arithmetic lowest. The girls were only allowed to speak English after six in the evening. Learning thirteen pages of *Universal History* by heart was typical

[1] p. 58.

of the work in subjects which make a call on the intelligence[1].
Miss Sinclair's novel *Modern Accomplishments* (1837),
though its didactic pietism makes it hard reading in the
twentieth century, paints a similar picture of the private
education of girls of the higher classes. It looked solely
to marriage: it starved the intellect, and induced a self-
centred attitude of trivial frivolity. Even the accomplishments in which it took pride were unreal; the pupils could
neither paint, draw, play nor sing properly; nor had they the
least desire to pursue these occupations except for display.

The text-books tell the same tale. Girls were excluded
from classics and mathematics, the only subjects of which
the educational value had been in the least thought out,
and were brought up on catechisms and epitomes, designed to give an appearance of familiarity with names and
events which it would be considered a mark of ignorance
not to know, but leaving the pupils utterly unaware of
the facts which these names represented. F. D. Maurice,
writing in 1826 in the *Metropolitan Quarterly Magazine*,
says of such text-books: "In these volumes are contained
'all that is really important' in history, viz. the dates of
the events which it records—in biography, viz. the time
when the gentlemen and ladies it signalises came into the
world and left it—in chemistry, viz. its nomenclature—
in astronomy, viz. a list of the fixed stars. All such slight
and unimportant particulars as relate to the nature of
those events whereof the period is so accurately ascertained,
in what causes they originated, what was their influence
at the time and what their ultimate consequences—all
trivial fond records of the persons who had the excellent
fortune to be born at such a time and place and to die
at such another—all knowledge of the chemical principles
and processes which are indexed by those barbarous names
—all study relating to the connection of those fixed stars
with the other parts of the system to which they belong and
the laws by which that connection is regulated, and the

---

[1] Miss Gadesden, in Roberts's *Education in the Nineteenth Century*,
gives interesting extracts from a diary of a schoolgirl at the school
of Miss Mangnall, of *Questions* fame.

wonderful discoveries by which the fact of their existence
was established—all these are subjects for the intellect, and
therefore in the works we have referred to they are carefully
and prudently omitted." "The imagination is a terrible
object of the dread, the hatred, and hostility of the mistresses
of establishments and the governesses of young ladies."

Herbert Spencer tells us something of the physical side
of girls' education. He had both a boys' and a girls' school
close to his house; the boys were always playing, but of
the existence of the girls' school, so silent was it, he was
long unaware. "The garden affords no sign whatever of
any provision for juvenile recreation; but is entirely laid
out with prim grass-plots, gravel walks, shrubs and flowers,
after the usual suburban style. During five months we
have not once had our attention drawn to the premises by
a shout or a laugh. Occasionally girls may be observed
sauntering along the paths with lesson-books in their
hands, or else walking arm in arm." Sir John Forbes had
asserted in 1833 that the following was an average sample
of the timetable: in bed, 9 hours; in school, 9 hours; at
optional work, $3\frac{1}{2}$; meals, $1\frac{1}{2}$; a formal walk, 1. These
demure walks, two and two, were as a rule the only exercise
taken, though Spencer informs us that some schools had
recently adopted gymnastics, which he proceeds to condemn as an artificial and inadequate substitute for spontaneous exercise. "Why," he asks, "this astounding
difference?" And he answers his question by suggesting
that " to produce a robust physique is thought undesirable;
that rude health and abundant vigour are considered somewhat plebeian; that a certain delicacy, a strength not
competent to more than a mile or two's walk, an appetite
fastidious and easily satisfied, joined with that timidity
which commonly accompanies feebleness, are held more
lady-like." Here we probably have the explanation of
many of the features in a girl's education. Possibly this
feeling represents an unconscious first striving by women
for the emancipation of their sex. In the fashionable
society of Louis XIV's time the men escaped all hard
work, but the women were, according to the ideals of

Madame de Maintenon and her contemporaries, still expected to exercise a practical management of the household. The old tradition survived on the negative side,
looking askance on woman sharing the sports of their
brothers, but broke down on the positive side through the
growth of a greater feeling of equality between the sexes.
Idle men did not see why their wives should not be idle.
Sport and the military tradition of aristocratic society
prevented men from adopting the Chinese badge of social
rank—the growing of the finger nails to a portentous length
as a sign that the owner of these monstrosities could not
be earning his bread by the labour of his hands—but there
was nothing to prevent the growth of a corresponding
tradition among women.

Coming to the less expensive establishments, we have
a description by Miss Clough, in an article in *Macmillan's
Magazine* for October 1866 of the schools frequented by
the daughters of parents earning £100 to £300 a year. "The
position of the teachers is often very painful. They are
poor themselves, struggling for subsistence; the parents
are economical, and there is constant haggling between the
two. The schools are often small, and this increases the
difficulty. The children being of various ages, the labour
of bringing them forward, even in a few simple subjects,
is excessive. There may be, perhaps, some twelve or
twenty children, from the ages of six to sixteen, two
teachers at most, and the parents meanwhile objecting to
much expense with regard to books, and therefore com-
pelling cheap and small compendiums to be used." She
goes on to note the "few dry facts taught," the "monotony
which is very dulling to the intellect." "Habits of close
attention and accuracy are rarely acquired." The curriculum consisted of the "three R's," grammar, geography,
history, and a little French and music.

With regard to the "superior schools," she pronounces
them too small, while the small numbers in each class and
the multiplication of classes led to loss of power. The pupils
came ill prepared. They were expected to take too many
subjects, mostly modern languages and accomplishments.

Mathematics, Latin, English literature, and science were almost without exception extras and rarely taken up. Such schools were too expensive for parents of moderate means. Writing at a time when examinations were beginning to standardise the education of boys, she wishes for some similar standardisation of the education of girls.

Fortunately the pioneers of female education were not an aristocratic *intelligenzia*, but a hard-headed, hard-working, religiously-minded, and common-sense group of middle-class women. Female education owes a great debt to Maurice and Kingsley for determining who should be its first adherents. Women educators of the nineteenth century were stirred not so much by a sense of women's rights as of women's duties.

Through his sister, who was a governess, Maurice had been led to interest himself in the work of the Governesses' Benevolent Institution. "In the practical working of that society and in the knowledge of the circumstances of governesses which they so acquired the importance of some standard by which to test the qualification of ladies engaged in teaching had become apparent." Maurice had since 1840 been professor of English literature and modern history in King's College, London. In 1847 he induced his fellow professors to form a committee, of which Kingsley was a member, to conduct an examination. The results showed that it was desirable to provide some knowledge on which to examine before expecting the candidates to undergo an examination, and so Queen's College was founded. A college in the modern sense it hardly was; it stood midway between a college and an organisation for promoting extension lectures. Its students included women of mature years and mere schoolgirls; its instruction was given by means of lectures, and perhaps we should regard them to-day as "popular lectures." "For such a purpose no endowment could be got and Queen's College was a venture depending for its success on the unselfish devotion and energy of its founders[1]," the small band of King's College professors. It prospered sufficiently to be incorporated in

[1] Maurice, *Life of F. D. Maurice*, vol. 1, p. 468.

1853, and counted among those who attended its lectures the two pioneers of girls' public schools, Miss Buss and Miss Beale. As time went on, it did not keep pace with the progress in the ideas of women's education; for instance, it still preserved a man principal, whereas Bedford College, which was incorporated at a later date (1869), has developed into an essential part of London University. But the importance of Queen's as marking a new idea cannot be over-estimated.

The progress in secondary education has been found in this country to follow the progress of university education. The revival of the old universities preceded the reawakening of the public schools; the founding of the provincial colleges preceded the institution of county and municipal schools. So it was in the case of female education. The early attempts at higher education came before the first of the new type of girls' schools; and the spread of women's colleges was followed by the spread of girls' schools. The causes are easy to see. The colleges supply teachers for the schools; they furnish them with an aim; and they create a desire for education. It may be well therefore to trace the rise of colleges first.

Bedford College in London ranks next in seniority to Queen's among women's colleges. It started in an unpretentious manner when in 1847 Mrs Reid established classes in her own house; it proceeded to take a more organised shape under a Board and Council of Management, and to obtain the help, like Queen's, of a number of distinguished male lecturers, and, after Mrs Reid's death, it obtained formal recognition in 1869 by a charter of incorporation. When women's colleges were first started there was no idea of women becoming candidates for university degrees and consequently no motive for placing them in university towns. But, though no such thought was in the mind of Mrs Reid, Bedford College was in fact situated in the seat of a nominal university, and its nominal character proved an advantage. London University, being merely an examining board, could admit women to degrees without raising any of the problems of co-education which were presented in the case of a teaching university; and, when this was done, Bedford stood in the same relation to the

University as King's and University Colleges. And, when the University was finally reorganised and became a real teaching institution, Bedford was able to take rank as a "school of the university in the faculties of Arts and Science."

But we are anticipating. The Schools Inquiry Commission marked an epoch of great importance in women's education. It suggested that girls' foundation schools would soon become a reality, and the leaders in the movement for female education saw the necessity of being prepared with women teachers and women's colleges to which the pupils of these schools should proceed. It was at this moment (1867) that Miss Emily Davies developed her scheme for founding a college "designed to hold in relation to girls' schools and home teaching a position analogous to that occupied by the universities towards the public schools for boys." It began in 1869 with a small house for six students at Hitchin. The choice of its abode was deliberately designed as a taking-off place for Cambridge. The prospectus distinctly stated: "The Council shall use such efforts as from time to time they may think most expedient and effectual to obtain for the students of the College admission to the examinations for the degrees of the University of Cambridge, and generally to place the College in connection with the University." In those days subscriptions for women's education were very hard to obtain; but in 1873 a nearer approach to Cambridge was effected and the College was transferred to Girton. Here again the peculiar system of English universities by which the College teaches and the university examines made the transition easier. Girton came within two miles of Cambridge but not into the town. At this distance the dons who favoured the scheme could give it their assistance and the University could not ignore its existence; but Mrs Grundy was satisfied. Whether the sacrifice of cab fares on Mrs Grundy's altar commends itself to the authorities of Girton nowadays is a different matter.

But already the sacred space within the statutory distance from Great St Mary's had been invaded. Curi-

ously, however, the founders of Newnham intended that
women should be educated *in* Cambridge, but should not
enter for the university examinations. Still, when Girton
had stormed the examination-rooms and Newnham the
residential area, they proceeded to share the spoils.
Newnham candidates were sent in for the triposes and the
university *pomoerium* was extended to take in Girton.

Miss Clough, who first presided over Newnham, is an
example of the kind of women who first realised the need
of women's education and forwarded it, not from any
desire of display, but from a sense of duty. Long ago in
1837 she had taught in the Welsh National School in
Liverpool, where she had neither instruction nor precedent
to guide her but found out her own ways of teaching by
the light of common-sense; she lived quietly with her
brother Arthur the poet; and sometimes she visited elementary schools elsewhere to get experience. "It is from
a sense of duty," she wrote, "that very many first enter
on this work [of educating the poor], but I would rather
speak of the great benefits we may ourselves derive from
this employment, of the many holy thoughts and aspirations after self-improvement that are awakened by engaging
in the instruction of others. Then it is, perhaps, that we
first learn to love our native land and to desire heartily
that its people may grow up, not a curse or a shame to it,
but rather a blessing and a glory. Our family ties, our
friendships hardly teach us this, but it is when we are
thrown upon the simple connection or bond of being fellow-
countrypeople, of speaking the same mother-tongue and
living in the same place, that we become truly national."
One of the marked features of her work at Liverpool was
the interest which she continued to display in her pupils
after they had left school. In 1852 she left Liverpool for
Ambleside and started a school in which the future
Mrs Humphry Ward was one of her pupils. It developed
as a school for the daughters of small tradespeople and
farmers—a type of school of which, as we have seen, far
too few existed—and furnished the experience which led
to the writing of the article in *Macmillan's Magazine* in

1866 from which we quoted earlier in the chapter. In the highest work of a schoolmistress, her influence over her pupils and the effect she had on their characters, her innate qualities made her most powerful; but, owing to her lack of training, she could never be "methodical," and her school might not have commended itself to the inspector of those days, to whom the anise and cummin were more than the weightier matters of the law. In 1861 her brother Arthur died, and in the following year she removed to Combe Hurst near Wimbledon, where she became acquainted with Miss Emily Davies, Miss Bostock, and Miss Buss, and came into the full centre of the movement for women's education.

In 1856 a woman candidate had presented herself for the London medical diploma and had been refused admission. In 1862 the same thing happened when a woman wished to sit for the matriculation examination. A proposal to admit women to matriculation was rejected in Convocation by the casting vote of the Chancellor, Earl Granville. The promoters of the movement now organised themselves. In 1863 they secured that girls should be allowed unofficially to take the Cambridge Local papers; in 1865 the practice was given an official trial for three years and at the end of that period was accepted permanently. In 1867 Miss Clough gave the evidence before the Schools Inquiry Commission which formed the basis of her article in *Macmillan*. One of her proposals was the establishment of courses of lectures in big towns which could be attended by the more advanced pupils in girls' schools. A committee for organising such lectures was set up and various prominent men came forward to give them. This was virtually the start of the University Extension system, which was thus given practical shape by women. In its turn this movement gave rise to the demand for a higher examination for women, and in 1869 the Cambridge Higher Local Examination was instituted. Out of the need of preparing women for this examination Newnham developed. Henry Sidgwick, professor of moral philosophy at Cambridge, started lectures, and among the distinguished lecturers were Maurice on history, Skeat on English, Mayor on

Latin, and Marshall on political economy. In order to allow students who were not natives of Cambridge to attend these lectures, Sidgwick took a house in Regent Street on his own responsibility and invited Miss Clough to act as its head. Beginning with five students in 1871, it moved the following year to Merton Hall, "a rambling old house buried among apple trees in a large garden on the edge of the town." In 1879 it was decided to build and the older portions of the present Newnham College were erected.

Girton and Newnham at first worked on somewhat different lines. Girton objected to separate examinations for women and demanded that they should be allowed to enter for the same examinations as men. Whether or no this is educationally the sounder plan, it had obvious advantages as a matter of policy. Men's examinations had already an established reputation, and, if women could gain the same honours as men in them, it was easily understood by the outside public for what those honours stood, and the suspicion that women's examinations were not only different in kind but inferior in quality was avoided. In 1870 Girton obtained the informal use of the papers in the Previous Examination and in 1873 of the tripos papers, and was thus able to say that its students had fulfilled all the requirements for degrees demanded of men. In 1881 the university gave a formal recognition of this arrangement. But between 1873 and 1881 much else had happened; in 1873 twenty-two out of thirty-four professors formally opened their lectures to women, and in 1879 they were admitted to college lectures; in 1878 London University obtained a supplemental charter by which it was empowered to admit women to degrees on the same terms as men. In 1880 it so happened that a new university, Victoria, was founded on the federal principle, and its charter provided for giving degrees to women, though the conditions were left to its constituent colleges. The next university founded, that of Wales, from the first admitted the two sexes on an absolute equality; and all later foundations have followed the same precedent, while the new colleges and universities already existing have fallen into line. The approximation of Newnham to Girton and the foundation of the women's colleges at Oxford, of which the first two, Somerville and Lady Margaret, date from 1881, completes the tale of developments in the university education of women. It was not till after the War that Oxford opened its degrees to women and Cambridge in the present year has again refused. Since 1887, when the first proposal to this effect was made at Cambridge, it has been discussed several times at both universities; but till the War was always rejected by the votes of non-residents in Senate and Convocation. Undergraduate prejudice combined with the conservatism of their parents united to produce this result; and when the country parson had revisited the scenes of his youth, replenished the empty purse of his offspring, and registered his vote against awarding to a woman who has taken a first class in the tripos the letters which reward his own third in the special, his son united with the rest of his college in signalising the success of their efforts by a bonfire. The argument most frequently used at these debates was that the M.A. degree conveyed the right of having a final voice in university legislation; but, in view of the way in which this right has been used, it is more than probable that it will be one of the first abuses to which the recently appointed Commission will devote its attention.

Women's colleges in their earlier days were not quite what they are now. Perhaps undue imitation of men, not because men's pursuits would naturally be sought for their own sake but because they are men's pursuits, is now a little too prevalent. It is a passing phase, which will disappear when woman's position has become well established and no novelty. In the modern universities we have already reached the stage when, if a woman's name is the only one in the list of first classes in any subject, there is no more demonstration of surprise in the newspapers than if it had been a man's. Examiners may pass "A. Smith" without knowing whether the "A." stands for Alfred or for Anne. But in 1880 the head of a woman's college was necessarily in a state of constant alarm lest any of her *protégées* should give the enemy the least occasion to blaspheme. A male undergraduate, whirling a rattle on the towpath, is of course deemed to be only acting according to his kind; but a burst of laughter coming through the windows of Regent Street might have postponed the success of the cause for a decade. In fact her biographer thinks it fortunate, in the days when the "capable woman" was suspected, that Miss Clough "did not dress well or walk well, and had a certain timidity and irresoluteness"; that "there was nothing of the direct, vigorous and masterful about her which young people and indeed crude people of any sort mistake for strength." "It sounds rather a fantastic comparison, but I often think her sayings were like the work of the early painters, all the more effective because the artist has not yet subdued his medium; sheer force of character and feeling has risen over the difficulties." And, if her rule was such that one of the students suggested that Newnham should take as its crest Mrs Grundy rampant and two students couchant, yet she goes on to suggest that "in nineteen cases she was troubled for nothing, but in the twentieth she may have avoided a disaster."

We now return to an earlier period and describe the rise of secondary schools for girls. Two protagonists stand out in this connection, Dorothea Beale and Frances Mary Buss, and round their lives the events of the movement may be clustered.

Miss Beale was born in 1831. Fortunately ill-health compelled her to leave school at thirteen—she herself is responsible for the word "fortunately"—and in a cultured house she had opportunities for omnivorous reading such as a clever boy of the time, much more a clever girl, might envy. It was no idle browsing, but solid fare such as first-rate historians, Euclid, science, reviews, biography. At sixteen she went for a year to a school for English girls in Paris—to be driven home by the Revolution of 1848. Then she attended the newly founded Queen's College and later took an active part in the teaching of that institution. In time she became dissatisfied with its working and closed her connection with it in 1856. For a year she was on the staff of the School for Clergymen's Daughters, an evangelical foundation, in which she was expected to teach Scripture, arithmetic, mathematics, ancient and modern history, geography, English, French, German, Latin and Italian. The result was to make her miserable for a year, which fortunately did no lasting harm, and to make her feel the need of a reform in girls' education, which has done lasting good. Of course she left at the close of the year; if she had been the woman to stand such a curriculum, she would not have been the woman to make a success of the College at Cheltenham.

Cheltenham Ladies' College had been founded in 1853 to educate the sisters of the boys whose parents flocked to Cheltenham to send them to the boy's College. Its first few years were not too prosperous and in 1858 a new headmistress was sought. It was almost an accident which made Miss Beale think of applying, and quite an accident which led the committee to appoint her. Indeed they had hardly done so before they began to repent; for Cheltenham was the favourite abode of the strictest sect of the Evangelicals—not the Evangelicals of our days, but the old-fashioned Calvinists to whom the orthodox view of predestination was more precious than all the promises of the Gospel. It was rumoured that Miss Beale was High Church, and a kind of inquisition into her beliefs was set up. Of course Miss Beale was not High Church, but she was a deeply religious woman who felt her religion to be so close a personal communion with God that she would not allow it to be twisted into the procrustean bed of cold intellectual formalism. Such a religion the committee did not understand, but they came to the conclusion that it was hardly of a kind to warrant the cancelling of an appointment already made. So they practically told her not to talk too much about it, and Miss Beale was not the kind of person who would want to parade her religion in public. So she commenced work.

We must not think of her in those days as the dictator of a female Eton and Trinity rolled into one, or as the national institution which she subsequently became. She had a long and strenuous struggle before success became assured. The idea with which she started was not to make girls' education a copy of boys'. She was not preparing for the university; she had not her eye on external examinations. She was guided entirely by what she thought girls needed; but she thought they needed something equally substantial, though not identical, with what was needed by boys. She began by pruning "accomplishments," though she reintroduced the teaching of the piano in spite of the opinion of her Council concerning "the singular and extraordinary notion that dexterity of fingering on a single instrument is *the* most important part of female education," to which notion they are inclined to attribute "the acknowledged deficiency of many of the fairer sex in logical qualities and reasoning powers." She laid great stress on English history—not taught after the manner satirised by F. D. Maurice; and hoped to make of German the equivalent of what Latin was in boys' schools. She dare not introduce Euclid at first; "had I done so, it might have been the death of the College." Though the pupils were not sent in for public examinations, an examiner from Oxford or Cambridge visited the College annually. By 1864 the period of uncertainty was over; there were a hundred and thirty pupils, and a boarding-house was opened to retain girls whose parents were leaving the town.

In this year Miss Beale resorted to a change as regards the hours, which had hitherto been arranged on the plan usual in boys' schools. She now experimented with a morning lasting from nine till one o'clock, broken by a half hour's interval, keeping the afternoons for individual music lessons and such extras. The plan was adopted by Miss Buss in the following year and became the standard allotment of hours with the schools of the Girls' Public Day School Company.

The Schools Inquiry Commission was such a landmark in girls' secondary education that we will break off the account of Miss Beale to trace the career of Miss Buss up to that event. She was four years older than Miss Beale; like her was educated at an absurd school of the old type and like her made up for it by private reading. Her mother had been forced through her husband's death to start a school; and Miss Buss began to teach at the early age of fourteen. She again reproduces Miss Beale's career by going to Queen's College, but she found her vocation earlier. With the help of the Rev. David Laing she gave a semi-public character to the family school in 1850, and, as her biographer Miss Ridley puts it, speedily ousted *Child's Guide* and *Mangnall's Questions* and the idea that even such mild gymnastics as jumping over a stick held a few inches from the ground was unladylike.

We have now reached the Commission. Its terms of reference contained no indication that it was intended to deal with girls' education; its framers so completely forgot girls that they forgot to exclude them. The promoters of girls' education saw their opportunity and petitioned the Commissioners to investigate the subject, and the Commissioners consented. Miss Buss and Miss Emily Davies were invited to give evidence in 1865 and Miss Beale in April 1866. Miss Beale was doubtful if girls could go so far as boys, at any rate in subjects like higher mathematics, and she was against an over-assimilation of the education of girls to that of boys on another ground, that the education of boys itself was largely based on tradition and might soon be modified. On the former point Miss Davies was more confident. She had for two years been acting as hon. secretary for the girls' side of the Cambridge Local Examinations during the period in which they had been used for the examination of girls informally and experimentally, and she was convinced of the identity of standard.

The Commissioners' Report drew public attention to what had hitherto been within the interest and knowledge of the few. "Want of thoroughness and foundation; slovenliness and showy superficiality; inattention to rudiments; undue time given to accomplishments, and these not taught intelligently or in any scientific manner; want of organisation—these may sufficiently indicate the character of the complaints received." By his work in making himself responsible for the part of the Commission's enquiry which dealt with the education of girls, Mr James Bryce did yeoman service to the cause. But women too had suggestions and proposals. Miss Clough was for establishing a university board for female education, a system of central day schools with which private schools should be associated for certain subjects and the system of extension lectures in large towns which we have already seen was shortly afterwards started. To a book of essays[1] published in 1869 Miss Wolstenholme contributed a well thought out discussion of the needs of women's education, entitled "The Education of Girls, its present and future," which began with the remarkable recognition that we are the worst educated nation in Europe. The upper classes sacrifice everything to accomplishments, and of true learning they say, "It will not help her to get married." The lower middle classes neglect education, because it has no pecuniary value: "we cannot appraise the value of a cultivated mind; presumably therefore it has no value." Teachers are not themselves well taught, and they do not know how to teach others. It is noticeable that Miss Wolstenholme takes for granted the need of a professional training of teachers as much as the need for their improved general education—this was certainly not an imitation of masculine education! Women must master the secrets of combination and co-operation; they must do away with the superstition that one person can teach everything (and everything included a great deal if the School for Clergymen's Daughters was a typical example.) External examinations are a necessity if the mass of worthless schools are to be brought into line. The replacement of governesses by schools is necessary if effort is to be used to the best advantage. Governesses' work "means giving an infinitesimal fragment of time and a divided and a distracted attention to each of the pupils and subjects in turn." Small schools involve these evils almost more than does private instruction; therefore schools must be big. "We wonder much how many schoolmistresses ever framed

[1] *Women's Work and Women's Culture*, edited by Josephine E. Butler, 1869.

a consistent course of study which should stretch over six years. We wonder still more how many have successfully carried it out in the case of even one pupil." In a word organisation is needed. But to the most obvious way of securing large schools, by copying the boarding-school system of boys, she is opposed. "Perhaps the best that can be said of them is that the inherent evils may by skilful teachers be reduced to a minimum; but it can never be considered very desirable to bring together great numbers of young people and throw them into the intimacy of an English boarding-school, without far more careful oversight than it is easy to secure, whilst any approach to the system of perpetual espionage would be at once hateful to our English notions and, as we believe, fatally mischievous to both teachers and pupils." Hence there is needed in every town a "High School"—a term soon destined to become familiar—and possibly also a "secondary school" under municipal or government control which would serve as a model to the private schools for which there would still be abundant room. For country districts she suggests schools which did not themselves take in boarders but licensed small boarding-houses under the charge of married ladies. She supports mixed schools where funds do not allow of separate boys' and girls' schools. "It is not proposed to argue that a system of mixed education would be of unmixed advantage; it is quite sufficient to show that the balance of advantage is in its favour." Finally more women's colleges of the Hitchin type are required and education must be brought to people's doors by extension lectures. "Equality of education must precede equality of industrial training"; and it is not only industrial training for which education is needed; it is wanted no less for the home, where it will increase the influence of mothers and will further the rational intercourse of husbands and wives.

We ask the reader to pardon us for quoting from this essay at so much greater length than from the report of the Commission; but it is important to know what women thought about women's education without seeing it after it has been refracted through the minds of men. For, however much men helped by collecting funds, by giving lectures, and by sharing in the business management, it was women who determined what women's education was to be, and it largely worked out along the lines of Miss Wolstenholme's essay, which may therefore be taken as fairly representative of women's views.

The Endowed Schools Act did something directly for girls' education. "In framing schemes under this Act, provision shall be made as far as conveniently may be for extending to girls the benefits of endowments." To ensure that the Commissioners appointed under the Act carried out this part of their instructions an Association was formed "for Promoting the Application of Endowments to the Education of Women." Schemes were gradually made, and, wherever the funds were not exhausted by the boys' schools, girls' schools were set up. The first were four founded out of the surplus funds of King Edward's School, Birmingham, which were at once filled. These were all of the second grade, but in the reorganisation of the wealthy Bedford foundation first and second grade girls' schools were set up. Both these were among the eight wealthiest foundations with regard to which the Schools Inquiry Commission had presented separate reports; among the other schools in this list, Dulwich, St Olaves, Tonbridge and Monmouth were made to set up girls' schools, and in 1898 Miss Zimmern calculated that there were over eighty endowed girls' schools.

But the process of securing the transfer of endowments was slow and in the meantime private endeavour had to step in. Naturally it is with schools of the first grade that private endeavour is most effective. In 1871 Mrs Grey formed a National Union for the education of women which in the following year established the Girls' Public Day School Company. In five years fourteen schools were founded and many more have been since added. The importance of the work does not end here, since their old girls have become mistresses all over the country and impressed the methods of these schools on many others which are unconnected with the Company. On the whole it may be said that, as regards curriculum, the wish to demonstrate the intellectual equality of the sexes, and for this purpose to prepare girls for the same school examinations and the same university courses as boys, has led to an acceptance of the usual boys' curriculum; but that as regards organisation and method, women have struck out on new lines. In the first place they have thrown the weight of social prestige on the side of day schools. This is of far-reaching importance; it means, apart from the educational ideal of keeping school and home in touch, the possibility that every town can develop a really fine school, unhampered by a crushing competition with fashionable boarding-schools which draw away the best pupils from every locality. This again means that parents of moderate means have access to the very best education possible. Hours are different. Discipline is different; perhaps more strict, but more secured by personal influence. Classrooms are, or were till recently, brighter. A working spirit has always prevailed. There has always been a great friendliness between teachers and taught. The average schoolmistress thinks more about methods than the average schoolmaster. She is less conservative and more aware of new ideas. She knows more of other types of education beside that in which she is herself occupied. Literature, art and other cultural subjects are taught with more genuine enthusiasm and welcomed with less regard to their examination value. The school is a more civilising influence. There is no tradition from the ages of barbarism to wear down. Headmistresses looked to what girls naturally were; headmasters have looked to what boys after a hundred years' tradition of idleness, bullying, housing in hovels, and worship of physical strength, had become. It is lamentable to think how the advantages of education are lost by a girl in a mixed school. The docility of girls makes them easy victims to the examination grind. A headmaster, brought up in the tradition—which he probably does not acknowledge even to himself—that, in order to get the right amount of work done, you must set twice as much as you want, to allow for the waste of boys' "ca' canny" methods—for schoolboys were the real authors of modern trade union methods, and public schoolboys can still give points to the miners—institutes for his conscientious girl pupils a veritable Egyptian bondage, harms their health, crushes their vitality, destroys their interests, and forces them *discendi causa doctrinae perdere causas*.

Miss Buss's school was to a large extent the model of the "High Schools," as the schools of the Company are commonly called. In order that it might thoroughly conform to her ideal, she now took the extraordinarily self-sacrificing step of turning it into a trust, "thus in addition to the loss of personal freedom risking a present certainty and the prospect of future affluence, to accept for the next three years a greatly diminished income with doubled or trebled work; giving up at the same time assured honour and widespread reputation for misunderstanding, suffering, and disappointment[1]." After such an example the cause of private schools against public schools was lost. Under the new scheme there were to be two schools, the North London Collegiate School in Camden Street of the first grade and the Camden School of the second. Subscriptions came in slowly; but £20,000 from the Platt Charity could be assigned to the schools now they were on a public footing; the Clothworkers Company also came to their assistance; and the new scheme finally took effect in 1879. As one of her obituary notices put it:—"A personality of singular charm and of what the slang of the day calls 'magnetism,' wholly without pedantry or self-consciousness, persuaded Royal Commissioners, City Companies, Lord Mayors and Royal Princesses, physicians and even universities, that women might be thoroughly educated without any danger to themselves or to the State."

Miss Buss was indeed a great personality, and some of the chief features which are brought out in Miss Ridley's biography may be noted. Her attitude to her pupils was motherly, at a time when "prunes and prisms" were the tradition. She needed to punish little; she could talk any

[1] A. E. Ridley, *Frances Mary Buss*, p. 93.

pupil into a determination to be reasonable for the future; henceforth in that pupil's case she might have to deal with faults of carelessness and thoughtlessness but not with faults of wilfulness. She remembered every pupil years afterwards. She was generous in helping girls in money difficulties and her generosity to the school passes words. She bore patiently periods of waiting, hopes, fears, and suspense. She won the affections of her staff. All her life through she was able to absorb new ideas.

As regards her policy, she was opposed to boarding-schools, and gave up her boarding-house as soon as she could, thus sacrificing a source of deep interest to her principles, as she sacrificed her pecuniary interests. She greatly believed in the influence of the school buildings and in absolute orderliness and tidiness. She could smile at her own enthusiasm in this matter, as when she said "I spend my life in picking up pins." On this feature of girls' schools which, perhaps partly through her influence, has become universal, the mere man does not pretend to pass judgment. Cloak-room and corridor rules, which seem to be to headmistresses the mark of a standing or a falling school, would provoke a mutiny among boys. But all will agree that when orderliness passes into hygiene, it ceases to be a fetish. She made her pupils come to school dry. "It is an amusing symptom of the hygienic influence of the North London School that, in my quest for properly shaped shoes, I find it best to fall back on the neighbourhood of Camden Road[1]." She virtually had a private system of medical inspection and records in her school long before anyone dreamt of the Medical Inspection Act. On the results she determined what calisthenics each girl needed. She wished headmistresses to have the same independence from their governing bodies as headmasters. School-masters will perhaps like to know what is the female counterpart of Thring's tact in reinforcing discipline by a sense of humour. Thring had just introduced tidy desks and was starting what to the boys must have appeared an autocratic and cranky attack on a cherished privilege which

[1] *Op. cit.* p. 222.

was supported by the prescriptive right of centuries—he had forbidden them to cut their names on them! No boy could believe he really meant it. No boy could at least resist the temptation to determine the point by the scientific method of experiment, even at the risk of a flogging. The first two criminals were haled before Thring. He might have secured his desks by flogging the boys; but that was not the method of a disciplinary artist. He took them to the woodwork room and made them carve their names on the hardest piece of wood which it contained. It took them the afternoon. Miss Buss too had the artistic instinct which declines the use of the sledge-hammer when a finer weapon will do the work. Our mothers know that fainting-fits were in their younger days the chief of the minor trials of governesses. We leave Miss Ridley to tell the tale. She ordered the "very coldest water that could be procured." "There is no sort of danger in this kind of attack, and the most certain cure is a sudden dash of very cold water in the face." The water was on its way. "Ah! I feel better now, thank you!" "If you feel a little faintness coming on, just retire to your own room without saying anything about it. Shut your door, open all the windows and lie down quietly. You will soon find yourself well again."

Her theory of intellectual education for women was thus summed up: "It may be—I am much disposed to think it is—that intellectual training effects greater moral improvement in women than it does in men because a woman's faults of character, on an average, turn more on irrationality and lack of nerve control, while the man's faults centre in his profounder self-absorption and slower sympathies." Educational theorists have not ceased arguing whether the curriculum suitable for a pupil is that which develops his strong points or that which counter-acts his weak points. Probably a different answer should be given according as we are considering efficiency or personality. If you are thinking of a person's capacity to do things, it will, by the law of diminishing returns, pay to teach him what he can learn easily. But efficiency in this narrower sense may be completely cancelled by faults of temperament which have not been checked by the formation of counter-habits. A particular kind of work which gives a low measure of efficiency may be of supreme value as a corrective. To cure a man of consumption does not directly train the muscles which he will use as a navvy; but, unless you cure his consumption, he has no chance of becoming a good navvy. Hence Miss Buss attached considerable importance to Science, a subject which has no aesthetic content, though French and history were her own specialities, and the North London School became famous for its scientific results.

Meanwhile the Cheltenham College continued to make great strides. Miss Beale, though reluctantly, realised the practical necessity of sending her girls in for external examinations. Her first experience of the "locals" had brought out a weakness in the mathematics of the school, which, once detected, was soon rectified. Pupils began to pass the London Matriculation examination, and complaints of overwork began to be heard. Parents had to be taught that overwork too often meant that school work was expected to be an extra to a full round of social engagements. But Miss Beale's faith in day-schools was not shaken, and parents were gradually trained to see the matter in its true light. In 1875 new buildings were undertaken, the college having reached three hundred, and in 1882 further extension was necessary. In 1875 too the governing body was reorganised in such a way as to recognise the fact that the college was a national and not merely a local institution. It started merely as a school, but it developed into something which has no counterpart in boys' education in modern times. Its nearest parallel is the Renaissance ideal of an institution which should be school and university in one. At the one end it has its Kindergarten, at the other its students working for the Higher Locals and London degrees. It is now organised, under the supreme control of the Principal, into a series of departments under responsible heads. The college course for girls over sixteen is preceded by the work of its secondary school department from twelve to sixteen and that again by the work of its preparatory and Kindergarten departments. It is a miniature educational system in itself. Many of its pupils of course pass on to the older universities, and a special hall at Oxford, St Hilda's, has been built for them; but in itself it offers a full course for the London degrees. Though Miss Beale was a believer in day-schools, boarding-houses grew up, as was inevitable in the case of an institution unique in the country. With its five hundred pupils it has almost eclipsed the boys' college.

The building up of this great institution was more completely the work of one individual than any educational development of which we can think in the nineteenth century, save possibly Dr Barnardo's Homes. Miss Beale had a good eye for form mistresses, but hers was the controlling spirit. Organisation with her, as with every great headmaster or headmistress, did not mean what it often means in a government department, sitting in an office and devising general rules which approximate to the right way of dealing with all cases but which exactly fit none. The girls at the top of the school she knew intimately, and she strove to know all. She taught and did not merely direct teaching. Little energy was frittered away in red tape. She inspired her pupils with the devotion, not unmixed with awe, commonly felt only for a sovereign. But her internal life was one of prayer and meditation. She was like the mediaeval monarch who wore a hair shirt under his royal robes. In her teaching the class caught her enthusiasm for the subject-matter, whether it were literature or the joy of intellectual discovery in mathematics. Her literature lessons were her chosen vehicles of revealing her views on life and conduct. "Miss Beale might be unacademic to a fault in these lectures, but she had that power of inspiration which made every poem she prized, every character she admired, live immortally for those who heard her speak of them. The actual reading—specially of poetry—was a delight to both teacher and hearers. Miss Beale had a strong dramatic instinct, a keen enjoyment of poetry and the right use of words. She had also a wonderful voice, which she managed well, and though always quiet and restrained in manner carried her audience with her unweariedly[1]." Her Scripture lessons were to her the event of the week and she reserved Friday evenings entirely to their preparation. By the time Miss Beale and Miss Buss died, the public had come to realise that a great headmistress should be treated with the same respect as a great headmaster. Arnold had his bitter opponents, Thring his critics; but no one would have dreamt of regarding either as a fitting object of mild witticisms. In the case of great headmistresses familiarity does not breed contempt; the smiles were only on the faces of those who had never met them, and those who knew them best respected them most.

By 1881 Miss Buss was able to write to Mrs Grey: "There is now no such thing as a 'woman's education question' apart from that of education generally; and the real question which has still to be fought for many a long year, I fear, is one as old as education itself: how is the child of either sex to be trained to the measure of the stature of the perfect human being." Suffice it therefore to say that the Act of 1902 spread girls' education as widely as it did boys', and that the Act of 1918 will give them the same advantages as boys in respect of continuation and central schools, which, though now classed as elementary, fulfil the functions which the Schools Inquiry Commission vainly tried to get performed in their own day by what they described as the sadly deficient third grade of secondary schools.

In one respect, however, we do not think that the question of the sexes as regards education has been solved. We refer to the problem of co-education. Co-education is vigorously at work in all grades of education. At the infant or Kindergarten stage there is nothing else and no one would probably want anything else. In elementary schools up to the age of twelve, provided the children come from good homes, the system seems to work well. The absence of home-work prevents the danger of over-pressure; and the mistresses seem to play a relatively more important part than in mixed secondary schools. But even

[1] Elizabeth Raikes, *Dorothea Beale of Cheltenham*, p. 262.

here it might be argued that too often the size of classes
reduces personal influence to a minimum and that this is
the reason why it makes so little difference which sex
appears to be influencing it. Again at the other end it
seems acceptable at the university stage. But it must be
remembered that at Oxford and Cambridge and to some
extent in London, the colleges, which are the real teaching
organisations, are not mixed, though the university is,
and that everywhere the lectures are not the supreme
educational instrument which the students sometimes
imagine them to be. Some sort of tutorial system exists
whereby there is closer contact of mind with mind between
male tutor and male student and female tutor and female
student. But at the age between twelve and eighteen
experience throws much doubt on the merits of co-education. Ideals are then forming, and the ideals of the two
sexes are quite different. No man can be a good schoolmaster unless he "understands boys"; every man admits
that. No woman can be a good schoolmistress unless she
understands girls: we suppose every woman would admit
that. But does any man claim that he "understands
girls?" He largely understands boys because he has been
a boy and because he still has something of the boy in him;
we surely mean more by the phrase than when we say that
a man understands dogs or horses. Unless we believe in
transmigration, we know that he has never been a girl.
With regard to young children of either sex, Nature seems
to have implanted in women a maternal intuition which
enables them to understand them. Men seem not to have
this intuition, nor do women as far as the adolescent boy
is concerned. And, what is equally important, girls cannot
find in masters the friends they find in mistresses. A
"just beast" is no good for girls. "Old Smith" would be
quite happy if his boys voted him "a decent old sort";
but girls incline to hero worship. Masters who are of an
age and temperament to make good "elder brothers" of
their boys can stand in no known relation to their girl
pupils. Some of the schools of the Society of Friends appear
to work the system with perfect success, but we imagine

it is done by a wonderful power of mutual delegation of functions between masters and mistresses rendered possible by the strong corporate solidarity of such a community. The early Christians could doubtless have run a mixed school with success in the catacombs. Strange as it may seem, it is easier in a boarding-school than in a day-school because masters and mistresses are compelled to see more of one another. In a day-school it seems to tend to emphasise the idea that the relation between teacher and pupil is limited to the class-room. The girls seem to suffer far more than the boys. The head is practically always a man. He makes it a boys' school to which girls are also admitted. Boys in their teens are a barbaric race; they glory in physical strength; they lack imagination and sympathy; and they despise what they do not understand. Little boys and little girls are conscious of no great difference in instincts and tastes. University men and women are conscious of a difference and feel bound to respect it. During the intervening years boys half-unconsciously exercise a forceful mastery over girls. The girls cannot assert themselves; and they lose the power of self-government which their sisters in girls' schools learn as much as boys. Later on, perhaps, they come to talk about the equality of the sexes, but they are no longer equal, because the boys have stolen a march on them.

Having thus traced the growth of female education, we must ask the question, What has been the result? Slight passing disadvantages, perhaps; but the suffragettes who have arisen as the bye-product of the emancipation of a sex count for little against the bolshevists who have arisen as the bye-product of the emancipation of a class. Apart from this transient inconvenience, who can doubt the gain? The empty-headed, silly woman could find no interest but frivolity; she could not be a solid factor in the bringing up either of her sons or of her daughters; she was powerless to influence her husband; if she remained unmarried or became a widow, she could not support herself; her peculiar gifts were lost to the State. Society is built up by that which every part supplieth; legislation needs women's sympathy as well as men's sense of justice; administrations should be human as well as businesslike; patience is wanted as well as driving-power. In the war educated women showed more of the Spartan mother than did the older type. They did not feel less, but they saw further.

The growth of girls' education has not been without its influence on that of boys. There being no tradition, girls' education had to be thought out from first principles. The true basis of curricula had to be examined, and it is possible that girls' schools have strengthened the fight against allowing the teaching of literature to be degraded into a memorising of notes, and the teaching of music and art into a mechanical drill in technique. Women have discovered that girls at school are not totally different beings from girls at home, and the methods of discipline and influence in the one are not based on entirely different principles from those adopted in the other. The traditional discipline of boys could not bear a sudden transition; but there is a growing recognition that the boy is not all hobbledehoy, though maybe he camouflages other elements in his nature in deference to the traditions of his school, and only reveals that he cares for things of the mind and taste when he goes up to college. In one particular the opinion of women has throughout been diametrically opposed to that of men. Women have always believed in the professional training of teachers. Miss Wolstenholme regards training and the degree as reforms to be pressed for equally. Miss Clough attended the lectures on teaching at Queen's. The Maria Grey Training College founded in 1877 commemorates Mrs Grey's services to education. Miss Buss helped in the establishment of training classes by the College of Preceptors in 1873, the first attempt of the kind in secondary education, and she began the agitation in 1885 which led to the foundation of the Women's Training College at Cambridge. "Could anything be done," she asked, "to avert this growing danger that the teaching profession should fall into the two classes of those who are highly educated and not trained and of those who are trained but not highly educated?" Miss Beale established a training department as an important section of the work at Cheltenham.

Should any male reader be tempted to think that, in suggesting that boys' education has ever learned or could ever learn anything from that of girls, we are taking a purely theoretic standpoint, we will ask him to consider whether Thring is not a proof to the contrary. Thring is a type of the forceful dominating headmaster who understood and governed boys: but Thring was an enthusiast in the cause of women's education, and it is remarkable that the reforms which he effected in boys' education are just on those points where girls' education has pursued a different path from that which had been traditional in the case of boys—the importance of the average pupil, the influence of a beautiful and comfortable environment, the need of getting down to the real human being in boys and piercing through the defensive crust of convention, the use of art, literature, and music as educational instruments, and the importance of thinking out new methods and not accepting traditions on trust.

REFERENCES

Alice Zimmern, *The Renaissance of Girls' Education*, 1898.

Frances Power Cobbe, *Life of, as told by herself*, 1904.

F. Maurice, *Life of F. D. Maurice*, 1884.

F. D. Maurice, *Lectures to Ladies on Practical Subjects*, 1855 (introductory lecture).

F. P. Cobbe, *Female Education and how it would be affected by University Examinations*, 1862.

Catherine Sinclair, *Modern Accomplishments*, 1837.

Emily Davies, *Higher Education of Women*, 1866.

Josephine E. Butler, *Women's Work and Women's Culture*, 1869 (essay by E. C. Wolstenholme on "Education of Girls").

Anne J. Clough, article in *Macmillan's Magazine*, October 1866, "Hints on the Organisation of Girls' Schools."

Herbert Spencer, *Education*, 1859 (chapter IV).

B. A. Clough, *A Memoir of Anne Jemima Clough*, 1897.

Annie E. Ridley, *Frances Mary Buss*, 1895.

Elizabeth Raikes, *Dorothea Beale of Cheltenham*, 1909.

Report of the Schools Inquiry Commission, 1869 (especially J. Bryce's report).

Sara A. Burstall, *Public Schools for Girls*, 1911.

CHAPTER X

POPULAR AND TECHNICAL EDUCATION

HITHERTO we have been considering mainly the improvements in the existing supply of education: henceforward we shall principally be tracing its spread to classes of the population which hitherto had been unable from lack of funds or lack of tradition to avail themselves of it.

The new universities claim our first attention. Of the foundation of London University and its subsequent reduction to the position of an examining body we have already spoken. The requirement of a College certificate of attendance was abandoned in 1858; at the same time, in order to give some indication to candidates whether they were pursuing their studies on right lines, the intermediate examination was added. The two original colleges continued to do good work of a real university kind; and even the external examinations, though falling short of the university ideal, encouraged many persons to pursue higher studies who would not otherwise have done so. One especial advantage in the new degrees was the encouragement of study in subjects which lay outside the restricted range of classics and mathematics, to which the older universities almost confined themselves. It is true that these subjects were not studied by methods which brought out their full educational value; "cram" was tolerated in order to secure that the subjects should be studied at all. Among the subjects which thus received encouragement was natural science, but the unwillingness to accept a course in scientific subjects alone as a qualification for the time-honoured degree of B.A. led to the institution of a special B.Sc. degree; and the newer universities have herein all followed the London precedent. Whether this divorce was advantageous educationally is doubtful;

certainly it was not justified by the historical meaning of the word "arts," for the original "liberal arts" included three branches of natural science—arithmetic, geometry, astronomy—as well as three linguistic subjects—grammar, logic and rhetoric—and one fine art, music.

The second of the new universities, Durham, attempted to reproduce Oxford and Cambridge, and was not a university of the newer type. Strangely enough, Oliver Cromwell was the original author of the idea of setting up a university for the North of England at Durham out of the cathedral funds; and it was a little strange that the Church should herself revert to the plan of old-time spoiler. A university with residential colleges, situated on the banks of a river in an old cathedral city, clearly belongs to the old order; but its absorption in 1882 of the Newcastle medical school brought it into touch with the life of a large modern industrial town and it now combines within itself the two elements, the old represented by the Arts side permeated by a strong clerical influence and housed under the shadow of the cathedral, and the new by the Armstrong College of Science situated in busy Newcastle.

It is with the foundation of Owens College, Manchester, however, that we come to the rise of the special type of university college, and afterwards of university, which the nineteenth century made its own. The history of Owens is largely reflected in that of its successors. It is possible that, had the Universities Tests Act been passed twenty years earlier, we should never have seen this type. But Owens College was just in time to win indisputable success before the Act was passed. It is curious that the College must be jointly assigned to Owens, a radical and nonconformist, and Faulkner, a tory and churchman. Owens wished to make Faulkner his heir, and Faulkner suggested the idea of a college. Owens left £97,000 and wisely laid down that the money was mainly to be spent on staffing before elaborate buildings were erected. It started in 1851 with five professors, two lecturers and sixty-two students. At first its prospects did not appear promising. By 1857 the number of students had sunk to thirty-three and the newspapers pronounced it "a mortifying failure." But from the appointment of Greenwood (1857–1889) as principal, it never looked back. In 1861 it absorbed the Working Men's College, founded in 1858 on the lines of F. D. Maurice's efforts in London. By 1864 it had 127 day and 312 evening students. It is curious to reflect that, even in 1868, when money was required for building, both Disraeli's and Gladstone's governments refused to give it State assistance. Probably the government exactly reflected the popular failure to realise that anything was being done which in the future would be regarded as a landmark in educational history. Outside their own towns the modern universities in their earlier days were treated with worse than opposition—they were ignored. Manchester as a city may look back with pride to the days when it saw its university through, unhelped and untalked of from without. The College devised a new constitution in 1871, opened its new buildings in 1873, began to admit women in 1874, and proposed to become a university in 1875. The previous year Yorkshire, however, had taken steps to start a college at Leeds; for it is a law of nature which rests on the surest inductive evidence that if Lancashire has anything to its credit, Yorkshire will not be long left behind, and that if Yorkshire has found anything good, Lancashire will not be left in the cold. Neither Lancashire nor Yorkshire, however, wished to pursue a dog-in-the-manger policy, and it was eventually arranged that the new university should be federal, and should be so constituted as to embrace Owens College from the start, the Yorkshire College at Leeds as soon as it had completed its organisation, and a college at Liverpool as soon as it could be found. The new university received its charter under the name of the Victoria University in 1880.

The Yorkshire School of Science was opened in 1874 and was, even more definitely than Owens, primarily a technological institution; but from the start W. E. Forster, the author of the Education Act of 1870 and M.P. for Bradford, foresaw that it might develop into a university. With the prospect of becoming a constituent college in

Victoria University, the College developed an Arts side and dropped the words "of Science" from its title. The growth of the older studies and the technological branches side by side is shown by the dates at which various departments were added; biology, engineering, mining, and classics in 1876; English and history in 1877; French and German in 1878; philosophy and dyeing in 1879; the inclusion of the medical school and its complete equipment in 1884; art and accountancy in 1887; leather, agriculture, a teachers' training department and organic chemistry in 1891; metalliferous mining in 1898; electrical engineering and law in 1899; economics in 1902, not to speak of later developments. The Clothworkers Company gave buildings for textile industries and dyeing in 1880 and a new set of buildings for arts and science was erected in 1885.

University College, Liverpool, was founded in 1881 and was designed from the first as a constituent college of Victoria. In 1884 Liverpool, like its predecessors, took over the pre-existing medical school. Among the characteristic schools which it had already developed, before the time when it sought incorporation as a separate university, were those of agriculture, commerce, law, marine biology, tropical medicine, hygiene, and dental surgery.

The federal system was for a time accepted as the natural form of organisation for provincial universities. It was adopted in Ireland and in Wales. The Welsh Colleges were founded in the early "eighties" and, like all other university colleges before they attained university rank, began by preparing for London degrees. Their development into the University of Wales in 1893 will be traced in the special chapter on Wales.

Before the end of the century the federal system was found to have grave disadvantages. What these were comes out in the discussion which arose when Liverpool proposed to defederalise Victoria University. This step was hastened by the incorporation of Birmingham University as a single institution. Birmingham has had two colleges. The first, Queen's, was founded as a medical and theological school; but the medical school grew while the theological withered away. In mid-Victorian days we presume that the atmosphere which suited Mr Bob Sawyer was uncongenial to the budding curate. But the College from which the university sprang was Mason College, founded in 1870 by Josiah Mason "to promote thorough systematic education and instruction adapted to the practical, mechanical, and artistic requirements of the manufactures and industrial pursuits of the Midland District," "to the exclusion of *mere* literary education and instruction, and of all teaching of theology." The present generation is in danger of forgetting that, till the day when Joseph Chamberlain resigned from the Home Rule Cabinet in 1886, Birmingham stood for everything which was modern, radical, practical, businesslike, efficient, *bourgeois* and anti-clerical in English life and politics. Manchester was modern, but it was not consciously hostile to what was venerable. Birmingham was the natural home for a university which should have nothing to do with a "mere" literary education. But even Josiah Mason was obliged to make concessions in order to secure recognition for his college from any institution empowered to grant degrees. The college was opened in 1880 and in a supplementary deed of 1881 he allowed Latin and Greek and "such a course of study as shall qualify for degrees in arts and science in the Victoria University or the London University or any other university of which the institution shall form part," though it was still to bear the name of the Mason Science College. The deed clearly contemplates the destiny of Mason College as being to enter Victoria or to form part of a new federal university. But by 1900 the idea of entering Victoria as junior to Manchester, Liverpool and Leeds did not satisfy the ambitions of Birmingham. Joseph Chamberlain was the most powerful man in the British Empire and was identified, as no other statesman has ever been identified, with his native town. So Birmingham became the first university in England which was instituted for a single provincial city. Though it no longer felt any revolutionary thrill of pleasure in defying tradition by incorporating the sentiments of Tom Paine in its title-deeds, you cannot look at its buildings without feeling that you are dealing with something new and unprecedented, of which you must take time to judge. The buildings of most modern city-universities mean nothing. They are just intended to keep out the rain and wind. But Manchester and Birmingham speak, and they say just opposite things. The Gothic quadrangle of Manchester speaks very quietly; it whispers to you that perhaps you find the bustle of modern life too wearing. "I know you cannot leave it for long; but step aside for a few minutes; in ten steps you are out of the twentieth century and you can remember that man has two sides to his nature; whenever you wish, in another ten steps you can be back." But the huge semi-circle of Birmingham, surmounted by its Eifel Tower, speaks to you through a megaphone. "You are great, Birmingham; indeed you are great; but it is I, Modern Science, who have made you great and keep you great; therefore I will mount up and look down on your city and watch you, lest you fall behindhand in the race of competition, for which the prizes go only to those that make the application of knowledge to industry the aim of every moment of their lives and cast all else aside."

The example of Birmingham gave a spur to the Colleges of Victoria. Time is money in these northern towns, and the waste of time involved in travelling to Manchester for business meetings of the University caused the government to fall mainly into the hands of those on the spot. In order to carry on the internal management, Liverpool and Leeds professors had to leave their classes; and, naturally, meetings were reduced to a minimum, and long delays took place before necessary things were done. The examinations became more like those of an examining body such as London, the teaching being adjusted to the examinations rather than the examinations to the teaching. Before the close of the century Liverpool was petitioning for separation. Leeds, however, felt that it was not strong enough to stand on its own feet. A counter-agitation was started, and carried some weight with graduates who felt that Victoria degrees had attained a prestige which would not be associated with the degrees of single-college universities. Till the system was tried, there was some genuine alarm lest a system by which a teacher had more weight than anyone else in passing or failing and giving classes to his students would open the door to personal idiosyncrasies and favouritism. Even under-cutting as regards standard between the three universities was prophesied. Manchester however supported Liverpool, the two Colleges gained the day, and none of the fears of the alarmists have proved well-grounded. The academic conscience and tradition of standards has proved equal to the trial, and the work of external examiners, who were instituted as a necessary safeguard, is now mainly confined to fostering an interchange of views between various universities.

Since Victoria was separated into three universities, all have added new departments and removed any surviving doubt as to their claim to be worthy of the name of university. Sheffield (1875) and Bristol (1876) university colleges have been also constituted universities, and Nottingham is looking in the same direction, though it is interesting to note that Leicester and Derby have put in a plea for a federal university, just as Leeds and Liverpool did in the case of Victoria. As they all more or less reproduce the history of the universities which we have already considered, it will not be necessary to trace their growth individually.

London University has at last reorganised itself as a true teaching university. The movement in this direction commenced in the two original colleges, University and King's, which felt that they represented the true intention of the University, which had been snowed under by its examining functions. The Royal Colleges of Physicians and Surgeons also wanted the right of conferring medical degrees, since the University had been so sparing in granting the degree of M.D. that students were driven elsewhere in the most important years just before they began to practise, in spite of the fact that London hospitals afforded an unrivalled field for getting experience. An association for promoting a teaching university for London was formed in

1884, but the university, though favouring the idea, could not be induced to agree on any concrete scheme for realising it, and it was necessary to resort to the usual expedient of a Royal Commission. The Commission reported in 1889 that the university should be reformed on a teaching basis, that the right of becoming constituent colleges should be confined to institutions situated within the County of London, that the colleges should be adequately represented on the governing bodies of the University, that the medical organisations should not be given the right of conferring degrees but that the university ought to grant medical degrees more freely, and that the work of external examining should be retained but subordinated to the internal work of the university. It was left to the university itself to frame a scheme to give effect to this policy. The problem of producing order out of chaos in London was, from the point of view of sheer organisation, the most complex that has ever presented itself in academic history. There were more students in London than in any city in the Empire, yet they were scattered amongst a host of utterly dissimilar institutions. There were whole-time students and evening students; general students, professional students, technical students; men, women, boys, and girls; middle-class students and artisans. The two old colleges; the women's colleges; the medical schools attached to the hospitals; the Inns of Court; technological institutions like the Government School of Science, South Kensington, and the City and Guilds Institute; working-men's institutions such as the City of London College, founded in 1838, with 2000 students, Maurice's Working Men's College with 500 students, and the Birkbeck Institute; various training colleges for teachers and theological colleges; all these existed without any organic connection, with totally different histories, and many of them almost unconscious of each other's existence. We are not altogether surprised that the university entirely failed to devise a scheme of union. Public opinion came to look on London University as a steam roller that had broken down and stuck in the mud, if we take a metaphor suited to its unwieldy bulk, or as Humpty Dumpty after his fall, if we think rather of its fragmentary condition.

University and King's in despair now reverted to an earlier project of leaving the existing university by the roadside and starting a new teaching university which, in memory of the Elizabethan worthy who had first conceived the idea of a teaching university for London, should be called the Gresham University. Parliament vetoed this proposal and set up a new Royal Commission, which in many words said ditto to the previous commission. "On a general review of the evidence laid before us on" the subject of internal versus external examining, "it would appear that the stress laid by witnesses on the importance of placing examinations in the hands of teachers has been in proportion to the extent to which they were regarding the higher and more progressive departments of study and the effect on the individual minds of the taught rather than the conditions to be imposed upon pass students, or the necessity of exacting for the professions a rigidly uniform standard of qualification." The last clause refers to the fact that the medical schools were the only teaching institutions which still supported the external system. Eventually a constitution was worked out and accepted in 1900, but in complexity it rivals that of the British State and it would be impossible to expound it in detail without writing a second volume. It is chiefly based on the fact that the greater part of the teaching institutions with which it is connected are of a specialistic kind. Hence its main principle is organisation by faculties, the various institutions being recognised as "schools of the universities" in one or more faculties. University and King's Colleges have been incorporated within the University (the former in 1907, the latter in 1910), and the University maintains several other teaching institutions of its own for specific purposes. The women's colleges, Bedford and Holloway, are schools in the faculties of arts and science; the medical schools of the hospitals in the faculty of medicine; and in various faculties the East London College, the Imperial College of Science and Technology, the Royal

College of Science and Royal School of Mines, the City and Guilds College, the South-Eastern Agricultural College, and the London School of Economics are recognised. An interesting feature which has been carried out as a result of the 1895 commission, which would have been impossible at an earlier period, is the formation of a faculty of theology which includes six "schools," two Church of England, two Congregational, one Wesleyan and one Baptist.

After this record of isolated events and facts, the reader naturally asks what has been the combined effect of the whole movement. In the first place, higher education has been opened to all classes. The child of a working-man who wins a scholarship from the elementary school may by the aid of scholarships continue his or her education till twenty-three or twenty-four and enter any occupation to which he is suited. The working-man who grows up a working-man may receive any form of scientific or industrial education which fits him for his craft, or evening instruction to improve his general culture. Ability can move more freely where it can be most effective and the nation makes a better use of its original supply of brains. In the second place, education is brought nearer to the doors of those who desire it. Every city of 300,000 inhabitants has its university and a map showing the distribution of universities will readily bring out that every big area, save possibly the extreme south-west, is served. In the third place there has been a revolution in the conception of the subjects which are suited for university studies. The humanities have indeed been spread more widely than ever before, since there is no single university in which there are not a considerable number of "arts" students. There is a more thorough study of the subjects required for the old professional faculties—theology, law, and medicine. But these changes are overshadowed by the revolution which has been produced in the attitude of the industrial world towards technological work. American manufacturers discovered the use of university men in their works before England; but England is rapidly following suit. Engineering, mining, metallurgy, chemical industries, textiles, leather, dyeing, even brewing, look to the universities for researchers and managers. Even the oldest and most conservative of all industries in the world, agriculture, has begun to send its pupils to college. Short-sighted critics sometimes complain that culture is being sacrificed to materialism. They forget that a system which confines educational prestige to the humanities makes directly for the production of what the Germans call *Hungerkandidaten*, young men with a degree but unable to earn a living. An unsuccessful intellectual class is the breeding-ground of revolutions. The Jews of old taught every boy a trade as well as the law and the prophets. Every university man should be taught a profession. It is true that in the two old professions of the Christian ministry and of teaching general culture plays a large part and that a graduate with a good record *and a certain innate fitness for those occupations* is well-advised to devote more time to the humanities than to theology or pedagogy; but he must be sure that he has the innate qualities. There are, besides these professions, a very few openings for the picked few, and it is well that only those who are likely to be among that picked few should take up a course of studies which does not obviously lead anywhere. But the great bulk of those who receive a higher education with special reference to their occupation would never receive a higher education at all, if the only kind open was of a purely cultural character. And even the most specialised technological education at the higher stages results in a considerable bye-product of cultural education. Applied science can only be built up on a good foundation of pure science, and pure science in its turn needs a previous training in mathematics and in the exact use of language, and benefits by a knowledge of modern foreign languages. Further, the longer that education is continued and the more that technical instruction is accepted as a natural part of the university course, the less effort is made to encroach on school days, which are left freer for a general development of those parts of our nature which fit us for the right use of leisure, and for instruction in those subjects which bear on citizenship.

It is no loss to accept brewing and dyeing into the university curriculum if we thereby restrict the range of book-keeping and type-writing in schools.

The extension of universities and university colleges was mainly the work of private generosity and municipal patriotism; but the time came when Parliament recognised it as a matter of national concern, and to-day it would be impossible for the work to be continued on an adequate scale without help from public funds. The first treasury grant of £15,000 was voted to university colleges in 1889. Most provincial universities are considerably aided out of the rates; and, in addition to direct grants, access to them is aided by municipal exhibitions. The final step was taken at the close of the War when the two old universities of Oxford and Cambridge applied for state aid, and a Royal Commission under the presidency of Mr Asquith was set up to consider on what terms it should be granted. State aid of course means a certain measure of State control. This has mainly been exercised in securing that universities should maintain a really high standard of university work, and in particular in the encouragement of research. After all, State control is no new thing in academic history: nothing that is now likely to happen will compare with the sweeping changes effected by the Crown in the century which followed the Reformation or possibly even with those which resulted from the Victorian commissions.

The extension of education, other than elementary, to the working classes and the supply of technical and technological education considerably overlap, though of course there is a considerable area of working-class education which was intended primarily to be cultural and a considerable area of technical education which by its nature removes the recipient from the category of working men in the ordinary use of the term. We propose to treat briefly the spread of cultural education to working men up to the time of the Technical Instruction Commission first, then to devote more space to the organisation of technical instruction, and finally to make a short survey of the spread of working-class education in more recent times.

Birkbeck's movement, the first of its kind, was technical in much of its subject-matter, though it was distinctly cultural in its results. But, by an almost inevitable transformation, the Mechanics' Institutes became less and less working-class and more and more middle-class in their membership; and many survived only as institutions for providing libraries, reading-rooms, and occasional popular lectures. The decline was marked after 1848. But there were numerous exceptions; the highly successful Birmingham and Midland Institute was established in 1853. Those which retained their original purpose were able to take advantage of the South Kensington grants after 1859, of grants from the City and Guilds Institute after 1879, and of the "whiskey money" after 1890. Thus there has been continuity from beginning to end and the original Birkbeck Institution is now a part of London University[1].

The Co-operative movement, as an effort of the more thoughtful and independent workmen, who were considerably fired by the enthusiasm of Robert Owen and of the Chartist leaders, produced a certain educational stimulus amongst its adherents and led to the foundation of a number of evening schools and lending libraries.

The Young Men's Christian Associations were a cultural agency which can be said to have furthered the cause of education in the wider sense. They originated with the assembly of a few young men, mostly drapers' assistants, under George Williams in 1844, and developed rapidly in the decade between 1855 and 1864. Their object was primarily religious, but from 1845 educational lectures were given in Exeter Hall for the next twenty-one years; mutual improvement and literary societies were formed; and from 1849 reading rooms and libraries were instituted. Their main function may be defined as an organisation of the rational use of leisure.

The University Extension movement may next be noticed. In the middle of the century the term had not acquired its present significance, but was applied to any

[1] For a longer account see Sir Michael Sadler, *Continuation Schools in England and Elsewhere*, pp. 21–31.

steps which might be taken for the admission of poorer students to the older universities or for the foundation of newer institutions of higher learning. In its modern sense it arose, as we have seen in the chapter on women's education, out of the invitation given in 1867 by a committee of ladies in the north of England, to Mr James Stuart, a fellow of Trinity, to lecture to their organisation. He followed up his course to the ladies by arranging similar courses to working men in several northern towns, and the main features of University Extension—the course of lectures as opposed to the single lecture, the printed syllabus, and the written exercises—were thus fixed before the movement received official recognition in 1873 from the University of Cambridge. London followed in 1876 and Oxford in 1878. The movement spread rapidly. In the North of England in particular it appealed to working men; and many were the instances where severe economies were practised and long distances covered to be able to attend the lectures. Probably the payment of a fee caused them to be more highly valued than would have been the case had they been gratuitous. It is easy nowadays to criticise the system; in spite of the written exercises and the voluntary examination at the end, it trusted mainly to the efficacy of oral addresses to large audiences. The lecturers were generally men who knew how to present a subject clearly and in a manner calculated to excite the interest of a popular audience; yet, except with trained hearers, lectures to large assemblies are bound to lack many of the elements which go to make up real teaching. The lecturer is only indirectly able to infer whether his points are understood; and, what is more important, the listener is liable to confuse a vague impression for a clear understanding. The first thing to do with the untrained mind should be to make the learner realise the precise meaning of everything which is presented to him, and conversation and questioning are usually the only methods by which this can be secured. But we must not under-rate the importance of the Extension system as a means of arousing interest in intellectual matters, which is a condition precedent to true intellectual training. Even if it goes no further, a man with intellectual interests is a nobler being than one with none. In particular an appreciation of literature and a wider outlook on the development of human history could be given without making severe intellectual demands. Economics, a subject of profound interest to working men, is on the other hand a subject to the profitable study of which previous intellectual training and accurate thinking are indispensable; and natural science is so technical that the lecture system rarely attempted to deal with it. Outside the north of England the Extension lectures could get good audiences, but they appealed less to the working man, and the hearers were more largely people of leisure, especially women who had been brought up in the days when girls' schools gave little satisfaction to minds keen for information and women's colleges were few. The summer meetings of extensionists at a university town began in 1888. The movement has by no means lost in popularity up to the present day, but the development of a better system of intellectual training by means of Tutorial Classes has diminished its importance as a means of adult working-class education.

Of Maurice's Working Men's College enough has been said in a previous chapter. One lasting effect of his work was to interest many minds in the universities in the lives of their fellow citizens in the slums of great towns, and so to revive that connection between the universities and the masses which was so large a factor of their influence in the Middle Ages but had been completely lost since the Reformation. This influence is specially associated with the name of Arnold Toynbee, who was appointed a tutor of Balliol in 1879. Unhappily his career was cut short in 1883; but in this short space of four years he had helped to create a new atmosphere. At the university he was engaged in humanising the teaching of economics. Orthodox economics till that time was for the most part unctuously optimistic. Its tone savoured of that adopted by the exponents of "design" in the early years of the century. In the one case natural and in the other case economic laws were so arranged as to lead to the greatest happiness of the greatest number with the least possible trouble or inconvenience to anyone. The reign of tooth and claw was ignored by the one, the squalor and misery of the slums by the other. Toynbee turned attention from economic theory to economic history, from the ideal to the reality. He emphasised the meaning of economic laws in their effect on the lives of men. Outside the university he gained the confidence of the working classes by his lectures and his social work in Whitechapel, where his friend Barnett was vicar of St Jude's.

In 1884 Canon Barnett, as he afterwards became, founded the first university settlement in the slums and called it Toynbee Hall in memory of his friend. It had a large number of successors, which benefited the slum-dwellers by the cultural influences which they brought to bear and the university men who came to reside there by the knowledge which it gave them of the conditions under which the submerged tenth lived. The problem of the slum has not yet been solved; for it is one of the saddest social laws that the classes who suffer most are least able to remedy their lot, and it is probable that in the future, even when the working classes as a body improve their position by their own efforts, the help of the intellectual classes whom Barnett and his imitators enlisted in the cause will be needed to work out practical steps for the rescue of the class which has sunk too low to know of any path along which it can seek its own redemption.

Polytechnics bring us more closely to the sphere of technical education and the modern State system of education. In their initiation, however, they were as much a private and philanthropic effort as any of the other institutions which we have been considering. In 1880 Mr Quintin Hogg obtained a building in Regent Street, known as the Polytechnic, which had been used by Pepper of *Ghost* fame as a kind of scientific entertainment hall, and converted it into an institution which has preserved the name, but given it an entirely new sense. His objects were partly religious, partly social, and partly educational;

his methods may be described as a combination of those of Maurice and those of the Y.M.C.A. He aimed at getting the young men of the shopman and artisan class; and, when polytechnics became an organised type of institution, the age was defined as being from sixteen to twenty-five. His institute comprised a library and a gymnasium, and its activities included concerts, debates, a natural history society, a savings bank, excursions, swimming, and rowing. Its teaching side developed more rapidly than he had ventured to hope. The first year he had 6800 members, who paid ten shillings a year or three shillings a term. The classes were mainly in connection with the City and Guilds Institute, the teachers being registered by the Institute and paid by results. Among the industries taught were brick-laying, metal-plate work, electrical engineering, plumbing, watch and clock making, carriage building, photography, tailoring, and printing.

It so happened that a royal commission on the parochial charities of London had reported in 1880. The original purpose of most of these charities was shown to be unsuitable to modern needs, and an act of 1883 appointed a body of trustees to deal with all except those of five large parishes. The charities of a secular character were found to bring in an income of £50,000 a year. After allotting a part to such educational purposes as free libraries, the trustees assigned the rest to the promotion of polytechnics. They laid down as their principles that the institutions which benefited should give instruction in the principles of the arts and sciences which underlie crafts and in the application of such principles to particular trades, that they should be a supplement and not in substitution for the workshop or place of business, that they might give instruction suitable for intending emigrants and hold lectures and concerts, encourage gymnastics, drill, swimming, and other forms of bodily exercise, and institute clubs and societies, libraries, museums and reading-rooms, that their educational facilities should be equally open to both sexes, that the fees should be small, and that drinking, smoking and gambling should be prohibited.

Among other institutions which benefited by these charities one may be singled out for special notice. The scheme suggested by Sir Walter Besant in *All Sorts and Conditions of Men* materialised in the "People's Palace," which received £7000 from the Drapers' Company and developed on its educational side into the East London College which now forms a "school" of London University in the faculties of Arts, Science, and Engineering. There is after all something to be said for our haphazard way of letting our educational institutions grow. If London University had been planned as Berlin was and had been made according to pattern, it would have been fully equipped and would have had magnificent buildings, with departments for every kind of learning and facilities for every kind of research, but would it have included a college in the East End to bring university education to the doors of the people? Just because the English educational system is so hard to describe and bring to rule, it is flexible enough to meet all needs.

We now turn from the movements which aimed primarily at bringing education, whether cultural or vocational, to the working classes, to the series of steps by which technical instruction was carried forward with an eye rather to national efficiency in the arts of production and exchange than to the raising of the culture of its recipients. It is becoming usual to use the words "technological" and "technical" to distinguish the two grades which, in the sphere of general education, are known as university and secondary: but as both grew up together and to a large extent independently of other forms of education, it is simplest in a historical summary to treat them in a single section.

The demand for technical instruction was the result partly of the scientific movement and partly of the fear that England was falling behind its industrial rivals. Great Britain had established its industrial supremacy during the Napoleonic wars, while the Continent was fully engrossed in the struggle, by developing its mines, its metal industries, and its textile manufactures. It had therefore been able to turn to the fullest possible advantage the invention of machinery for spinning and weaving and the discovery that coal could be used to develop steam power. England had the benefit of being first in the field, and its rivals had to look for some counter-advantage. To some extent this had been found in developing the skill of the workers even as early as the great Exhibition of 1851, which first suggested that this country was in some respects falling behind, and led to some demand for the technical instruction of workpeople and for a development of scientific teaching. It was in this year that the School of Mines and of Science as applied to the Arts, known since 1890 as the Royal College of Science, was founded. In 1853 the science section of South Kensington was added to the art department of the Board of Trade, and in 1856 this Science and Art department was transferred to the Committee of Council on Education. We have already seen how it distributed grants to local science classes and science schools and conducted examinations in science for teachers (1859–1867) and for pupils (since 1861), and how these Schools of Science were reorganised by Huxley in 1872. This last change was due to the Devonshire Commission on Scientific Instruction (1871–1875).

But a marked accentuation of the demand for technical education took place about this date. Two powerful rivals entered the field, Germany and the United States. After its unification in 1870 under the far-seeing rule of Bismarck, Germany had found two great weapons for wrenching Britain's industrial supremacy from her. One was scientific research as applied to industry; the other was technical instruction. The United States, which were fast changing from an agricultural into a commercial nation, followed suit. The more observant English manufacturers and merchants began to realise that our technical instruction was a mere skeleton and that any training which would produce scientific researchers among the highly educated classes was non-existent.

The report of the Royal Commission on Technical Instruction issued in 1884 shows the progress which had been made up to that time. The institutions for technical training were of course far fewer than now—otherwise the labours of the Commission would have been in vain— but a start had been made. We will summarise their account of existing institutions, following their order, namely, first London, then the rest of the country.

University and King's Colleges are mentioned first. The former had recently built chemical, physical, and en gineering laboratories, had instituted a department of applied chemistry, and employed a professor of engineering who, in American fashion, was engaged in private practice as a consulting engineer. King's was not far behind, though its engineering was of a more directly practical type.

The Normal School of Science and Royal School of Mines, South Kensington, the foundation of which in 1851 under a slightly different name we noticed above, had been reorganised in 1881. It was primarily intended for the training of science teachers and for "the instruction of students of the industrial classes selected by competition in the annual examinations of the Science and Art Department," but fee-paying students were also admitted. Its regular three years' course was unspecialised and consisted of mathematics, mechanics, physics, chemistry, geology, astronomy, mineralogy, and drawing; in the last year students specialised in mechanics, physics, chemistry, biology, geology, agriculture, metallurgy, or mining. It offered twelve exhibitions of £50, six free studentships, twenty free places for intending teachers, and free places for local exhibitioners.

The School of Design, which had since 1857 been conducted at South Kensington as the National Art Training School, contained 128 students and gave preliminary or "art teachers'" certificates and certificates of the third grade. An elaborate system of examinations was conducted by the Science and Art Department to encourage the teaching of art throughout the country, comprising twenty-five branches of art and divided into grades suited respectively for elementary school pupils, for secondary school pupils, for teachers, and for art masters.

In 1877 the London City Livery Companies, after enquiry abroad, had set up a committee to prepare a national system of technical instruction. As a result, in 1880 they founded the City and Guilds Institute, which subsidised existing educational establishments, encouraged evening classes in the chief towns, maintained model technical schools in London and inspected and examined classes elsewhere which were likely to become the nuclei of technical colleges. The Royal Commission took Finsbury Technical College (1883) as an example of their technical schools. It was intended as a "model trade school for the instruction of artisans and other persons preparing for intermediate posts in industrial works." It consisted of a day and an evening school, the latter giving systematic instruction to those engaged in the staple industries of the district, *e.g.* cabinet-making. Exhibitions were offered to pupils of middle-class schools. Mathematics, practical mechanics, physics, chemistry, electrical technology, freehand, model and machine drawing, workshop practice, French and German were taught; and there were evening classes in carpentery and joinery, metal-plate work, brick-laying, drawing, painting, modelling, and design. The City and Guilds Central Institution in Exhibition Road, South Kensington, which was completed in 1884, was meant to train teachers of technical subjects, managers of works, engineers and industrial chemists, and was conveniently situated for the science schools and museums of South Kensington: it now forms part of London University.

The Commission also notice Cooper's Hill, established in 1871 for Indian Government engineering students but afterwards thrown open to engineering students generally; the Royal Naval College, Greenwich, intended for giving instruction in marine engineering and naval architecture, which was mostly frequented by government students; the Crystal Palace School of Practical Engineering; and the newly founded polytechnics.

Outside London the institutions noted are chiefly those which have now assumed university rank, whose progress has already been noticed earlier in the chapter. A few words must, however, be added as to the progress of science and technology at the older universities. The Commission found little to write about at Oxford save the new Museum in the Parks; but science was already throwing forth vigorous shoots at Cambridge. Till 1871 there had been no practical teaching in science at that university except in chemistry. Then the Cavendish laboratory was built for physics, and Lord Rayleigh presided over it at the time when the Commission visited Cambridge. What it has subsequently become under his guidance and that of Sir J. J. Thomson, the present master of Trinity, it is unnecessary to describe. Already, the Commission note that Maxwell had introduced physical problems into the papers for the mathematical tripos, and that Michael Foster had brought the biological sciences to the fore, and they are able to notice among the names of distinguished Cambridge scientists those of Stokes, Humphry, Liveing, Dewar, Vines, Coutts-Trotter and Balfour. But they are compelled to remark that still "few students have time or inclination for original research": Sir James Thomson and others could now tell a different tale. Indeed the discoveries by Oxford and Cambridge physicists and chemists which helped to win the war will probably not be fully known for some time.

In the more strictly technological sphere the Commission noticed specially James Stuart's mechanical workshops for forty-two students. "The system of tuition is arranged on the basis of an actual mercantile establishment. The rate of wages for each student is fixed, the cost of material and the time employed being accurately noted and entered in a ledger so that the cost of every article produced can be ascertained."

The Mechanical Sciences (or Engineering) Tripos was the first noteworthy technological development at the older universities, but it would take too long to enumerate all the new studies which they have encouraged in recent years. Where a subject is not admitted into the degree course it has a diploma. New laboratories are constantly being built. Practical arts such as agriculture and forestry, the oriental languages needed by Indian and Egyptian civil servants, social, economic and hygienic subjects required by public officials, are all taught. Post-graduate research work, long in being recognised, has found that the libraries of Oxford and Cambridge give facilities unrivalled except in London. Though the number of universities which are doing the work expected of such institutions fifty years ago may be multiplied still further, yet the higher research work will tend to find natural centres as in America, and the old universities have at last recognised their possibilities as such centres.

The Royal Commission, whose report we have been largely engaged in summarising in the last few pages, forms a landmark in the history of technical instruction. It was appointed in 1880 and reported in 1884. The Commissioners enquired not merely into the provision of technical instruction in the narrower sense, but also on the teaching of science, on which it must necessarily be based, from the elementary school upwards. Its report woke the country to the need not only of specialised technical instruction but of getting the preliminary work done in secondary schools, and indirectly to the necessity of providing a better supply of secondary schools generally. Its direct outcome was the Technical Instruction Act of 1889, but it played no small part in leading up to the Bryce Commission on Secondary Education and to the Education Act of 1902. These, however, properly belong to the chapter on the development of our modern State system of education.

It remains to take a glance at the further development of working-class education since 1889 so far as it has depended on private initiative, though of course the State has stepped in with financial assistance whenever any institution justified its existence. Such assistance has secured the permanence and progress of pre-existing institutions. The Mechanics' Institutes and Working Men's Colleges, however flourishing for a time, had struck on two rocks, the difficulty of obtaining funds when the first enthusiasm had passed away, and the lack of a sound elementary and secondary system of education as a basis.

They were dependent on obtaining the voluntary services of good lecturers, had no whole-time staff, and ran the risk of being supposed to give "popular" instruction instead of promoting continuous and serious study. In the case of the surviving institutions founded by these movements, all this passed away. The polytechnics, which were still in the heyday of their first enthusiasm when State aid came, were preserved from undergoing any subsequent decline. The State left them complete freedom as regards the social side of their activities, but required on the educational side that they should have a whole time principal and staff, proper laboratory and workshop instruction, classes of a reasonable size, and a test to secure that those who were admitted had been properly prepared. Thus they have become in the fullest sense a part of the educational system of the country.

Further institutions have been founded to meet the requirements of London. The Goldsmiths' Company presented their Institute at New Cross to the University in 1904; it was opened as Goldsmiths' College in 1905. The Northampton Institute, besides providing for whole-time and evening students, introduced the "sandwich" system for seasonal workers by which they could take their courses during the less busy half of the year. This apparently new device was in reality following a very old precedent; the Scottish universities sat for a single session, which covered the six winter months, to allow their students to work on the farms during the summer. In these Institutes internal degrees are open to evening students, and the literary side of education is found to be in demand as well as the scientific.

In 1899 an experiment was made in the direction of bringing adult working-class education into touch with the older universities by the formation of Ruskin College at Oxford. It is managed by a council consisting partly of university men and partly of representatives of the trade unions, who finance it. Its object is not to provide a degree course for its students but to give a civic training to men who are likely to take a lead in working class movements.

Economics, sociology, and politics thus form the staple of its course of instruction, and there are no formal examinations or diplomas. Economy is aimed at, before the war the students doing their own house work and the cost not exceeding £52 a year. The chief danger to this institution that has revealed itself is that, though in intention non-political, education may receive a party bias.

The most definite organisation, however, of adult working-class education in a form likely to secure a continuous course of studies and definite intellectual training has been secured by the conjoint activities of the Workers' Educational Association and the University Tutorial Classes Committees. The Workers' Educational Association was formed in 1903 to arouse interest amongst the workers in education, to find out demands, and to organise the supply. It consisted of a central authority, district authorities, and local branches. Under its auspices a conference of working-class and educational organisations was held at Oxford in 1907 which, "affirming the growing desire on the part of workpeople for higher education, and anxious for the further co-operation of Oxford in the systematic teaching of historical, economic and other liberal subjects," appointed a committee which reported in the following year in a volume entitled *Oxford and Working Class Education*. The report, after a short historical account of the various movements for working class education and of the work of universities in the past, proceeded to discuss the defects in the system of extension lectures by which the universities had for the last forty years been trying to supply teaching to the workers. They came to the conclusion that the system by which each centre was expected to be self-supporting made a large attendance necessary if a deficit was to be avoided. The results were, first "that both the lectures and the subject to be studied must be chosen not solely or chiefly on account of their educative value, but with a view to the probability of their drawing such large numbers that the lectures will 'pay'[1]," in other words that the lectures became popular in the worst sense

[1] *Op. cit.* paragraph 59.

of the term; secondly that with such large classes "individual students rarely receive the personal guidance and supervision which is offered to an undergraduate in Oxford [1]," in other words that tutorial work was out of the question. In order to obviate these disadvantages they proposed the new system of tutorial classes by which "in certain selected industrial towns classes should be established of not more than thirty students; that these classes should pursue a plan of study drawn up by workpeople and representatives of the university in consultation; that Oxford should appoint and pay half the salary of the teachers by whom such classes are taught; and that such teachers should receive a status as a lecturer in Oxford [2]." In order to secure that the teaching should really meet the demands of the workmen, the classes should be organised by the local branch of the Workers' Educational Association. A continuous course of study should be followed for two years. The type of method suggested was one in which an hour's lecture was followed by an hour's discussion. There should be close contact between the lecturer and the students; a fortnightly essay and regular home reading should be expected; and the lending of books should be carefully organised.

Work was immediately started on the lines of this report, and the example of Oxford was speedily followed by the other universities and university colleges. A Central Joint Advisory Committee was then formed by the tutorial classes committees of the several institutions. The Board of Education agreed to contribute £30, subsequently raised to £45, to the support of each class, and the Gilchrist Trustees gave valuable financial assistance. Summer schools came to be held regularly and the number of classes increased from eight in 1908–9 to 145 in the year preceding the war, the students increasing from 237 to 3234.

It is difficult to foretell on what lines adult working class education will develop in the new period which began with the close of the war. The supply of an efficient system of secondary schools, the improvement of the machinery for

[1] *Op. cit.* paragraph 60.   [2] paragraph 88.

choosing county scholars and "free placers," and the other steps for substituting an open highway for the "ladder" by which the elementary school pupil can climb to the university, have till recently been the main educational demands of the workers. "Equality of opportunity" was the phrase which summed them up. But it is plausible to argue that the adult workmen of to-day who join tutorial classes are precisely those who, had they been born twenty or thirty years later, would have been caught up by the scholarship system and would in the end not have been manual workers at all. If the system of selection could ever be made perfect it would thus mean that all the best intellectual material would be gone, and the working class of fifty years hence would really be a mentally inferior class and not a body of persons who had had less opportunity to develop their native aptitudes. Nevertheless the present course of events seems to suggest that we are about to pass through a stage of political development in which the government of the country will largely rest in the hands of such working men as become trade union officials. The labour leaders of to-day are the men of innate capacities who grew up when no ladder existed: they are therefore able to combine sound intellectual qualities with real experience of their trades. But the education of future labour leaders cannot be properly envisaged till we know who are to succeed the Clyneses and Hendersons. Will they be boys of working-class parentage who have received a higher education and have never worked at the trades of whose unions they are officials? Will they be the accidental omissions of the scholarship system? Will they be—we hope not—persons who from a belief in the natural antagonism between manual workers and brain workers have refused to train their intellects as if they were by so doing committing an act of treason to their class? Dare we hope that there will be many who, after receiving a high academic training, will pursue manual occupations for a time so as to represent the experience of their class? Or will the scholarship system work so efficiently that they will really be taken from those who were incapable of profiting by an academic training, and, if so, will they have other practical abilities which will make up for the absence of the qualities which schools and universities value? We admit that the problem seems so far to be an insoluble riddle; but on it turns the whole problem of future adult working-class education, and the continuation schools only seem to mitigate but not to solve the difficulty.

REFERENCES

Report of the Royal Commission on a University for London, 1889.
Report of the Royal Commission to consider the Draft Charter for the proposed Gresham University in London, 1894.
P. J. Hartog, *The Owens College, Manchester*, 1900.
Various petitions relative to the charter of Liverpool University, 1900.
M. E. Sadler, *Continuation Schools in England and Elsewhere*, Manchester, 1908.
J. W. Hudson, *History of Adult Education*, 1851.
H. J. Mackinder and M. E. Sadler, *University Extension*, 1891.
R. D. Roberts, *Education in the Nineteenth Century*, Cambridge, 1901.
Sir Philip Magnus, *Educational Aims and Efforts*, 1880–1910, 1910.
—— *Industrial Education*, 1888.
James Stuart, *Reminiscences*, 1912.
R. D. Roberts, *Eighteen Years of University Extension*, 1891.
Second Report of the Royal Commission on Technical Education, 1884.
Oxford and Working-Class Education, Oxford, 2nd edition, 1909.
Annual Reports of the Central Joint Advisory Committee on Tutorial Classes.
Article in *Encyclopaedia Britannica* on polytechnics.

CHAPTER XI

EDUCATION IN WALES

AS Wales established a State system of secondary education eleven years before England, and as this precedent possibly hastened England's acceptance of the principles which were embodied in the Act of 1902, this seems the natural place to insert a chapter on the history of university and secondary education in the Principality.

In the Middle Ages Welshmen flocked to Oxford in considerable numbers; and later Queen Elizabeth, mindful of her Welsh descent, founded Jesus College specially for them. The first project for a special university for Wales was formed during the Commonwealth. The object, however, was not to foster Welsh nationality, but the reverse. The Puritan government regarded the Welsh as a race of obstinate royalists and episcopalians, and the university was to be a means of converting them to proper republican and anti-episcopal principles. The Restoration put an end to the project; and, before anything more was heard of a Welsh university, the absentee Georgian bishops had alienated the mass of Welshmen from the Established Church, the Methodist Revival had made religion, in a changed form, their main interest, and the Romantic movement had revived Welsh poetry, established the Eisteddfod, and inspired a keen interest in the antiquities, language, and literature of the people.

When the great age of school foundation closed early in the seventeenth century, it left Wales poorly supplied with grammar schools. Like their English counterparts, they mostly sank· into insignificance by the nineteenth century, and none of them was fortunate enough, like the nine "public schools," to improve its fortunes. Such small schools existed at Bala, Bangor, Beaumaris, Bottwnog, Brecon, Cardigan, Carmarthen, Cowbridge, Denbigh, Deythur,

Dolgelly, Haverfordwest, Hawarden, Lampeter, Llanrwst, Presteign, Ruabon, Ruthin, St Asaph, Swansea, and Ystrad Meurig. The seventeenth century, so full of interest in connection with Welsh elementary education, has practically nothing to show in connection with Welsh secondary education.

The religious revival was the root from which the modern educational movement in Wales sprang. Before the end of the eighteenth century the need of training candidates for the ministry had led to the foundation of theological colleges, which of necessity had to supply what was lacking in the secondary education of their students. Somewhat later the Anglican Church followed suit, as Bishop Burgess of St David's found that most of his clergy had had no other education than a year at Ystrad Meurig, a school which, like others at the time and till much later, received adults as well as boy pupils. He consequently promoted the foundation of Lampeter College in 1827, and there was a demand that it should acquire something of a university rank.

The forties saw a great educational revival. At first it centred round elementary education, and was led by Sir Thomas Phillips of Newport, Sir Hugh Owen, and the Rev. Henry Griffiths. In 1846 Owen founded the Cambrian Educational Society. As regards elementary education, the movement received an unfortunate check through the excitement created by the adverse report of a Commission on Welsh elementary schools, which was popularly called "Brâd y Llyfrau Gleision" (the treason of the blue books). The movers, however, directed their attention to higher education. In 1849 Phillips, in a book called *Wales, the language, social conditions, moral character and opinions of the people considered in their relation to education*, which is the best authority for the history of Welsh education up to that date, urged the foundation of Durham university as a claim for the establishment of a university for Wales. Historically the two projects were closely connected, as the Commonwealth had conceived them both. Moreover, Scotland had four universities and Ireland one. The only immediate outcome was that Lampeter received the privilege of conferring the degree of B.D., an unsatisfactory solution, both because the right to grant degrees has elsewhere been confined to institutions of university rank and because Lampeter was a strictly denominational foundation. Shortly afterwards a petition was sent up to Parliament by Welsh clergymen resident in Yorkshire for the first time definitely demanding the establishment of a real university.

In 1854 Owen called a conference to press for the institution of colleges on the model of those recently set up in Ireland. This project was temporarily shelved in favour of one for founding a training college. The success of this appeal showed that popular enthusiasm could easily be roused for educational objects. Advocates went round the country, eloquently pleading in wayside chapels; money poured in freely from poor congregations; and it was clear that the rural communities of Wales were as zealous for education as the artisans of Glasgow and Lancashire. Welsh education was a spontaneous growth, owing nothing to the State and little to wealthy manufacturers, but created mainly by country congregations or those of small market towns. No sooner had the training-college project been realised by the foundation of Bangor Normal College in 1852 than the university scheme was revived at the Eisteddfod of 1853. At this point the religious difficulty entered, Churchmen being satisfied by the granting to Lampeter of the right to give B.A. as well as B.D. degrees. Owen's first idea was to set up two colleges, one in the north and one in the south; but a site at Aberystwyth presented itself and the geographically central position led to its acceptance. The College was opened in 1872 and prepared for London degrees. Owen continued for the rest of his life to be the soul of the movement for maintaining the College as he had of that for founding it.

It is easier to stir enthusiasm in order to raise a capital sum than it is to maintain a steady flow of annual subscriptions. There was likewise a period when students came in none too freely, the number sinking from a maximum of 93 to 57, and these coming almost entirely from the few neighbouring counties. In 1879 the Welsh members therefore brought forward a motion in favour of government aid for Welsh higher education. It was defeated in Disraeli's House; but in the following year Gladstone obtained a large majority at the general election. Gladstone was a resident in Wales and knew something of its needs. When Hugh Owen continued to press for an enquiry the new government set up a Committee under Lord Aberdare to enquire into the whole question of secondary and higher education in Wales. The part of its report which dealt with schools will be considered when we come to the Intermediate Education Act; as regards higher education, it reported in favour of setting up two colleges which should receive government grants. One was to be in the populous industrial area of Glamorganshire; the other should either be the existing college at Aberystwyth or a college situated in North Wales. The evidence on the matter of a full degree-giving university was somewhat divided; but the argument which decided the Committee was that Lampeter already possessed this privilege and that Lampeter was a denominational institution. They looked therefore to a future federation of Lampeter and the two proposed colleges into a full university.

The government adopted the Committee's proposals as to state-aided colleges. Till their site should be determined a temporary grant was made to Aberystwyth, and a valuable precedent was created which was subsequently extended to England. Arbitrators were appointed to examine the competing claims of Cardiff and Swansea to be the site of the South Wales college. They decided in favour of Cardiff, and the college was opened in 1883. Twenty-five years later Swansea also established its claim that its technical college should be reorganised as one of the constituent colleges of the university. North Wales refused to be satisfied by the existence of a college as distant as Aberystwyth and, after the claims of thirteen competing towns had been examined, Bangor was selected and the college was opened in 1884. The government grant was now withdrawn from Aberystwyth and given to the two new colleges; but Aberystwyth fought hard for existence, and eventually the government agreed to give a grant to all three.

It is remarkable how rapidly, after one gap had been filled, the Welsh educational enthusiasts set themselves to discover and fill another. Secondary schools came next. The Aberdare Committee had reported that only 1540 boys and 265 girls were receiving secondary education apart from those in private schools. Excluding Monmouthshire which possessed a fine educational endowment, only two of the old grammar schools, Christ College at Brecon and Friars School at Bangor, and one new foundation, Llandovery College, were really flourishing. Bangor and Brecon both owed their position to Daniel Lewis Lloyd, afterwards bishop of Bangor. His career is typical of Wales in the nineteenth century, though in England we should have to look several centuries earlier for parallels. Born in 1843 on a farm in Cardiganshire, the most Welsh of all Welsh counties, he received his education at the two small schools of Lampeter and Ystrad Meurig, went up to Jesus College, Oxford, and was appointed curate at Dolgelly, where, by one of those curious makeshifts to which the old grammar schools had to resort, the curate was also on the staff of the school. Lloyd thus drifted into the scholastic profession. In 1873 he was appointed to Friars where, in the days before the Schools Inquiry Commission, the irremovable headmaster is said to have flogged away almost all his pupils and to have enjoyed a life of leisure to the end of his days. Lloyd was at Brecon from 1878 to 1890, and, in days before county scholarships, he used to tour the elementary schools in search of promising pupils. Enthusiastic, fiery-tempered, and forgiving, he knew everything of individual boys, to whom he was a hero. Llandovery, now the largest boarding-school in Wales, had among its headmasters the present archbishop of Wales and the present bishop of St David's. Monmouth School was reorganised as a result of the Endowed Schools Act, being one of the six largest endowments on which the Schools Inquiry Commission had presented detailed reports. These four schools together accounted for two-thirds of the secondary school boys in Wales.

Such a provision for secondary education was obviously quite inadequate. Moreover, it was too closely associated with the Church of England to satisfy a community where the Nonconformist majority was brimful of educational zeal. In England the effective demand came from the professional classes; farmers, artisans, and shopkeepers only began to think of a good secondary education when they found a supply offered to them. Hence till 1902 the really effective portion of English secondary education was modelled on the lines of the reformed public schools. In Wales the demand was for something which should form the next rung of the "ladder" from the elementary school. Those were days when every clever and ambitious boy in Wales wished to become a minister, and when his success in reaching a theological college was the pride of his family. In their early days the university colleges were compelled to do a large amount of secondary school work: indeed at the time of their foundation many persons were inclined to regard it as their function to take boys from the elementary schools and pass them on to Oxford. The theological colleges were obliged to conduct preparatory schools of their own.

The Aberdare Committee came to no very definite conclusions as to the solution of the problem. They were anxious that Wales should have equal facilities in the shape of first-grade schools with England; but neither commissioners nor witnesses were clear how such a type of education, which with a scattered rural population necessarily involved boarding-schools, could be provided at a cost which should be within the reach of parents of moderate means. They saw too that the provision of first-grade schools only touched the fringe of the problem: and that the main demand was for schools of a less ambitious type which would be readily accessible to day-pupils in every district. Provision for girls was more urgently needed even than for boys; but the Committee was a little too early to adopt the solution of mixed schools. They saw that rate or State aid or both were essential conditions of financing the schools adequately; but they evidently felt that, in expressing such an opinion, they were making an unprecedented proposal.

It was left to the Welsh private members to carry a scheme through Parliament. A private members' bill must necessarily be simple and of a kind to appeal to the public. The Intermediate Education Act of 1889 fulfilled these conditions. It set up a uniform type of schools, not very expensive, and numerous enough to be accessible to every district. A government bill, embodying the findings of a Royal Commission, would probably have been more complicated, and would have provided for more differences of type; but it is by no means certain that, without the light of subsequent experience, it would have provided the types which were really needed, and it may be assumed with confidence that it would not have made the same popular appeal as this easily comprehended measure. Provision was to be made by counties. The original schemes for the various schools were to be drawn up by three representatives of the County Council and two nominees of the government. When once the schools were founded, they were to be administered by a governing body for each school (or pair of schools in cases where the boys' and girls' schools were separate); but all these local bodies were to be in some measure under the control of a central governing body for each county. Except in populous areas the schools were "dual," which in practice has come to mean mixed. The County Councils were empowered to raise a halfpenny rate—the first ever avowedly raised for secondary education—and the Treasury was to pay pound for pound. By 1895 thirty such schools had been founded, and by 1902 the number had risen to ninety-five. Monmouth, Llandovery, and Brecon refused to give up their independence; but the bulk of the older schools voluntarily converted themselves into county schools under the new act.

The Welsh Intermediate Education Act was clearly a model for much of the English Act of 1902. County Councils received even larger control under that Act; rate aid and treasury aid both appear; and the type of school set up was meant to be very similar. The faults in the early working of bureaucratic administration of education will have to be considered shortly: for the moment let us consider only the benefits which resulted from the creation of a new type of school. For the first time schools were established whose normal function was to take the most promising pupils of the elementary schools, to continue their general education, and to pass on those who eventually proved most apt to the local university. When Huxley spoke of the "ladder," the metaphor, though unintentionally, suggested a strait and narrow way, by which elementary schoolboys could singly climb with difficulty the ascent to which their more favoured neighbours could crowd up through a broad staircase. These schools provided something more than a "ladder" in this sense. The elementary school pupil who comes out top of his school finds transfer to the secondary school the natural and normal event. The discovery of the nation's brains is no longer left to the merest accident. In rural Wales, at any rate, the parent is rare who puts his boy to work at fourteen in order to earn an immediate wage if the chance is open to him of proving a real success at the university.

It is noteworthy that the whole conception of a series of steps from the elementary school to the university is of British origin. It was unknown in France and Germany, to which English legislators were looking for educational models during the period of the Royal Commissions and for some time later. If the idea was taken from anywhere, it was from Scotland; and, outside the British Empire, the only great country where it is to be found is of British origin, namely the United States. Democratic education is as British as are democratic political institutions. Critics of the Welsh system are sometimes inclined to compare its efficiency with that of the Prussian system to the detriment

of the former. The comparison misses the point. The Prussian Gymnasium provided a connected secondary school
course from nine to nineteen. It was bound to teach more
than can a course which at the earliest begins at twelve.
But the efficiency was won at the expense of entirely
debarring the working classes from its advantages. The
boy who began in an elementary school ended there. It
was assumed that all boys of a certain social position would
complete their educational career and that no boys of a
lower social position would carry it beyond fourteen. Such
a system made organisation delightfully simple. Latin
could be begun at nine, French at eleven, Greek at thirteen,
geometry, algebra, and natural science at the earliest age
at which experience showed that they could be digested,
and a ten years' connected course of history, geography,
and literature could be so devised that no period, no
country, and no author of importance should be omitted.
The elementary school course, on the contrary, cannot be
arranged for the benefit of the few pupils who will ultimately proceed to the university. But education needs
two factors for success, efficient teaching and innate
capacity. The democratic system widens the area of selection so enormously that, even assuming that capacity is
twice as common among the classes which have pushed
their way upwards than among the rest of the population,
this increased field probably secures at least five times as
large a proportion of able pupils; and, in the long run, this
will compensate for the shortened period of secondary
schooling. The pupils transferred from the elementary
schools start with a handicap which they may not have
made up by the age of eighteen, but they may easily be
ahead by twenty-three.

The use of the term "intermediate school" suggests that
the framers of the scheme hardly contemplated that the
schools would be in the fullest sense secondary. It seems
to have been thought by the Aberdare Committee that
sixteen would be a usual age for entering the university
colleges. Experience has falsified expectations. Though
few pupils remain at school beyond sixteen except those

who are proceeding to the university, yet the age of
entering the Welsh colleges is now normally exactly the
same as that which prevails at Oxford and Cambridge, so
that the future university students complete their secondary school course.

The establishment of the schools thus soon produced a
supply of students for the colleges who could at once enter
on degree courses. It was felt that the time had come for
the federation of the colleges into a national university.
From their inauguration Viriamu Jones, the first principal
of Cardiff, had never lost sight of the idea. On the foundation of the South Wales College he had relinquished the
principalship of an organisation in being—Firth College,
Sheffield—to venture on an untried experiment among his
own people. He supplied an enthusiasm which never
relaxed till he worked himself into an early grave. He
strove vigorously to keep education in touch both with
large employers of labour and with workmen's organisations,
which is as much the secret of success for a college in the
industrial area of Glamorgan and Monmouthshire as in
the large towns of the North of England. He fought for
intermediate schools, for university extension, and for
the formation of a national university. He held that the
dependence of the colleges on the external examinations
of London tended to create a false estimate, in the minds
both of students and of the general public, of the place of
examinations in university education. "We are an over-
examined people; the bloom of originality is too often
brushed from an original mind by our examination
system." In 1888 a conference of the three colleges had
already agreed to ask for a federal university on the lines
of Victoria—the lines which within a few years Victoria
sought to alter—but except on federal lines it is difficult
to see how there could have been a university at all. An
alternative scheme was, however, suggested by R. D.
Roberts, who held offices in connection with the extension work of Cambridge and London, by which the
university should send forth itinerant lecturers and give
its degrees to candidates who attended evening classes.

It is an idea which London University has more than any other been able to attain, and it is an idea of which we shall hear more in the future. But it had two great defects. First, it is a very different thing to have a university throwing out tentacles in all directions and to have the tentacles without the university. If either is to be created first, it must be the nucleus. Where could the higher work, which inspires the rest, go on if the university had no local habitation? Secondly, it presumes a university of part-time students. Part-time students will be technological students, for whom there is no division of interest; for they learn by night the principles of what they do by day. But the arts or pure science student who is studying for half his time is serving two masters—with the usual result. It is true that hitherto the extension work has been the weak side of the Welsh university; but this is possibly a reaction against the movement to make it the whole of its work. Lord Aberdare and Viriamu Jones fought hard for a teaching university built up on the three colleges, and by 1891 their policy was accepted; and the charter of the new university received the royal approval in 1893.

With this event the constructive period in the history of Welsh education closes and the critical begins. The whole organisation existed; it was left to test its working by experience and to modify it as that experience suggested. The criticisms which have been brought against the schools and against the university must be considered separately.

Criticism of the schools generally resolves itself into criticism of the Central Welsh Board. This body came into being as follows. One of the conditions on which the government agreed to give grants to the intermediate schools was their submission to an annual inspection and report. The governing bodies were anxious to avoid too rigid control from Whitehall, which still carried the burden of Robert Lowe's sins. In 1892 therefore the Treasury assented to the creation of a central board for Welsh inter-mediate education, only reserving the right to the Charity

Commissioners, to whom the board reported, to conduct a further inspection or examination if it should seem necessary. Viriamu Jones strove hard that the University Court should become the central authority, with a view to securing the co-ordination of secondary and university education. He was supported by the veteran principal of Jesus, Sir John Rhys; but the governing bodies would not accept the proposal, and in 1896 the Central Board, consisting mainly of representatives of the County Governing Bodies, together with a few representatives of teachers and of the University, was set up. There can be no doubt that the new body committed the very fault which it had been created to avoid; for it tended to regard written examinations as the one test of the efficiency of a school and to give or to withhold grants purely on the results of its annual examinations. It had no exact counterpart in the educational machinery of other countries, and it seems to have interpreted its function as similar to the delegacies or syndicates appointed by the English universities for the conduct of local examinations. Inspection was wholly subordinate, and Wales exhibited the phenomena which we have already noticed in connection with England, the establishment of a series of examinations—preliminary, junior, senior, and honours—the annual testing of all pupils except those at the very junior stages, the repeated sending in of candidates for the same examination to secure more distinctions for the school, compulsion on candidates to enter at the earliest possible age, over-pressure, and ill-digested knowledge. These evils were accentuated by the fact that Welsh pupils are more ready to work and had less tradition of "ca' canny" devices than their English cousins, that the very zeal for education among parents —who often had never been at a secondary school themselves and had not learned by experience that more effective work may be done in seven hours than in eleven —increased the danger of over-pressure, and that, most of the schools being mixed, the girls were encouraged to risk their health and mental freshness by conscientiously endeavouring to do what their brothers could only manage with the utmost difficulty. On the whole, however, these evils were first discovered in Wales because State secondary education was thirteen years older than in England, and probably their discovery has done something to demolish the examination fetish in the larger country.

Another criticism often brought against the Central Welsh Board is its supposed neglect of the practical subjects. This may be partly explained by the bookish conception of education which prevailed everywhere at the time when the Board was set up. The Act defined "intermediate" education as one "which includes instruction in Latin, Greek, the Welsh and English language and literature, modern languages, mathematics, natural and applied science, or in some of such studies, and generally in the higher branches of knowledge," while technical education was defined as including "any subject applicable to the purposes of agriculture, industries, trade, or commercial life and practice, including science and art classes." This was the universal conception in 1889. The laboratory had taken its place alongside of the class-room; but that any true education could come from the saw or the spade was undreamt of. But what of art and music? Where were ye, Nymphs, when arts which had taken their place in the national culture ages ago were omitted? The answer can only be found by an analysis of the mixture of idealistic and utilitarian motives which influenced parents. They did not, as a rule, choose for their sons occupations which would bring in wealth; there is much truth in the saying that every able young Welshman wished to be a teacher or a preacher. Such ambitions may partly arise from a desire to escape "shirt-sleeve" occupations; but they likewise imply in the community which cherishes them a respect for the things of the mind. Technical education, which appeals to the desire for wealth, was not therefore in great demand; but, among the things of the mind, a technical motive was at work, favouring those subjects which were needed in the ministerial or scholastic callings; and, as these were precisely the subjects which had formed the staple of traditional schooling, they were

eagerly seized. When the claims of art, music and hand-
work as essential elements in the education of the whole
man began to be pressed both in Great Britain and in
America, the difficulty that these subjects in no way assist
the pupil in his subsequent university course proved, in
Wales as in England, the most serious obstacle to their
recognition. Neither country has yet solved the problem.
The literary ideal of education, which in England in the
past was a peculiar possession of the classes which sent
their children to schools conducted on public school lines,
is, however, now so threatened everywhere by the rising
tide of commercialism, that twenty years hence there will
probably be no complaint that there are more aspiring
teachers and preachers than there are class-rooms or
pulpits to be filled, and a future generation may be glad
that in rural Wales the old Victorian ideal still persists
among all classes.

Wales was affected as well as England by the Board of
Education Act of 1899 and by the Education Act of 1902.
The former, by handing over the powers of the Charity
Commissioners to the newly-constituted Board of Educa-
tion in London, substituted a real for a nominal master
over all the Welsh authorities, including the Central Welsh
Board. The Act of 1902 made the County and County
Borough Councils, acting through their Education Com-
mittees, the Local Education Authority for all classes of
school, and they thus took the place of the old County
Governing Bodies and often encroached on the powers of
the Local Governing Bodies.

The effect of the former change was seen in due course.
The idea of devolution was in the air; but, whereas in
regard to things of the body it is very difficult to disentangle Welsh administration from English (a letter from
North to South Wales, for instance, goes by way of
Shrewsbury and Hereford), in things of the mind the
two countries are very different. Hence there has been
some tendency to try devolution first in educational
matters. The Board of Education, which shared with all
bureaucracies the love of power, cleverly secured it by a

superficial concession to this desire. It established a separate Welsh department which turned into a reality the nominal powers formerly vested in the Charity Commissioners; but this branch had no real independence, and was under the direct control of the President of the Board. The Welsh branch of Whitehall in consequence had overlapping jurisdiction with the Central Welsh Board, and the question of "dual inspection" led to a long controversy. Some sympathy can be felt with Whitehall. It had experienced a sudden conversion. It was conscious that, in its unregenerate days as the Committee of Council, it had been given over to the idolatry of examinations. Its officials, like all converts, were now the most zealous preachers of the doctrine which they had once persecuted. Preliminary and junior examinations were hewn down and burned in the fire; it was proclaimed as an article of faith that two examinations only might be accepted, one at sixteen and the other at nineteen; and possibly they were feeling their way to see if these examinations might not, as in Germany, be controlled by the State. In England the old heathenism had plenty of adherents, but no college of priests: in Wales the Central Welsh Board seemed to occupy the latter position. It was summoned to recant, but it took some time to recite the new creed properly. The Inquisition began its work; the order of merit in which the successful candidates in the honours examination had been placed was the first victim; the newly-instituted examination between the senior and honours examination had a short life; the junior examination was sentenced to death but the execution of the sentence was deferred. Ultimately the Central Welsh Board subscribed to two articles of the new creed; first, that inspection is more important than examination; and secondly, that music, drawing, woodwork, needlework, laundry, and housewifery are canonical subjects in the curriculum. But Whitehall is watching it carefully, and any day an indictment may be laid against it as a relapsed heretic.

Meanwhile it was being whispered that the university was guilty not only of the worship of examinations but of

another false goddess, Red Tape. On this occasion the
Board of Education, perhaps from a little uneasiness lest
it had not cleared its own precincts entirely from the latter
form of idolatry, did not formally figure at the trial, which
was carried on before a Royal Commission over which
Lord Haldane presided. Their report appeared in 1918.
The difficulties inherent in the federal system, which had
led to its abandonment in Victoria University, were ten-
fold greater in Wales. Liverpudlians had urged as a reason
for separation from Manchester that the time consumed
in travelling prevented their representatives from attending
university meetings. What would they have said if their
only means of reaching a sister college had been by the
Cardigan Bay Coast route? But there was a reason in the
case of Wales, which there was not in the case of Victoria,
why the abandonment of the federal system would have
entailed a great loss. A federal Victoria embodied no idea;
the Welsh university stood for the spiritual unity of the
Welsh people. It was felt that administrative difficulties
must somehow be got over without sacrificing this advantage. The Royal Commissioners seem to have arrived
at a happy solution. The colleges should be given a large
measure of independence as regards courses, syllabuses,
and examinations; and the university should be made
more than a combination of the three colleges. The reformed
system of London on its internal side may have suggested
this solution. The colleges were to be what University and
King's Colleges were to London; but there would also be
a technological organisation for South Wales, an extension
system, a close connection with the National Library and
the National Museum, a university press, and a central
body for arousing and directing interest in national
archaeology, history, and literature; in fact the university
should be a brain controlling many limbs. The independence of the colleges would destroy the external character
of the examinations and would do away with the need
for much of the "red tape"; and the university would be
set free to devote itself to constructive work.

The experience of Wales in the matter of her university

may be of value to England at some future date when she seeks to set up provincial colleges for her rural areas. At present the prospect of an Eastern Counties University with colleges at Norwich, Lincoln, and Ipswich, seems as remote as in 1850 seemed the prospect of a northern university with colleges at Manchester, Liverpool, and Leeds: but the latter is now a matter of history, and why should the former be impossible? Cardiff is of course similarly situated to one of the English city universities; but Aberystwyth and Bangor have no counterpart in rural England. Yet there are indications that the age of great towns may be a passing phase. Mr H. G. Wells has seen visions of a time when London may be as accessible from Exeter as twenty years ago it was from Streatham. Works are being built as far away from big towns as conditions admit in order to avoid high rents. Electricity will hasten the process. Finally agriculture is always bound to assert itself. It is the oldest of industries and the most essential. And it will be mixed farming. The specialised wheat farming of Manitoba will pass away and the mixed farming of East Anglia will remain. If any change takes place, agriculture will become more intensive and more like the garden farming of Japan. Old King Coal reigns only till science has found a means to use other sources of energy, and who doubts her power to tame them? But Mother Earth will be the supply of man's food till the sun grows cold.

The University of Wales is sometimes accused of not being national. Before examining the charge, let us take the senses in which it undoubtedly is national. In the first place it is closely bound to the rest of the national system of education. There can hardly be a parish in the land which does not contain one of its graduates and some boy or girl who will some day be one of its graduates. It presents a goal to which hundreds of lads in isolated farm or mountain cottage aspire. It must contain a much greater percentage of poor students than the most democratic of English universities. Secondly, it is the centre of research into the national history, language, and antiquities.

The contributions of its staff to knowledge contain a high proportion of what is specifically national. It is true that it is not a wholesale manufactory of bards, but what university is? *Poeta non fit* can be no more overcome than the law of gravitation. In the third place it is closely bound up with the specific interests of rural Wales from theology to agriculture. May we hope that it will, in consonance with history, develop forestry into a great national industry? And it has no firmer friends than the slate quarrymen.

What then is meant by the charge? Sometimes it only means that the critic objects to some action of the university and uses "anti-national" as the worst name he can call it. But the criticism is not all of this kind. Perhaps the sense in which the university could be made more national is that the people at large should see more of it. London University, thanks to the smallness of its academic diocese, has been the first to bring its teaching to people's own doors. It is far more difficult in a scattered area. If a professor at Manchester or Birmingham announces a public lecture, all the constituents of that university area can with a short railway journey attend. Aberystwyth and Bangor can only solve the problem as Mohammed solved it in regard to the mountain. A beginning has been made by means of tutorial classes. Sir Henry Jones has adumbrated a scheme by which every village shall, if it wishes, see a representative of the university. When the university is accused of not being national, it probably means that the working men want, not merely to know that the clever boy of the village is working at one of the colleges, but to hear a teacher from that college in their own village hall. Let the critics think out a scheme: it needs men and money. But it will not be a substitute for the present system by which the able boy is removed to one of the university towns for eight months in the year: it will be an addition. The able boy is needed as one of the future lecturers. It is a difficult problem, but, if it is ever solved, it will be the finishing touch to the work of the university in rural areas.

REFERENCES

Departmental Committee on Intermediate and Higher Education in
    Wales (Aberdare Committee), *Report*, 1881.
W. Cadwaladr Davies and W. Lewis Jones, College Histories Series,
    The University of Wales and its Colleges, 1905.
K. V. Jones, *Life of Viriamu Jones*, 1915.
Royal Commission on University Education in Wales, *Report*, 1918.
Annual Reports of Central Welsh Board.

CHAPTER XII

THE MODERN STATE SYSTEM

THE aim of this chapter is to trace the steps by which, within the last twenty years, the State has come in a large measure to control and to supply secondary education. The central point on which attention is to be fixed is the Education Act of 1902. This Act largely carried out the recommendations of the Royal Commission which reported in 1895, and was anticipated as regards technical education by the Technical Instruction Act of 1889. Its results need to be traced till we come to the next great landmark, Mr Fisher's Act of 1918.

Though the Act of 1902 was the first avowed recognition of the principle that secondary education is a fitting object of public expenditure, the State had in fact, though not in name, been aiding secondary education before that date in three distinct ways.

(1) The grants of the Science and Art Department, South Kensington, originally meant to help classes rather than schools, had come to dominate a whole body of schools. It is true that an "organised science school" was not necessarily, in the ordinary sense of the term, a school at all; in fact, where it was connected with a school, it consisted only of a particular department or of particular classes of that school. But the system of South Kensington grants brought with it the consequence that, provided the instruction given in a school was mainly scientific, that school was eligible to receive considerable financial assistance from the State. The only conditions were that the parent's income should not exceed £500 (originally £400) a year and that thirteen hours a week (originally more) should be given to science. At the time when the Commission reported in 1895, payment by results in these schools was being abolished; henceforth three grants were

to be given—an attendance grant, an examination grant which was to be in respect only of the higher courses, and a variable grant dependent on inspection and oral examination. Inspection was to cover all subjects taught, literary as well as scientific. In other words science schools were assuming a more definitely secondary character. The past system of South Kensington, however, was severely criticised by the Commission. Their grants had narrowed the curriculum and the method of determining them had encouraged "cram." South Kensington schools "suffer from a permanent examination fever[1]," and the Commission recommended that the Science and Art Department, which had since 1884 been virtually independent, should be fused with the Committee of Council under the new designation of "Board of Education." This recommendation was carried out by the Board of Education Act, 1899.

(2) The Technical Instruction Act, 1889, was another means of introducing State subsidies to secondary education by a side-wind. It permitted county councils to spend money not merely on technical education in the strict sense, that is, direct preparation for a specific occupation, but on such general education as was necessary to enable the pupil to profit by a true technical course. The county councils, which had been brought into existence in the previous year, were allowed to raise a penny rate for technical instruction understood in this broad sense. Probably little would have come of the Act but for a fortunate accident. In 1890 the government proposed a scheme of legislation for the purpose of reducing the number of public houses. In order to compensate publicans whose licenses were taken away, an additional tax was imposed on all alcoholic liquors. The bill imposing the tax was passed, but that authorising its intended application met with such opposition from the prohibitionists, who would not listen to any proposal for compensating the publican, that it was dropped. Parliament found itself in the most unusual position of possessing a sum of money

[1] Bryce Commission: *Report*, p. 100.

with which it did not know what to do. Arthur Acland,
afterwards Minister for Education (1892–1895), and the
leading educationalist on the West Riding County Council,
suggested in a lethargic and half-empty house that the
money should be handed over to the county councils and
ear-marked mainly for the purpose of technical instruction.
This was agreed to; and the county councils were thus
enabled, or rather compelled, to provide for technical
education without the necessity of levying a rate, which
most of them would have been very reluctant to do. It
was the experience which they acquired in this branch of
education which paved the way for their appointment as
the secondary and elementary education authority by
the Act of 1902. The sum so handed over every year was
always known as the "whiskey money." So curious a
source of revenue, however, entailed one unfortunate
result: the funds available for technical education increased
whenever drinking increased and diminished with a spread
of temperance, so that, if the total abstainers could have
persuaded the whole country to "go dry," there would
have been no funds left! The Commission found in 1895
that 93 out of 129 county and county borough councils
were spending the whole of the whiskey money on education but that in only thirteen cases was a rate levied. Of
the £317,000 directly administered by county councils[1],
£188,000 was spent on technical education in the strict
sense, £17,000 was used to subsidise secondary schools,
£39,000 was given in scholarships, £14,000 went to evening
continuation schools, and £22,000 was devoted to the
training of evening school teachers[2]. No large proportion
of the money therefore went to aid secondary education
in the strict sense of the term, but the bulk was spent on
the education of pupils of secondary school age, not of
adults; and the Commission notes that county council
grants had tended to modify the curricula of schools.

(3) School Boards, chiefly in large towns, though intended to supply only elementary education, had been led

[1] *I.e.* not by county borough councils and not handed over to the
councils of towns   [2] *Report*, p. 35.

by the deficiency in the less expensive forms of secondary education to overstep the strict limit of their functions, and had set up "higher grade" schools. The Commission noted that many schools had assumed this name which differed from other elementary schools only by charging a higher fee[1]. But the real higher grade schools, of which there were about sixty, kept their pupils to a higher age: they were in effect what the Schools Inquiry Commission had wished to term "third-grade secondary" schools. The secondary part of their work could as a rule only be financed by turning the upper classes into an organised science school under South Kensington. The Commission of 1895 held that higher grade schools could not, "speaking generally, share in the grant distributed by the Education Department nor be supported out of the rates, although in a few instances this seems to have been attempted[2]." But the actual words of the Education Act of 1870 did not seem to impose such a restriction, for an elementary school was defined as one "in which elementary education is the principal part of the education given." Acting on this apparent permission, the London School Board began to use the rates freely for such post-elementary education till it was brought to a sudden stop in 1899 by the action of Mr Cockerton, the Local Government Board auditor, who surcharged all expenditure incurred on pupils over fifteen years of age. This decision was upheld by the courts in 1900: thus no way was left save by legislation to avoid the abandonment of the schools which were already in existence. A temporary act was hurried through to allow the expenditure for the current year, and the government promised to introduce a comprehensive measure dealing with the whole organisation of education as soon as possible. This was duly brought forward and passed, and became the Education Act of 1902.

Before dealing with this Act, we must, however, return to the Royal Commission of 1895, generally known as the

[1] When fees were abolished in elementary schools in 1890, these schools were still allowed to charge the difference between their original fee and that of other schools. [2] *Report*, p. 10.

Bryce Commission. The question really before this body was whether or no there should be a State system of secondary education. It practically reported that private endeavour had failed to produce an adequate supply. It was true that the Endowed Schools Commissioners appointed under the Endowed Schools Act had before their disappearance in 1874 made no less than 902 schemes for reforming individual schools, and that their successors the Charity Commissioners had made an addition of 295 schemes. Great improvements had thus been effected: for instance, in the West Riding there were thirty-six efficient schools (eight of which were first-grade) against twenty-eight (of which only three were first-grade), mostly inefficient, in 1865. But the deficiency in the supply of secondary schools which had been pointed out by the Schools Inquiry Commission had only in part been remedied. Many of the small grammar schools were crippled by lack of funds and some were situated in such small places that their removal was desirable. The number of secondary school pupils at the outside was not more than 2·5 per thousand of the population. It varied greatly in different counties, Warwickshire, with the numerous schools which had been set up at Birmingham out of the King Edward's foundation, having 5·2 against Lancashire's 1·1. Schools were very deficient in the purely agricultural areas such as Devonshire, and in such districts education was little valued.

For these reasons they were of opinion that an adequate supply of inexpensive secondary schools could only be secured by State intervention. They were also influenced by the fact that the State was already virtually subsidising secondary education of a scientific kind and that thereby an unfair discrimination against the more literary type of education had come into being almost unnoticed. There was in fact a danger of the old grammar schools being entirely supplanted by the more modern technical and scientific forms of education, and this prospect the Commission did not welcome. "Such schools represent especially the tradition of literary education. There is little danger at the present day that we shall fail to recognise the necessity of improving and extending scientific and technical instruction. It is less certain that we may not run some risk of a lopsided development in education, in which the teaching of science, theoretical or applied, may so predominate as to entail comparative neglect of studies which are of less obvious and immediate utility[1]."

There was not entire unanimity in favour of State intervention among the witnesses. No doubt this was due in a large measure to the atrocious policy which the Committee of Council had been pursuing in regard to elementary schools for the last thirty-five years. Temple, at that time bishop of London, and surely a progressive educationalist, was so haunted by visions of examinations and payment by results that he could not reconcile himself to the change. The fact that the responsible minister would necessarily be a party politician, coming in and going out with his party, did not inspire confidence. Finally there was the fear of bureaucracy, that is to say, of the permanent officials gathering into their hands more power than was intended and, as the Report put it, "managing secondary education on the same centralised system as primary." This has to some extent come to pass. Still, the Commission was probably right in regarding State control as the lesser of two evils, and their prophecy that the combination of secondary and elementary education under one department would do more to liberalise elementary education than it would to mechanise secondary[2] has, on the whole, been fulfilled. Elementary education had grown up under government auspices and teachers trembled at the thunders of Whitehall; secondary education had been accustomed to enjoy independence and continued to assert it. It is not often that a change of name brings a change of character; but the Board of Education in its most bureaucratic days never converted the negation of education into a system, as did the old Committee of Council in the sixties.

Educationalists were undoubtedly groping for some arrangement by which secondary education could be con-

---

[1] *Report*, p. 48.   [2] *Report*, p. 104.

trolled and financed by the State without becoming subject
to the party system. The Commissioners were clearly aware
of the difficulty, but they were afraid to face it. This was
inevitable. Since the war we have become critical even
of the most fundamental principles of the British constitution and of parliamentary government. Up to 1914
they were sacrosanct; every statesman prided himself on
being constitutional, and it was not likely that any
reputable politician would undermine the constitution
for so small a thing as educational efficiency. The problem
is with us still: it is doubtless responsible for the attraction
of schemes of devolution to many minds: and it is therefore
worth while dwelling on the exact nature of the difficulty
and the form in which it presented itself to the Commissioners.

It has always been regarded as an integral part of the
Constitution that departments which spend the public
money should be represented by a minister responsible
to Parliament. Under the party system this means that
the education minister comes into office with his party,
goes out with it however efficient he may be, and is rarely
likely to be turned out however inefficient he may be. The
system, which was designed to secure parliamentary control, works out in a manner quite the reverse. The minister
himself is responsible to Parliament, that is to the party
whips, who have no interest in real educational efficiency,
with the result that the permanent officials, who are the
real authors of educational policy, are responsible to
nobody. During the war the party system was in abeyance
and the novel departure was made of appointing a real
educationalist as President of the Board. The contrast has
made us realise the loss which education sustained by the
fact of the first seven presidents having no interest in
education before they held the post or after they quitted it.

A proposal was laid before the Commission which, if it
had been possible to adopt it, would have left State education in educational hands. It was suggested that the
minister should be assisted by a council composed of
permanent representatives of the Crown and members

elected by the universities and the teachers. The Commission came to the inevitable conclusion that the proposal was inconsistent with the Constitution. And indeed it was; for either the minister must obey the council or the council must obey the minister. If the minister obeyed the council, he would sooner or later come into collision with the party whips. If the council obeyed the minister, the public would in time realise that the party politicians were over-riding their expert advisers and would draw their own conclusions. The only way out of this difficulty would be the restriction of the cabinet system, so that such a committee could be represented in the House by a chairman who did not go in or out with the cabinet. A far more drastic remedy has now come within the horizon of practical politics, namely to remove education and many other matters from the Imperial Parliament altogether and to hand them over to provincial parliaments; but it seems rash to assume that such local parliaments would avoid the party system any more than the Imperial Parliament.

The Commission went as far as it dared in suggesting that there existed a large province in education which lay quite outside the sphere of parliamentary politics, viz. all that is concerned with membership of the teaching profession, with inspection, and with examination, "the means by which educational ideals can best be made to penetrate the educational machinery, scholastic and political." So far as this province was concerned, they accepted the idea of a council. Such a body would undoubtedly have become exceedingly powerful; for, whatever is laid down by law, the persons who possess zeal and knowledge will, under such circumstances, always be able to win the day against those whose position rests only on law. It is possible that in course of time nothing would have been left to the officials of Whitehall save the working of the parliamentary machinery. The ministry and officials, however, were careful to see that no such body was set up; they indeed permitted two shadows of it, the Teachers' Registration Council and the Consultative Committee, to wander like ghosts about Whitehall; but they rejected all the proposals of the former and confined the latter to the writing of occasional reports.

After discussing the constitution of the central authority, the Commission naturally proceeded next to consider the local authority. They found that scholastic opinion was against all forms of local control, while the administrative and political witnesses were all in its favour. Here again the teachers' objection doubtless was that local elections were usually conducted on party lines and, in the case of school board elections, on denominational lines. But the opposite case was well put by one of the witnesses:— "While elementary education may properly be *imposed* on a nation, the higher education ought only to be organised in response to the people's demand; hence it ought to be mainly under popular control," and German secondary education was in consequence to be regarded as too centralised. The meaning we take to be that, if you are starting elementary education for the first time in a country, the people are *ex hypothesi* too ignorant to be entrusted with its initiation; but, if you have reached a stage at which an extensive system of secondary education is possible, there exists *ex hypothesi* a fair degree of enlightenment. In that case the parents have sufficient idea what they desire to doom your system to failure if you do not take account of their wishes.

The Commissioners, however, did not recommend handing over secondary education to the school boards, the existing authority for elementary education; the majority of the witnesses were unfavourably impressed by the smaller boards. Nor did they propose any new *ad hoc* body. The bulk of the electors would probably not have voted; and nothing expresses the public will less than a body about which the public is so apathetic that it will not take the trouble to exercise the franchise. Though the Commissioners were not very explicit, they seemed to favour the county councils, reinforced by expert co-opted members and possibly by representatives of the central authority and of teachers. The assumption that the local authorities for secondary and for elementary education would be distinct led them into difficulties over the higher grade schools which, though doing secondary work, were counted as elementary. In the Act of 1902 the Government cut the knot by making the county councils the authority not only for secondary but also for elementary education.

The Commissioners were anxious to bring the large public schools and other boarding schools under the central authority, though their non-local character made it impossible to bring them under any local authority. They believed that the best of the private schools would welcome inspection if it carried with it official recognition; ultimately recognition should be made compulsory. To allay the fears of non-provided schools, they suggested that the education authority should not be permitted to found new schools where the existing supply of recognised schools was adequate: but they contemplated that a certain number of such schools would be willing to be transferred to the authority. Unfortunately this part of the report remained a pious aspiration. Existing schools were found to have the deepest distrust of local authorities and a very limited trust in the central authority. Only financial necessity could make them part with their independence. The Act of 1902 was obliged to omit all reference to existing schools, and its effect was thus to remove deficiencies in the supply but not to create a true State system of secondary education. Much has, however, been done by administrative action to bring the bulk of the older schools in return for Board of Education grants, which began in 1901, under the central, though not under the local, authority. A State system cannot, however, be regarded as satisfactory so long as the schools which can afford to do so insist on boycotting it. They may be few in numbers and some of them might reasonably be suspected of doing so from an anti-democratic bias: but this is not the case with all, and the lamentable fact must be admitted that neither parents nor teachers have any great confidence in the State as compared with private endeavour. Till the State is capable of winning that confidence, it is desirable that it shall have rivals to stimulate it by competition; yet it is an unhappy sight to see the institutions with the greatest attractions of antiquity and prestige, which moreover educate a very high percentage of the most successful pupils, moving in an orbit of their own outside what without them can be called a State system but cannot be called a national system of secondary education.

As regards government and county council grants to the schools, the Commissioners recommended that there should be no "payment by results" and no differentiation in favour of scientific subjects. No legislation was needed to carry out this part of the report, and action was taken rapidly. In 1895 literary subjects were made compulsory in organised science schools; in 1897 payment by results finally disappeared from elementary schools; and in 1901 the newly constituted Board of Education began to make grants to secondary schools. Schools which did not wish to receive grants could nevertheless, by submitting to inspection, obtain "recognition." We will return to the present conditions as regards the number of grant-earning and recognised schools later.

Perhaps the most important recommendation of all has been left till last. The establishment of an adequate supply of secondary schools and of a system whereby they should be financed by public authority was a necessary condition of realising Huxley's ideal of the "ladder" from the elementary school to the university. It would be a mistake to suppose that there was ever a period when no boys from humble homes found their way to Oxford and Cambridge; and the success of some of the large town grammar schools, such as Manchester, Birmingham, and Bradford had considerably added to the number in Victorian times. But such cases were exceptions. The boy of outstanding ability in a large city stood a very fair chance of being discovered, in smaller towns he stood little and in rural districts none. The mass of pupils whose capacities were well above the average but not actually outstanding had few opportunities. The establishment of a State system rendered normal what had previously been exceptional. The witnesses who were examined by the Commission differed as regards the desirable number of free places in State-supported schools, the estimates ranging from one-third to one-twentieth. The Commissioners did not venture to suggest a percentage but contented themselves with expressing the view that free places should be given to "candidates of exceptional rather than of average ability." They discussed the difficult problem of the right selection of children aged twelve by competitive examination, and had to be content with leaving it as a insoluble. Scarcely any witness favoured the idea of free secondary education, which, however democratic it sounds, means in effect using the rates to pay for the education of the prosperous classes. So long as enough free places are given, every fee-paying pupil increases the total sum available for carrying on the school, and the fee-paying pupil is thus rendering an advantage to the free-placer. In order to give the fullest share in the system to the really poor, what is needed is not so much an increase in the number of free places as subsistence allowances which will induce the poorest class of parents not to refuse .the offer of a free place because of the loss of wages which their child incurs by remaining at school.

The chief extension of the free-place system occurred in 1907, when it was made obligatory on every secondary school as a condition of receiving the full government grant to admit 25 per cent. of free-placers. The Report of the British Association for 1918 contains an interesting review of the working of the system, which shows that it has on the whole been successful in fulfilling the aims of its authors. The few weaknesses which are revealed are such as we should expect in the working of any new system, and remedies are suggested; but a history of education is hardly the place to discuss them.

The Act of 1902 followed the Royal Commission of 1895 after a much longer interval than the acts which gave effect to the recommendations of the Public Schools and Schools Inquiry Commissions. Even so it might have been delayed still longer but for the situation created by the Cockerton judgment. For the first time elementary and secondary education were treated as part of a single whole. The two forms of education starting at the two ends had at length met in the middle. The elementary school age had risen till it had reached fourteen: a type of secondary school with a lower leaving age than the old grammar schools was now to be founded in considerable numbers.

As we are only concerned here with the effects of the Act on secondary education, we are able to omit all discussion of the great controversial feature which alone at the time interested politicians and a large section of the general public, the clauses which threw the voluntary schools on the rates. But, in order to understand the choice of the county councils as the authority for both kinds of education, it is necessary to refer to their predecessors in the sphere of elementary education, the school boards. The school board had controlled the education of a single town or village; it did not matter whether the town were London or whether the village contained only a few hundred inhabitants. The big boards worked fairly well, the small ones worked badly. In many villages it was impossible to find members with any educational views. But in any case, if the functions of the local educational authority were to be enlarged so as to cover secondary education, the smallest area which could be put under one authority must be large enough to support a secondary school. The smaller boards must therefore in any case disappear; but it would have been possible to substitute larger *ad hoc* bodies. But the school boards, which were elected on a crude system of proportional representation (the single transferable vote not having yet been thought of), were generally elected on strictly denominational lines. It is true that, once elected, the members usually laid aside their theological weapons; but it was feared that, under any system of *ad hoc* election, denominational firebrands would be elected rather than educationalists. On the other hand the county councils[1] had been successful in their management of technical education, and they were the one body in the sphere of local government in which the public had displayed any interest and which had attracted

[1] These include the county borough councils of towns with over 50,000 inhabitants.

men of real administrative capacity to stand for election. It does not appear at first sight to be a qualification for an education authority that its members have been chosen not with a view to their educational capacities but to their ability in managing roads, police and asylums; but it is our English way to adopt lines which appear to work well, regardless of logic. In order, however, to secure that the county councils should not be left without expert advice, it was enacted that their powers, other than financial, should be delegated to a committee, on which, in addition to their own members, they should appoint experts from outside, some of whom should be women. The suggestions of the Royal Commission as to the representation of the Board of Education and of teachers on the committee were not carried out by the Act.

The need of the Act was shown by the fact that up to 1912 the county and county borough councils had founded 330 new schools and taken over 53 existing schools. It stands therefore as a great landmark in the history of English secondary education; for by it the two great problems of an adequate supply of schools and of trans-ference of the best pupils from the elementary schools received their solution. This work is permanent. It cannot be prophesied with equal certainty that the choice of local education authority will stand the test of time; the school boards probably felt as secure of their position in 1895 as do the county councils now. There are already indications of a feeling that local interest is insufficiently secured by the centralisation of powers in the hands of a body which controls so large an area as the county councils, though this danger does not affect the county boroughs. The manage-ment of a school should of course largely voice the opinions of the area from which the school draws its pupils, but in a large county the county council is almost as non-local a body as the Board of Education. On the other hand a county council is more likely to secure differentiation of type than a body which controls only one school; and a lesser body is unlikely to found training colleges and schools for highly specialised purposes. But many of the county

and county borough authorities are on the other hand too
small for the latter purpose without combination. The
fact is that the nature of the unit for local educational
purposes is in each case the result of historical accidents[1].

The reader may wish to have some information as to
the numbers of schools of various types in the year 1912,
as ten years would appear to give time for the Act to have
produced its effect and the Act was the last important step
towards increasing the supply of schools. It is, however,
no easy matter to give the desired information. No complete list of secondary schools exists. The Board publishes
a list of grant-earning and recognised schools; but half the
schools represented on the Headmasters' Conference and
a fair number of those represented on the Headmasters'
Association have never sought recognition, and there are
besides a considerable number of private schools. The
number of schools represented on the Headmistresses'
Association which are not on the Board's list is much
smaller. In practice it is therefore necessary to ignore the
mass of private schools, except the few which have been
inspected, and the endowed schools, mostly small, which
are neither inspected nor represented on any of the three
above-mentioned bodies of heads of schools.

The problem is complicated by the fact that there are
no less than five bases of classification which are of some
importance:

(a) According to the sex of the pupils—boys', girls',
or mixed.

(b) According to the leaving age, where no hard and
fast line exists, and the most that can be done is to divide
according as the proportion of pupils over sixteen to those
between twelve and sixteen is over 25 per cent., between
25 and 10 per cent., or under 10 per cent.

(c) According to their relation to the Board of Education
—grant-earning, recognised, or independent.

(d) According to their relation to the Local Education
Authority—provided, subsidised, or independent.

(e) According to curriculum, where again no hard and

[1] There are 62 administrative counties and 80 county boroughs.

fast line exists, such as that between *Gymnasien, Realgymnasien* and *Realschulen* in Germany.

(*a*), (*b*), *and* (*c*).

The facts for English grant-earning and recognised schools are obtained by adding up the schools as given in the *List of Secondary Schools in England Recognised by the Board of Education as Efficient*, 1913. The similar list for Welsh schools does not distinguish between grant-earning and efficient. To give a greater completeness to the list, we have assumed that the remaining schools on the Headmasters' Conference would come into the highest class as regards leaving age, the remaining schools on the Headmistresses' Association and half those on the Headmasters' Association into the second class, and the remaining schools on the Headmasters' Association in the third class. But to prevent an unwarranted appearance of exactitude we have given only round numbers except in the first case, where there is not much likelihood of error.

Proportion of pupils over 16 to those between 12 and 16.

		Over 25 %	10–25 %	Under 10 %	Total
Grant-earning	Boys'	16	123	218	357
	Girls'	76	174	60	310
	Mixed	4	74	140	218
		96	371	418	885
Recognised	Boys'	22	13	6	41
	Girls'	42	10	3	55
	Mixed	1	2	2	5
		65	25	11	101
Welsh ...	Boys'	1	14	10	25
	Girls'	4	16	5	25
	Mixed	11	38	12	61
		16	68	27	111
Others ...	Boys'	66	40	40	146
	Girls'	—	20	—	20
		66	60	40	166
Totals ...	Boys'	105	190	274	569
	Girls'	122	220	68	410
	Mixed	16	114	154	284
		243	524	496	1263

It will be noticed that the leaving age appears to be higher in the case of girls than of boys. This is partly explicable by the deflection of boys from local schools caused by the existence of the great public schools and is a mere paper result; for in many cases the presence of a single additional pupil over 16 is sufficient to remove a school from one class to another. But the statistics as regards mixed schools and the number of cases, especially in the industrial districts, where, of two parallel schools, the girls' is in a higher class than the boys', show that the boy, whose education is thought of by the parent as vocational, is taken from school earlier than the girl, whose education is regarded as general. It is possible, however, that the better diffusion of talent among the teachers in the case of girls' schools, which is encouraged by the non-existence of anything corresponding to the large public schools for boys, may produce a half-unconscious recognition of the great mass of girls' schools as giving a more valuable education. The high leaving age of the small secondary schools of rural Wales is noticeable when one goes through the schools individually.

(d).

The following table shows a classification of grant-earning and recognised schools according to the character of the governing body.

	Grant-earning	Recognised	Welsh	Total
Founded by L.E.A.	329	1	6	336
Taken over by L.E.A. ...	53	—	—	53
Endowed schools	395	55	4	454
Welsh intermediate schools	—	—	99	99
Conducted by religious bodies	49	9	2	60
Proprietary, etc.	59	18	—	77
Private	—	18	—	18
	885	101	111	1097

Of the schools founded by local education authorities about one-fifth are boys' schools, two-fifths girls' and two-fifths mixed. Twelve of these girls' schools and two of the mixed schools come into the first grade as regards leaving age. Of the boys' schools five-sixths are in the third grade;

of the girls' schools two-thirds are in the second grade. Taking all these facts into account it is clear that the Act, necessary as it was for boys' education, was still more beneficial to that of girls.

(e).

The Board, when wishing to give an idea of the curriculum, states what languages are taught. In grant-earning schools Latin was taught in 757 schools, Greek in 183, French in 879 and German in 273. Another classification is into one, two, three and four language schools:

One language	(French, 100)	106
Two languages	(French and Latin, 359)	386
Three languages	(Latin, French and German, 207;	
	Latin, Greek and French, 47) ...	256
Four languages	... ...	137
		885

As the first grade recognised and independent schools are mainly four language schools, the figure of 137 may probably be doubled to reach the number of schools equipped on all sides existing in England.

It will readily be seen from these statistics that we do not possess a "system" in the French or German sense. State action has supplemented the existing supply without interfering with it: but it has secured an adequate supply of schools which, though wonderfully varied, appear to meet all needs. In time all the great boarding schools will probably consent to receive government recognition by submitting to inspection; for, as long as they are not dependent on government grants, their independence is in no way threatened, since, in the highly improbable event of the government insisting on changes in curriculum as a condition of recognition, they could at once sever their connection with the government and, if they carried the parents of their pupils with them, the Board of Education would be powerless. Till they do so, the hands of the government are tied in taking any action with regard to a very different class of school, the inefficient non-recognised private school. On the other hand it would be a misfortune

if the government attempted to crush out schools which
do not conform to existing conventions, such as Bedale's,
by reason of their very originality. Even if some such
experiments were to be "crank schools" in the worse sense,
it is always possible that here and there one such school
might reveal lines of future advance.

The period between the passing of the Acts of 1902 and
1918 was thus marked more by the silent changes brought
about by the activities of local education authorities and
the influence of inspection than by any outstanding
legislative or administrative change. This is, however,
perhaps the best point at which to treat the history of the
various attempts to secure a teachers' register.

The idea of a registering authority which should ultimately fulfil for the teaching profession the same functions
as those performed by the General Medical Council and
the Incorporated Law Society for the medical and legal
professions is as old as the Schools Inquiry Commission.
In a sense it was more pressing in 1869 than it is at the
present day, since there were then more unqualified private
schoolmasters and mistresses. We have seen that the
proposal to establish such an authority was omitted from
the Endowed Schools Bill during its passage through
Parliament. It was revived and strongly recommended by
the Bryce Commission, and the Board of Education Act,
1899, provided for its institution. Its subsequent fortunes
were not happy. A registration council was actually set
up and a register established in 1902. It was arranged in
two columns, one for elementary teachers and the other
for secondary. The National Union of Teachers objected
to this division as preventing the transfer of an elementary
teacher to a secondary school. The Board, rather than
make up their minds to an amendment of the scheme,
secured the passage of an Act in 1907 under which they
withdrew the register altogether. Their action was somewhat of a shock to progressive educationalists, as it seemed
to betoken vacillation, the absence of a fixed policy, and
a yielding to expediency. For some years the Board could
not be induced to take any further action: they vetoed the

proposals of the leading teachers' organisations on the pretext that they did not provide for the inclusion of certain specialist teachers such as those of domestic subjects and of physical training. It was not till 1912 that a new registering authority was set up. It is composed of an independent chairman and forty-four members, representing in equal proportions university, secondary, elementary, and specialistic teachers. At present the register is drawn up practically by taking things as they stand, a fee of one guinea and five years' satisfactory experience being all that was demanded of existing teachers. After 1920 it was intended that no one should be admitted unless he should have fulfilled the conditions which the Council should lay down; but the war upset the calculations of the promoters of the scheme. On the academic side the conditions are practically in operation; a degree, the Board's certificate for elementary teachers, or certain substitutes for the degree accepted in the case of specialist teachers. But the value of the register virtually depends not only on the requirement of training from all save university teachers, but also on making registration a condition of being allowed to teach in a recognised school. Compulsion could of course be introduced by stages, e.g. by first requiring that a certain proportion of the staffs should be registered and afterwards by allowing no new teacher to be appointed whose name was not on the register. The next few years are likely to see a solution of this long-standing problem.

The year 1918 stands out as a landmark in English educational history. At the very time when the Germans were inflicting on the allied armies a series of defeats which might well have been regarded as the precursors of the subjugation of Great Britain and France to the German Empire, the British Parliament was quietly passing Mr Fisher's Education Bill which had been crowded out by the Representation of the People Act during the preceding session. By the time the check of July had turned into a retreat, the retreat into a rout, and the rout into the *débâcle* of November, the Act was on the statute-book. The provisions directly concerned with secondary education are few. But the requirement of a continuation school training till eighteen of all persons who have not continued their full-time training till sixteen, or reached the standard of a school leaving examination, if it does not exactly make a secondary education compulsory on all, at least makes schooling during the secondary age compulsory. The Act also requires that free places shall be given to all who are fitted to receive a secondary education and desirous of receiving it; and time will show how far these two provisions taken together will increase the number of pupils in secondary schools. The provisions of the Medical Inspection Act are also made applicable to secondary schools. By another important Act of the same year provision was made for the pensions of secondary school teachers. But it is clear that this *annus mirabilis* marks the opening of a new period in our educational as well as our general history; and it is not the province of this volume to anticipate the history of this new period.

The advent of universal schooling is probably the greatest fact in the history of that most crowded century in the record of human development—the century from 1815 to 1918. If we look back over the centuries, we seem to find a tremendous acceleration in the rate at which progress travels. The landmarks of the past—the invention of tools, the taming of animals, the discovery of agriculture, the invention of writing, the use of metals—stand centuries apart. The first millennium B.C. reveals the first considerable acceleration; but the first millennium A.D. is a period during which, looking at the whole world, we hardly know whether there was advance or retrogression. From about 1400 A.D. advance has been becoming increasingly more rapid. Printing diffused knowledge among the upper and middle classes of the Western world; the geographical discoveries brought all mankind into a partial contact; science began to revolutionise the outlook of the intellectual classes and the standard of comfort amongst all. The world of 1800 A.D. differed more from the world of 1400 A.D. than the world of 1400 A.D. from the world of 600 B.C. But the nineteenth century seems to have progressed as rapidly as the four preceding centuries. The outlook of the educated European began to spread to all classes of European society and to a minority of the members of races outside Western Europe. Another century may see a practical homogeneity of the race. For, whatever had been gained up to 1800, was virtually the possession of a minority in each country. A bolshevist rising in any country of Europe in 1800 would, by sweeping away the "bourgeoisie," have sent back civilisation to 2600 B.C. in a few months. Not that it would have made these countries all that Russia is now; for the unsophisticated Roman or Greek or Arab would have had a sense of moral and social responsibility which the oppressed Russian peasant lacks. But the gains of twenty-four centuries were stored with the few. The nineteenth century has many bad features, obviously bad: its industrial system produced a submerged tenth lower in the scale of humanity than any large class which existed in England in the two preceding centuries; their environment was more squalid, their interests lower, their opportunities for development more stunted. But it developed the antidote. It realised that the civilisation which the intellectual classes had developed was maintained by being handed on from one generation to another by two means, the printed page and a deliberate education. A civilisation based on oral tradition and unsystematised transmission might be lost as completely as many a civilisation of the past must have been lost on the occurrence of some unrecorded Völker-wanderung. Greek and Roman civilisation was not lost, because it was written, and became a living force again when the Renaissance used the organisation of a systematic schooling to spread it. The country folk of Stuart and Hanoverian times had undoubtedly a not ignoble traditional civilisation; it was on the national ideals of the mass of the people that the more self-conscious civilisation of the intellectual classes was built up. But the agricultural and industrial revolutions almost destroyed this traditional civilisation; it was cut adrift from the conscious civilisation; class ceased to know class; but for the Wesleyan movement the religious basis of social tradition would have been lost; and there was a danger that a large portion of the people would become without tradition, without State, without religion, without means of self-expression. Story and song, music and dance, worship and patriotism gone, what but the primitive instincts is left? Education was called in to prevent the loss of what had been before; but it was the germ of an advance beyond anything that had yet been. It cannot be judged on what it has yet accomplished; for its work is only beginning. It is perfectly true that before the nineteenth century there had never been a nation all or practically all of whose members could read and write; but it would betoken a sad lack of vision to think that the nineteenth century produced a nation all of whose members were educated. The past century gave everyone the tools by which a man can make for himself a path to the inheritance of the world's stored experience but it did not teach everyone how to use them. It made a good beginning; the results already gained have made a new age in the future possible; but it had two tremendous difficulties to encounter. The first is obvious; the same imperious necessity which brought it into being limited its immediate success. It strove to humanise many whom industrial and social conditions were dehumanising. The second was its confinement to the years of childhood: even fourteen was obtained as a leaving age only at the close of the century. Childhood can only forge the tools by which intellectual education can later be won and form the habits on the foundation of which moral character can be built. The "teens" are the really formative period during which mind and character assume the shape which they will retain. At present we are in the main a half-educated people; with the majority of our countrymen education has been broken off in the middle, and only a few beyond the age of fourteen can finish their education themselves by their own thought and reading and their own power of learning from their experience of life without further guidance. Unfortunately the dreams of theorists in the seventeenth century, that every one is capable of an equal degree of education, have been shown to be fantastic hopes. There is no economic or political impossibility—the difficulty is psychological. Modern scientific research has shown and is showing more clearly every day that not only saints and men of genius but men above the average in character and ability are born before they can be made and cannot be made by the best education unless they have been born potentially what they are later to become. The progress that has been made in standardising the Binet tests has not yet been grasped by the bulk of educated people in its full significance: it has shown that every child is born with a very distinct limit to his individual educability, and that these limits are in the majority of cases lower than the optimists of the past would have anticipated. All the more need that distinct ability should be discovered, in whatever station its possessor has been born, and that all should be educated to the full measure of their ability! The twentieth century has awakened to its double problem; and the system of free places and that of continuation schools have been devised to meet its two sides; it will be the task of the rest of the century which is still young to work out its full solution.

REFERENCES

Report of the Royal Commission on Secondary Education, 1895.
Education Act, 1902.
British Association, *Report* for 1918, "On the Free Place system.'
Education Act, 1918.

CHAPTER XIII

CHANGES IN CURRICULUM AND METHODS

THE last twenty years have witnessed more rapid changes in curriculum and methods than have been seen at any time since the Renaissance. The contributory causes have been numerous. In the first place the changes in the schools have reflected the advances of the subjects themselves and their increasing recognition by the universities. Up to the close of the third quarter of the nineteenth century British universities lagged far behind those of the Continent in the matter of research; but by the beginning of the new century the relation of the universities to two at least of the important school subjects, natural science and history, had been revolutionised; and geography was rapidly taking its place as a coherent body of principles. Secondly, the adoption of new subjects, the challenge to existing subjects, and the frequent failure of the new subjects to fulfil the hopes which had been formed of them—a failure which was generally due to the crude mechanical methods by which they were taught—led to a deliberate attempt to improve the methods of teaching both old and new in order that they might survive in the struggle for existence. Thirdly, the growth of non-classical boys' schools and of girls' schools, for which no traditional curriculum existed, compelled educationalists to think out the whole problem of intellectual education from first principles. The British Association showed a keen interest in scientific and mathematical education. The exponents of new subjects united the teachers of those subjects into societies like the English Association, the Modern Language Association, the Historical Association, and the Geographical Association, with the double object of spreading a conviction of the importance of the subject represented by the particular association and of so teaching it as best to bring out its true value. The older subjects were no less eager to maintain their hold, and the Mathematical and Classical Associations have very considerably modified the spirit in which their two subjects are treated in schools. Finally, the measure of State control which has existed since the beginning of the new century, though it has not originated any new ideas, has exercised an influence in levelling up schools which might otherwise have been content to remain behind their time, and in particular the Reports and Inquiries division of the Board of Education did much to discover what was being done in other countries and to give publicity to it by means of the *Special Reports* which were entrusted to the editorship of Sir Michael Sadler. These general influences and their results will become more apparent if we now examine the changes which have recently taken place in the teaching of individual subjects.

Classics had attained the zenith of its power as an educative force for the ablest pupils at the top of the school much earlier in the century. While "pure scholarship" still retained much of its pristine glory, sixth-form classics were at the same time made the basis of a comparison of the ancient and modern worlds, and thus formed the introduction of the adolescent mind to that serious reflection on political, moral and economic problems which, perhaps more than anything else, is necessary for the leaders of opinion in a modern state. But, in the newer types of school, the duration of school life and the utilitarian needs of modern society, made a study of Greek up to the point when it would yield a return of this kind impossible; and it is doubtful whether it could ever do so except in the case of the picked pupil. Consequently Greek never gained an entry into the new type of school, and Latin, deprived of her partner, had a difficult struggle to justify her continuance. The entrance requirements of modern universities and of various professions demanded Latin but not Greek: and for some years, owing to our innate British conservatism, this compromise was generally accepted. Indeed the coming into being of the Board of

Education and the reaction against the narrowness of the
Organised Schools of Science appeared to give Latin a new
lease of life, and it became almost a necessity in schools
receiving a government grant. Up to the War, repeated
attempts to deprive Greek of its position as a compulsory
subject at the older universities and Latin at the newer
just failed to win the day. But it was generally felt that
the teaching of classics outside the older type of schools
was unsatisfactory. By the traditional method the first
three or four years yielded little return. The accidence took
a long time to master; the differences of construction
necessitated a long course of exercises in translation out
of English and of "made up" matter into English; and the
fourth year often saw only the power to hammer out
slowly portions of Caesar and Livy with the aid of notes
which translated all difficult sentences, even if the pupil
did not use the further and unauthorised assistance of a
literal translation. Thus the majority of boys never reached
the stage when they entered into the mind of a Latin or
Greek author, or when they derived the real benefit of
translating English into Latin, which comes of the necessity
of analysing the meaning of the English with the greatest
exactitude.

No mere cutting down of the reduced course was of the
slightest avail. The full public school classical course could
be cut down without removing anything essential. Verses
and Greek prose had long disappeared from the German
Gymnasien. But it was precisely in the case of the large
public schools that no great demand for cutting down
existed. Verses are no longer imposed on the less able
pupils; they have become optional in classical scholarships
and in moderations at Oxford; but they still secure marks
and give the versifier an advantage. But in the case of the
reduced curriculum, lack of thoroughness at the initial
stages virtually excluded the pupils from the power to
benefit by the later stages. The attempt to do in four hours
a week for two or three years what had formerly taken
about twelve hours for four or five years was inevitably
doomed to failure. Yet all the earlier attempts were to

produce text-books which aimed at following the old path but rushing along it at a faster rate.

Such was the situation when a few individuals seized on the "direct method" which had already thoroughly justified itself in the case of modern languages and applied it, *mutatis mutandis*, to the teaching of Latin and Greek. The Perse School, Cambridge, under Dr Rouse, has, since the beginning of the century, been the pioneer of the new attempt, and the Association for the Reform of Latin Teaching the medium for spreading the idea. At the Perse and in a few other schools the method has been an undoubted success and it has been shown that, by the new method, pupils can be brought even with the reduced hours to the stage when the classical languages bring real returns in greater numbers than under the traditional system. But the direct method succeeds at present only in the hands of real scholars who are at the same time first-rate teachers; and one of the factors in the present situation is that the increase in the number of schools in which Latin up to matriculation standard is taught has made it absolutely impossible for the bulk of them to obtain teachers of the class which is needed. In many small schools Latin is taught in whole or in part by teachers who have taken honours in other subjects or who have not taken honours at all. It is thus too soon to decide whether the new method will withstand the growing attacks of utilitarianism and whether the retention of Latin when Greek, from which the full classical course received the chief measure of its inspiration, is given up will in the long run continue to appeal to the bulk of humanists. It is likewise too early to predict whether the abandonment of compulsory Greek at the older universities will slowly reduce the numbers of classical specialists till the ancient languages become merely a part of the professional training of the theological student.

Mathematics stood in quite a different position from classics. It is true that the growth of natural science has drawn away from the more advanced stages of pure mathematics many candidates who fifty years ago would have

taken the Cambridge mathematical tripos; but it has
largely increased the number of persons who need to study
mathematics beyond the old standard for admission to the
university. Mathematics enjoys several other advantages;
it has a natural avenue in the universally taught subject
of arithmetic, which secures that a pupil whose natural
ability leads in that direction is almost sure to be discovered; and, being an exact subject, it is comparatively
easy to teach at least passably. The methods of teaching
it have undergone radical changes in the last twenty years;
but most of them were long overdue, some of them having
been anticipated in France by *two hundred years!* The
reforms in the teaching of elementary arithmetic since the
days when Matthew Arnold described it as "a special form
of the science peculiar to inspected schools" belong rather
to the history of elementary than to that of secondary
education. More radical was the reform in the teaching of
geometry which involved the abandonment of Euclid,
whose text-book had held its own for two thousand years!
The Port Royalists wrote a revised geometry in the seventeenth century, and Euclid had already been superseded
in every other civilised country. In Great Britain he
received his death-blow in a discussion at the British
Association in 1901. His long survival is probably to be
explained by the persistence of the idea that the study of
a work arranged in strict syllogistic form trained the
pupil in a type of reasoning which could be applied with
success to every kind of subject-matter whatever. Up-
holders of this traditional view had failed to disentangle
the essentials of this training from its non-essentials. The
rationality of everything in Euclid's proofs and order had
been taken for granted: Euclid had become the touchstone
of reason rather than reason of Euclid. After 1901, however, it was no longer heretical to hint that Euclid could
be guilty of a tautological definition, that his postulates
had been determined more by the build of Greek compasses
than by that of the human mind, or that some of his
axioms were less axiomatic than some of the propositions
which he thought it necessary to prove. Hitherto the

pupil who began by regarding geometry as a fascinating subject had found his progress barred by the *pons asinorum*—the cumbrous proof of Proposition V; but this terrible obstacle appeared to the innovators merely as betokening a naïve belief on the part of Euclid that a triangle could be turned on its back more easily if a piece were added at two of its corners than if it were left in splendid isolation. A more coherent course of practical work was rendered possible by the discovery that the absence of all reference to number was rather a defect in the geometrical practice of Euclid's day than a merit; while a far more logical arrangement of the order of propositions could be adopted as soon as it was seen that there was no logical reason why "theorems" should wait attendance on "problems" and that Euclid's order in the first book was hopelessly confusing. The result of the attacks was that examining bodies ceased to require Euclid's sequence of propositions and that a variety of text-books containing other orders sprang into being. Among the reformers there was of course a left and a right wing: the left wing allowed more propositions to be treated as axiomatic, accepted a few proofs which, though they were equally convincing to the pupil, were not regarded by Euclideans as conforming to the rules of the game, and aimed at reaching more rapidly the propositions which, like that dealing with the equality of the square on the hypotenuse of a right-angled triangle to the sum of the squares on the remaining sides, reveal a relation hitherto unsuspected by the pupil; while the right wing changed little in Euclid but the order.

The "reformed geometry" has made it possible, as Rousseau long ago demanded, to make a class think out the propositions as "riders," to begin problem work from the very beginning, and to substitute a real "feel" of the proofs for an empty form of words. The older "geometrical drawing" which stood in no relation to theoretic geometry has been incorporated. Quantitative problems at the early stages make the connection with arithmetic and mensuration obvious to the beginner. Probably for the average boy or girl, geometry, so far from having ceased to be a training in reasoning, has for the first time come to give such a training. But the maintenance of this position would involve so thorough an examination both of the nature of proof and of the steps whereby the growing mind can best be led to feel proof as proof, that it is impossible to attempt it here.

At about the same time changes were attempted in the teaching of elementary algebra. The traditional order in teaching algebra had been based on the order in arithmetic. After an unintelligent manipulation of symbols came the "four simple rules," and then and not till then simple equations and problems leading thereto, which are the first things which reveal to the beginner the *raison d'être* of algebra and are not treated by him as mere juggling tricks. The pedagogic and mathematical absurdity of this treatment is well exposed in Dr Adams's *The New Teaching*, but we fear that reform in the early teaching of algebra has not yet made as great strides as in the early teaching of geometry. At a later stage the earlier introduction of trigonometry and of logarithms and the tendency to remove cumbersome accretions in favour of those parts of mathematics which are real "tools" in the hands of those who can use them are the outstanding reforms, just as at a still later stage the putting of the calculus earlier in the course is a prominent feature in reformed syllabuses.

Of natural science we have already spoken in a separate chapter. It has made rapid strides since the "eighties," every extension of schools having added to the proportion as well as to the actual number of pupils who make it one of their main subjects. It suffered badly from the effects of written examinations in the early days; for examining bodies had not envisaged the possibility of a subject whose very essence consisted of practical work. A strong reaction against mechanical memorising produced the atmosphere in which the claims of the heuristic method were able to thrive. This method differed fundamentally from the reforms which have been proposed in other branches of the curriculum: the most that can be said against any of them is that they require specially competent teachers, whereas the heuristic method was based on unsound presuppositions. It assumed a matured power of holding in the mind a large number of considerations to be present in a child of ten; and it further assumed that the power of balancing those considerations could be learned by practice without the aid of imitation. Experience and psychology have confirmed the suspicions which those who had a practical acquaintance with growing minds all along entertained that till the age of adolescence science cannot be studied scientifically; while, even in the case of adolescents, it is now recognised that the handling of the reins which guide each individual in a class so as to encourage intelligent guess-work is a fine art too delicate to be reduced to formulae[1].

The teaching of modern languages is being absolutely transformed by the introduction of the direct method, hindered though it is by the lack of trained teachers and of Englishmen possessing a good spoken knowledge of French and German. The older methods, described by Dr Moberley before the Public Schools Commission, have, however, not yet been thoroughly driven out. The direct method was worked out in Germany during the "eighties" and was rapidly accepted in that country and in France; but it has been adopted by Great Britain only since the beginning of the new century. Probably it is used more successfully in girls' than in boys' schools, partly because women have cultivated modern languages more and partly because they are far more ready to give a fair trial to new educational methods.

The term "English" covers a variety of branches of the curriculum—composition, grammar, and literature.

The practice of English composition has been fostered in many ways. As Arnold treated "translation," as opposed to "construing," from foreign languages, it gave a training in English expression. Unfortunately, however,

---

[1] For more details as to improvements in the methods of teaching natural science, see Kimmins's lecture in Roberts, *Education in the Nineteenth Century*, ch. VII.

there has been a sad decline in this kind of "translation"; and in many of the newer schools the latinised or frenchified English which is used in the Latin or French lesson must go a long way to counteract the efforts of the teacher of English. The old Latin "theme" was a training in another side of composition; for it compelled the pupil to collect and arrange his ideas as much as an English essay would have done: but in the middle of our period it gave way entirely to translation from English into Latin. In sixth forms English essays have long been effectively used to introduce the pupil to historical, political, critical, and other problems: but the traditional essay set to the middle forms imposed the task not only of making bricks without straw but of combining them into a building without a plan. In other words, the pupils had neither ideas nor guidance in the art of arranging ideas. External examinations, however, began to require English essays, and the newer types of school had to respond to the demand. Cram-books of model essays began to be written, and kinds of essays were found to be capable of classification as readily as problems on clocks and bath-pipes. Pupils preparing for the more elementary public examinations were taught to catalogue the parts of an animal beginning with its head and ending with its tail or to recount the career of a man under headings as precise as those of *Who's Who*. Variety was slowly introduced; but the discovery of the great superiority of French teachers in the technique of teaching composition and their surprisingly good results has done more than anything to improve the teaching of the subject in this country[1].

Much of what is now called English Grammar was taught in the old grammar schools as part of the Latin teaching. Indeed we are now becoming conscious that most of what has passed as "English grammar" is merely the terminology of Latin grammar transferred to a language which it does not equally fit. Matthew Arnold, who was a firm believer in the "logical training" afforded by a study of Latin, was very anxious to see English grammar taught to all pupils

[1] *E.g.* P. J. Hartog, *The Writing of English*, 1908.

who did not learn Latin: Thring too wrote text-books and taught the subject at Uppingham. Modern questionnaires suggest that it is the best hated subject in the curriculum; possibly this confirmed the high opinion formed of it by the old disciplinarian school of thought. Another merit in the eyes of some teachers was that, being entirely formal and standing in no relation to the world outside the class-room, it did not necessitate any fresh reading to keep abreast of the times or to impart freshness of presentation. It has now become the natural target of all enemies of formalism and believers in making school work a live thing. But it has a great measure of support from the teachers of other languages, who prefer to ease themselves of the grind which might threaten a loss of interest to the early stages of teaching French or Latin. A practical step was taken in 1909, when the teachers of all languages united to agree on a standard grammatical terminology applicable to all languages ordinarily taught in schools. This amounted to an agreement that, as far as schools are concerned, grammar is merely a body of terms used to describe certain phenomena of language and not an explanatory science.

English literature owes its entrance into schools almost entirely to external examinations. The older schools believed that it could not profitably be taught in class, and tried to encourage it by school libraries[1], by holiday work, and by occasional readings given to a class as a kind of hour's holiday. The need of introducing it seemed axiomatic to opponents of classics. "Why teach Greek and Latin, even French and German, literature, and not teach the incomparable literature of our own tongue?" It was introduced, and taught exactly as Latin and Greek authors were taught. The author was snowed under by the notes. The notes, like the classical *eruditio* of Renaissance times, consisted of scraps of isolated information, philological, grammatical, historical, archaeological, biographical, critical. Rarely has a subject suffered so severely at the hands of its friends! In how many children has the

[1] *E.g.* Markby, *Practical Lectures in Education*, p. 59.

desire to read the English classics been killed by cramming such matter for examinations! An attempt is now
being made to improve the teaching by altering the character of examination questions; but it has yet to be shown
that a vernacular literature is capable of being made an
examination subject. Teachers are in a dilemma. If it is
not examined, while other subjects are, it probably will
not be taught at all; if it is examined, it follows that it
will be taught badly. Even in the universities, where it
now usually forms an honours course by itself, a constant
struggle is needed to prevent "English" from becoming
predominantly philological.

History was one of the earliest of the new subjects to
obtain recognition at the universities, and its importance
was admitted by the old-fashioned headmasters; their
difficulty was that they were not willing, like the supporters
of some modern subjects, to introduce the subject first
and find out how to teach it afterwards. The higher stages,
at which thoughtful essays could be obtained, and the
lowest stage of all, where history is pure story-telling, soon
assumed shape: but the middle stages have suffered from
a fair measure of rote memory-work. Dr Keatinge's source
method has in recent times attempted to solve the problem
of the middle stage, and it has exercised a considerable
influence on existing methods, though it has not often
been adopted in its entirety[1].

Geography was long a bye-word as a mere memory
subject. Its transformation in the hands of good teachers
since 1900 has been more complete than in the case of
almost any subject. Much of this is due to the efforts of
Sir H. Mackinder and the late Dr Herbertson at Oxford
and to the large number of students who have attended
vacation classes there and elsewhere. In the preceding
quarter of a century, the men of science, led by Huxley,
had done much to develop "physiography," which became
a favourite subject in junior examinations, but they had

[1] For a connected review of the teaching of history in the nineteenth century, see Withers's lecture in Roberts, *Education in the
Nineteenth Century*, ch. VI.

effected too great a divorce between the physical and the human sides of geography. The neo-Herbartians on the contrary tried to correlate geography so closely with history as to deprive it of all organic unity; but their efforts never got far beyond the domain of theory. The synthesis of the physical and the human is the ideal of the new school of geographers. Geography affords a striking instance of the effect on the teaching of a subject in schools which may be produced from the broadening of the subject itself by its non-scholastic exponents.

Drawing entered the lower grades of secondary education first and thence climbed upwards. It was as a utilitarian rather than as an artistic subject that it first appeared. Geometrical drawing was thus in favour; but it was kept strangely isolated from theoretic geometry till the last twenty years. The story of the mechanical teaching of freehand drawing, beginning with straight lines and curves, and continuing with the drawing of copies, belongs more properly to the history of elementary education, as it was due to a Pestalozzian tradition and was spread by the influence of Kay-Shuttleworth. Herbert Spencer's attack did not finally drive it from the schools for thirty or forty years. South Kensington has in the past dominated the teaching of the subject. The Public Schools Commission held that every boy should be taught either drawing or music; but Thring was the first enthusiastic supporter of the artistic subjects in the large public schools. Though the attitude of educationalists to the artistic subjects has now become thoroughly favourable, drawing has still two difficulties to face. The first is that, not being a subject required for the matriculation examinations of universities, many schools allow the pupil to drop it as soon as he possibly can and do not treat it with the same seriousness as they treat the intellectual disciplines; and this is as true of many schools of the new types as of the old-fashioned school. The second danger comes from a section of its own adherents. Latterly a kind of pedagogic futurism and cubism has arisen, which would have us allow children to draw unrecognisable daubs without correction as a means

of encouraging "self-expression." We might as well encourage unintelligible and ungrammatical English with
the same object. It is impossible to believe that this craze
will hold the field for long, though it is obviously popular
with the lazy teacher who would have the world believe
that his laziness is an application of the latest educational
theory.

Music also owes much to Thring. Few schools fail to
encourage it either as a class subject or as an out-of-school
recreation or as both, though, where it is treated as a class
subject, it, like drawing, often suffers from not being
a recognised subject for matriculation examinations.

The manual subjects are beginning to come to their own;
but naturally we expect to see them more developed in
elementary, technical and continuation schools than in
ordinary secondary schools. By a curious irony, they are
not allowed to benefit by being utilitarian; for, the moment
any utilitarian claim is put forward for them, we are told
that we are converting a secondary into a technical school:
yet, the moment they are left to stand on their merits as
a part of the training of an all-round human being, parents
at once forsake them for other subjects which may in the
abstract be supported as part of a general education but
whose appeal to them is purely monetary. Thus, while we
should have expected every human being to aspire to become a handy man, no social class seems to favour manual
training. To the head-worker it seems to have no marketable value; and the hand-worker suspects it as a surreptitious
device of the capitalist to prevent his children entering the
ranks of head-workers. Unfortunately it has not fared well
in the United States, where Dewey's idealistic conception
of the subject had to yield to commercialism; otherwise
his views would probably in a few years have produced a
strong impression in this country.

The improvement of methods of teaching every subject
is bound up with the question of the training of teachers.
A short account of the history of the movement in favour
of the training of secondary teachers is therefore in place
in this chapter.

Training of elementary teachers has long been the rule, and it is possible that the more rational opposition to the training of secondary teachers, as opposed to that which sprang either from sheer conservatism or from the dislike of an additional year's work, sprang from certain associations of training in general with the specific methods of training at one time in vogue for elementary teachers. It is undoubtedly true that training came into existence in connection with very mechanical methods of teaching. Under the monitorial system, when the teachers were themselves children, nothing but cut and dried methods could be taught them; and the object of training was precisely the same as that of military drill, to prescribe an exact method by which every act should be performed, and to turn that method into an automatic habit. Gradually the age of teachers was raised till the students were no longer boys but men: but still the fearful grind hindered any real development of initiative. The student was expected to teach all day in school, to prepare his lessons, to undergo a course of general study, and to be trained; save for meal times, he was at work from five in the morning till bed-time. We learn that at one time the method of training was as follows:—the student taught each class in turn; he then went into the training college and assumed the rôle of pupil in each class and was taught every lesson in the regulation manner; he practised some of them on his fellow-students; and at the end he was supposed to know exactly what to do in every lesson in every class and to be ready to go out and do it. Kay-Shuttleworth, the first secretary of the Committee of Council, did much for elementary education; in particular he substituted pupil-teachers for monitors and tried to increase the number of adult teachers. In a private capacity he founded Battersea Training College; and he trusted to training colleges to improve methods of teaching. But the mechanical side of training did not disappear. Kay-Shuttleworth wished to follow Pestalozzi, and it was quite easy to interpret Pestalozzi's principles, in the literal sense of his own phrase, as an attempt *méchaniser l'éducation*. Kay-Shuttleworth's conception of method was to reduce every subject to its logical elements; in reading you proceeded from letters to syllables, from monosyllabic to dissyllabic words, and so on. The method was thoroughly unsound, but it lent itself to a stereotyped procedure; and such a procedure was stamped on training colleges during the critical period when elementary education was taking shape in this country.

It is not our intention to recount the history of elementary training colleges in any detail; for till 1890 they were isolated from the rest of higher education, and convenience suggests that they should be treated along with elementary education. Their great defect was the confinement of the instruction strictly to the subjects which the student would have to teach; and matters were made worse by Robert Lowe who, from motives of false economy, would have liked to destroy them altogether, but, being unable to do so, forbade the founding of any more and limited the curricula of those which existed to little more than "the three R's." Between the time of Lowe and 1890 the Government once more came to see their necessity; and, whereas in early days it was found impossible to fill them, the demand now came greatly to exceed the supply of places. The old conditions had been far from satisfactory. The whole day was filled up; students had no private rooms in which to work; there were no facilities for exercise; the staffs were composed almost entirely of old students; the studies consisted largely in memory-work. The professional training was somewhat unreal; it encouraged the cult of "talk and chalk"; it was tested by "show" lessons before the inspector, in which it was generally believed that the best impression was made by choosing a scientific topic and working a number of "interesting" experiments which the class regarded in the light of conjuring tricks. As such lessons were unlikely to be given by the student in his subsequent career, there was in this an element which struck the outsider as worse than a mistake—as partaking of the nature of a sham.

It must be remembered that the demand for the training of secondary teachers began while that of elementary teachers was still in this unsatisfactory state. It can be readily understood what Temple meant when he said that the business of a schoolmaster was "not so much to teach as to make the children learn." He implied that the teacher was encouraged to be so active as to leave the pupils passive, whereas true education consists in the pupil learning how to teach himself. Or again we can understand the point of Thring's dictum, "The perfection of teaching is that it does not work by a given pattern."

The first believers in training among secondary teachers were mainly women. There must be some reason for this. All the great headmistresses from the very first were in its favour; it was long before any prominent headmaster supported it heartily. Women as a rule have more of the teaching instinct inborn in them than men; hence we should suppose that they need training less. Our own explanation is this. It was a tradition in the old boys' schools that the headmaster should never be in the room to hear one of his staff teach. Women can never hand over the reins in that way; many men would say that they must be interfering. The headmistress soon found out how badly the average beginner teaches—we are not speaking of discipline but of actual teaching. They also learned how much she improved with a little guidance. Contemporary headmasters, never entering a new master's class-room, never realised either fact with equal clearness, but tended to assume that, if discipline were satisfactory, teaching would look after itself.

The College of Preceptors was the first body to institute lectures on the science and art of education for secondary teachers, Joseph Payne acting as professor from 1873 to his death in 1876. Cambridge University instituted lectures during the eighties, and R. H. Quick, who had published his *Essays on Educational Reformers* in 1868, was invited to lecture. This move seems to have been inspired more by a desire to satisfy an outcry than by a conviction of any good which would accrue. The experiment could not be pronounced very fruitful; casual lectures are not training, in fact they sin against one of the first principles which the lecturer would lay down that an art can be learned only after practice. Not, of course, the advocate of training would add, by unguided practice. Training in teaching is like net-practice in cricket under a professional coach. The old system of education sent the teacher to the wicket without any practice at all; the lecture system assumed that discussions on forward and back play (the theory of education) and a study of the life of W. G. Grace (the history of education) would make a man a cricketer. Quick was a man brimful of ideas; but it is doubtful whether an "educational reformer," in the sense of a man who believes that education is right off the rails and needs getting back, was the best choice to commend training to a faithless and untoward generation. Such a man is of necessity searching for the right methods, sure that they have not been found; whereas a man with fewer alterations to suggest but perfectly sure of those few would have been more likely to command confidence.

We therefore think that the credit of being the real authors of secondary training in England must go to women like Mrs Grey, who founded the Maria Grey College in 1877, and Miss Buss, who secured the foundation of the Cambridge Training College for Women in 1885. Miss Buss foresaw the danger that training would be neglected by women whose classes in the tripos would readily obtain them posts and might be confined to such as wished to make up in some other way for lack of academic distinction. This has been another cause which has hindered the progress of training. If the training colleges get only inferior material, training will not be justified of its children. It is the same story as that of modern sides; headmasters first relegated to them all their less able pupils and then demonstrated from the results that modern studies were of less educational value than the classics. The spontaneous spread of training among women has since been considerable. It is noteworthy too that the schools of the Roman Catholics and of the Society of Friends, who are more free from tradition and more ready to examine an educational question on its merits than ordinary schools, have been favourable to training. Meanwhile the elementary training colleges were being transformed. The buildings were improved; each student was allotted a study-bedroom of his own; hours of work were reduced; playing fields were attached; the curriculum was widened; students were encouraged to sit for London degrees; women principals were required in the case of women's colleges; salaries were improved; and the colleges were encouraged to appoint graduates on their staffs.

An undoubted hindrance to the spread of training was a widely felt suspicion of educational theory for which some of its exponents were in a large measure to blame. It is a curious fact that we have almost completed our story of English secondary education during the last hundred years without having had a single occasion save in a digression on elementary education to refer to any influence exercised by the great continental exponents of educational theory. The three whose views have in turn been brought to Great Britain are Pestalozzi, Froebel, and Herbart. As a philanthropist, indeed as a confessor for education among the poor, Pestalozzi had an influence on the spread of elementary education which is above praise. But as a theorist, if indeed he can be called such, his influence, as we have pointed out, made for a mechanical conception of teaching. Froebel's work was almost unknown in England till the foundation of the Froebel Society in 1874. In spite of some tendency to set the *ipse dixit* of their founder above experience, Froebelians have, on the other hand, done an immense amount of good, and have revolutionised our ideas of the infant school. The influence of Herbart was later still in showing itself and coincided with the demand for training. The Felkins translated portions of Herbart's writings in 1892, and among a section of "reformers" Herbartianism became a craze. Pilgrimages to Jena to sit at the feet of Dr Rein, his great contemporary exponent, were as obligatory on the faithful as pilgrimages to Mecca in the world of Islam. The arrangement of lessons in five steps—Herbart himself only knew of four—was believed to be all that was needed (unless perchance it were the determination of curriculum on a culture-epoch basis) to bring about an educational millennium. To the old-fashioned headmaster Herbartianism appeared as the very canonisation of soft pedagogics. The truth is that very little of Herbart was left in popular neo-Herbartianism, which was inextricably intertwined with the notions that teaching was a process of exposition in which the teacher did all the work and that it must always be made, in a crude sense, "interesting."

The application of psychology to education was also a matter of suspicion to the practical teacher. The reason for this difference of attitude between the theorist and the practical man is now quite evident. The theorist saw that psychology, as being the science of mind, must be the foundation of education, which is the treatment of mind, just as physiology must be the foundation of medicine. But the practical man saw that the rules of procedure which he was bidden to follow in the name of psychology would not work. How did this contradictory state of affairs arise? Simply because psychology claimed to direct education before its own foundations were securely laid. Till far into the nineteenth century psychology meant the faculty psychology of Aristotle. When, for instance, the psychologist Bain wrote his *Education as a Science*, he might as well have written an exposition of medicine as a science based on the old Greek theory of the four humours. Nevertheless psychology, in spite of some wise criticisms by Temple in 1858, obtained a lodgment in elementary training colleges, but it meant little more than talking about everyday experience in a very technical jargon. The able student saw through it, while the man of less brains became conceited of his fine-sounding phrases. It is difficult to fix a date at which psychology entered on its modern scientific stage: the transition took place in Germany; the American, William James, was probably the first writer to popularise the new psychology in England; and Ward's article in the *Encyclopaedia Britannica* is usually regarded as the first important exposition by an English writer. The overthrow of the faculty psychology, however, was not enough to fit the science to be the basis of an educational theory; it rather left a void. Blasting is often necessary before the foundations of a building can be laid; but it is not usual to say that a house is built on a foundation of dynamite. The next stage in psychology was analytic, classificatory, and terminological, that is, it sought to state the results of common experience in exact language before starting to make new discoveries. This stage was quite neutral in its effect on education. It might, for instance, be psychologically more accurate so to define attention as to imply that we are in some measure attending every moment of our lives, but it still remained more convenient for the master to rebuke Smith minor for "inattention" than on the more accurately expressed charge of dispersed, discontinuous, and fluctuating attention, of a low degree of intensity, and only intermittently directed on the required object.

Suspicion of psychology and suspicion of Herbartianism became in many minds closely associated; for the neo-Herbartians claimed that Herbart had years ago superseded the faculty psychology by a new system of his own. Curiously enough, headmasters, though reluctant to admit that psychology could have any value in the training of the teacher, had been always willing to carry on educational controversy in terms of the old psychology, which was consecrated by the time-honoured authority of Aristotle: but the proposed substitute was anathema to them. The truth, however, was that the Herbartian psychology, which entirely ignored the innate and hereditary elements in the human mind and regarded education as a process of introducing ideas from without, had never had a wide vogue in the country of its origin, and was quite obsolete before the educational views of the Herbartians were introduced into England. If Herbartianism was the enemy, the headmasters might well have regarded modern psychology as an ally for purposes of the attack upon it.

Psychology has now become an exact, constructive and experimental science. Its educational bearings are obvious at every turn. One caution, however, is still needed. Its

work has so far been done, and for some years will probably continue to be done, mainly in regard to what we may
call the cruder psychological processes—sense-perception,
imagery, and memory. Only when these have been
thoroughly examined will the higher processes—conceptual
thought, imagination, and reasoning—be properly investigated. Unless the educationalist is careful, he may
come to regard the cruder processes as constituting the
chief subject matter of education, whereas it is the higher
processes which are its main objective. An instance of
this tendency is to be found in the extraordinarily crude
theories of the function of hand-work in education which
are sometimes put forward on the authority of medical
men. Then too there is the fact that educational psychology
is of German origin and that, while German writers are
unsurpassed in the collection of evidence, they are not
equally noted for discrimination as to the relative importance of the facts which they have collected. The study of
Meumann's standard work on the subject, for instance, is
of doubtful advantage to the student unless his teachers
encourage him to study the evidence and exercise his
critical powers continually on the conclusions. Nevertheless, the claims of educational theory can no longer be
denied; it is impossible to discuss educational questions
without it; and the alternative to admitting it to a place
in a course of training would be to shut out educational
discussion altogether.

We may now revert to the history of training colleges,
as we have reached the point when the story of elementary
and secondary training unites. In 1890 the Government, to meet the lack of accommodation in existing
elementary training colleges, adopted a suggestion of the
Cross Commission to found "day training colleges" or,
as they are now termed, training departments, in the
various universities and university colleges. At first only
a part of the students studied for their degrees, but in
1907 it was found possible to insist on this in all cases where
the department was attached to a university. The professional work, which was the same as in ordinary training

colleges, was at first done concurrently with the academic course, but in 1911 it was postponed to a special post-graduate year and the examining was left to the university itself. By this time most universities had already established post-graduate secondary training courses, usually conducted by the same staff as that which carried on the elementary training. A further step in the unification of our educational system was taken in the same year by the substitution for the old promise, which was not legally enforcible, required of every student on entering on a course of elementary training, that he would spend his whole life in an elementary school—for so it was interpreted by the Board—of a legal undertaking to teach seven years in the case of a man or five in the case of a woman in any grant-earning school, secondary or elementary, or training-college. Finally in 1918 students admitted to an elementary training department who succeeded in obtaining a degree with honours were allowed to transfer themselves to the secondary training department, for which the State also provides grants. The distinction is thus now mainly one between the specialist teacher of older pupils and the non-specialist teacher of younger children.

The Board of Education likewise from its first institution set about to liberalise the existing training colleges for elementary teachers. The Act of 1902 permitted county and county borough councils, singly or in combination, to establish or take over training colleges, a concession which has secured a supply of places equal to the demand and has removed the grievance which was previously caused through the bulk of existing training colleges being supplied by the Church of England.

The result of all these changes is that elementary training has begun to react on secondary training. In the new municipal and county schools, which largely absorbed the old higher-grade schools, graduates who had received an elementary training began frequently to appear on the staffs. Further, as the number of teachers required was increased, it became evident that the supply of "teachers by the grace of God" was inadequate to meet the demand;

and outside that select band, the trained teacher was found to be superior. It is true that at first his merits were of rather a routine order; he knew how to arrange his facts systematically, to give a consecutive narrative, and to drill his pupils thoroughly. The old-fashioned training hardly gave that power which the "teacher by the grace of God" possessed, of training the pupil to teach himself, of being suggestive rather than didactic. Here, we suspect, was the weak spot which men like Thring had detected in teaching by rule. The old trained teacher certainly tried to "make the pupil think," he generally believed that he had succeeded. But too often he was only exercising an art in which he undoubtedly excelled, the barrister's art of driving the pupil by a series of questions to state at the end what he wished him to state. As, however, the pupil did not know after the cross-examination was over how he had been got to the point of that particular conclusion, he was no better able by virtue of the process to think out any other problem when left to himself. Frequently indeed there were serious fallacies in the reasoning which neither teacher nor pupil detected. But, in spite of obvious defects, it was clear that training could develop potentialities more certainly and more speedily than unguided experience.

The mutual interaction of secondary and elementary tradition has been of undoubted advantage to both. The former, starting from a basis of small classes and older pupils, had laid stress on the work of the individual pupils; the latter, which in its early days had mainly to do with enormous classes of children aged not more than ten, had perfected collective teaching by means of oral exposition. Both have their place; and each body of teachers is learning to value the side which they had previously under-estimated. The secondary teacher has discovered the need of thinking out his procedure, of cultivating narrative power, and perfecting his explanations; the elementary teacher has discovered, especially since a reduction in the size of classes permits of less mechanical procedure, that methods which originally had children of ten in view do too much for pupils of twelve or thirteen. Training is now winning adherents among secondary teachers, while the ideals of what constitutes a sound training are being modified among elementary teachers.

A cause which is likely in the future to force an acceptance of training even in the most conservative quarters is the rise of new methods of teaching old subjects. No untrained teacher can hope to teach languages on the direct method; and the common-sense of parents sees at a glance that a method which enables a pupil to speak, as well as to read and write, a living language is superior to one which only gives the last two facilities. Often the same parent finds that his girl, who is taught by a trained teacher, is able to do all three well, while his boy, who is taught by an untrained teacher, cannot speak at all and is only able to stumble through a piece of translation from either language into the other. This is the kind of evidence which appeals to the practical Englishman, and it is a kind which headmasters will not long be able to resist.

The history of higher education in this country from 1800, when we had but two universities and those only just waking from a long sleep, nine large schools which were still sleeping, and a number of small schools which were well-nigh dead, up to 1918, when the number of educational institutions has become so great and their character so varied that we doubt whether any one person, even an official of the Board of Education, thoroughly knows the work of them all, surely shows what is the work of the State, of the public, and of the individual in improving and spreading education. The individual initiates, public enthusiasm vivifies, the State spreads. The true function of the Government in education is like the irrigation work of British rule in Egypt and Mesopotamia; it can control a huge system which is beyond the power of any smaller organisation. But individuals are the sources of the stream. We see this more clearly in the case of schools where even the names of the chief initiators are known than in the case of universities, the very reason for whose existence is that, by bringing individuals together in a small society, they may pool the brains of all. We see it too in the case of technical and workmen's education; it is due to the initiating work of Birkbeck, Maurice, Toynbee and Hogg that the State has been able to do its later work. But the State has irrigated, that is to say, it has, by means of Royal Commissions and otherwise, broken down obstacles which shut in the life-giving waters of the initiators' ideas; it has financed the construction of channels by which the surplus stores of educational talent could be transferred from an existing place of education to a region hitherto desert; it has spread the waters from universities to schools; it has even by means of reports provided them a channel from abroad. But the early attempts at a State-made teaching of science show the contrast in vitality between the live work of individuals when subsequently spread by the State and the sapless skeleton-like growth which results from the State's own work. But besides the individual initiator and the State organiser there must exist a public to welcome and to demand. It would have been useless to provide a complete system of secondary education for the rural population of England fifty years ago. Wales obtained its system of rural secondary schools first because it was ready for it. A demand can probably be created in time, but it is a slow process.

Let us hope that the functions of all three agencies will be recognised in the future. Let the State allow such freedom that new educational ideas may be developed by individuals. May public opinion not think that, because the State has undertaken the supply, there is no more call for the enthusiasm which enabled the municipal universities, the polytechnics, and the Welsh intermediate schools to be founded. And may the State not think that the work of extension is done or ever will be done.

INDEX

CPSIA information can be obtained at www.ICGtesting.com
Printed in the USA
LVOW10s0311090415

433660LV00001B/7/P